Aviation Project
Management Framework

Aviation Project Management Framework

Lifecycle and Practices

James Marion, Tracey Richardson,
Valerie Denney, and Carlos Chaves

BEP

BUSINESS EXPERT PRESS

Leader in applied, concise business books

Aviation Project Management Framework:
Lifecycle and Practices

Cover design by Cassandra Kronstedt

Interior design by S4Carlisle Publishing Services, Chennai, India

First published in 2025 by
Business Expert Press, LLC
222 East 46th Street, New York, NY 10017
www.businessexpertpress.com

ISBN-13: 978-1-63742-862-7 (paperback)
ISBN-13: 978-1-63742-863-4 (e-book)

Portfolio and Project Management Collection

First edition: 2025

10 9 8 7 6 5 4 3 2 1

EU SAFETY REPRESENTATIVE
Mare Nostrum Group B.V.
Mauritskade 21D
1091 GC Amsterdam
The Netherlands
gpsr@mare-nostrum.co.uk

Contents

List of Figures

Who Should Read This Book?

The Aviation Community

For executives and specialists, and especially for those aviation professionals who are transitioning into new roles as project managers, this book is an essential guide to navigating the complexities of aviation projects. The aviation environment is unique, characterized by its stringent safety regulations, high stakes, and intricate stakeholder networks. Whether managing aircraft maintenance, repair, and overhaul (MRO), aviation systems, or new product development, this book equips readers with the tools to address the industry's challenges.

Executives will find value in understanding how aviation-specific project management frameworks can align with strategic goals, ensuring that projects deliver value while maintaining compliance with rigorous standards. Specialists such as engineers and technicians will appreciate the practical insights into managing technical deliverables, coordinating multidisciplinary teams, and adhering to safety and regulatory requirements. For professionals transitioning into project management roles, this book provides a robust framework to integrate their existing aviation knowledge with project management best practices, fostering success in managing complex, high-stakes projects.

The Project Management Community

Generalist project managers will discover how to adapt their existing methodologies to the highly specialized aviation sector. This book serves as a companion to established project management standards, including PMI's PMBOK® Guide and agile frameworks, offering aviation-specific adaptations and case studies that highlight unique challenges such as safety certification, stakeholder alignment, and lifecycle decision-making.

For project managers transitioning into aviation, the book offers a roadmap to bridge the knowledge gap. It explains critical aviation concepts, regulatory landscapes, and the importance of safety and quality management. By understanding the aviation-specific nuances of scope, schedule, and risk management, project managers can confidently navigate their new environment. This book also provides practical checklists and templates to enhance their project execution capabilities, making it an invaluable resource for those managing projects in this demanding industry.

The Academic Community

Academicians and students will find this book a valuable resource, whether for teaching, learning, or research in aviation project management. Its structured approach and alignment with real-world challenges make it an excellent textbook for graduate-level courses. Educators can leverage its comprehensive coverage of aviation-specific project management practices, lifecycle models, and regulatory requirements to prepare students for careers in this field.

For researchers, the book offers a wealth of topics for exploration, from the intersection of safety and project management to the impact of emerging technologies like artificial intelligence (AI) and digital twins on aviation projects. The detailed case studies and frameworks presented in this book can serve as a foundation for academic inquiry, inspiring dissertations and further study into best practices for managing complex aviation initiatives.

Description

Aviation projects are high-stakes, high-risk, and highly regulated—yet existing project management standards often fall short of addressing their unique demands. As the field of project management evolves toward more conceptual and flexible approaches, aviation professionals are left without the concrete, process-driven guidance they need to succeed.

Aviation Project Management Framework **bridges this critical gap with a comprehensive, research-backed framework designed specifically for the aviation industry.** Drawing on real-world case studies and academic research, this book outlines a tailored methodology that accounts for aviation's distinct operational constraints, stringent safety standards, and complex regulatory environment.

Whether you're overseeing aircraft design, airport construction, maintenance operations, or regulatory compliance programs, this book equips you with tools and strategies that align with aviation's high-pressure, no-fail culture.

Perfect for project managers, engineers, regulators, and aviation executives alike, this essential guide empowers you to deliver successful outcomes in one of the world's most challenging and dynamic industries.

Introduction

The Challenging World of the Aviation Project Manager: What Do Aviation Project Managers Tell Us?

Aviation projects come in many forms. Airlines customize generic planes as they roll out of the assembly line. Construction firms build control towers and airport terminals. An airline may choose to upgrade software and systems associated with aircraft avionics. They also engage in periodic maintenance, repair, and overhaul activities that are temporary, unique, and fulfill the definition of a project. Finally, aircraft manufacturers charter product development projects to create new aircraft models. Aviation project managers, therefore, face a wide array of projects that would challenge anyone to effectively manage.

Without question, the aviation project environment is one of the most severe when it comes to risk, safety, regulatory matters, and a wide array of stakeholders.

What, then, do aviation project managers tell us? Project managers within the field of aviation understand that aviation is inherently dangerous, and any aviation products, components, or services produced by projects must always consider that human lives are always at stake. This puts a premium on safety and risk management.

Project managers within the field of aviation also tell us that aviation projects are informed by a nearly endless array of diverse requirements. Such requirements emerge not only from the clients who commission aviation projects but also from regulatory bodies, internal technical organizations, risk and safety standards, and, finally, from the significant body of stakeholders served by the aviation industry.

Aviation project managers must also navigate severe constraints—many of which are activities undertaken, and work products produced in aviation projects must be meticulously documented. Aircraft components also must be carefully sourced so that they meet specific standards and support safe operation. This requires considerable effort to vet and maintain strong supply chain partners. Furthermore, aviation project deliverables may require certification by regulatory bodies. The totality of this high-risk and highly constrained environment therefore requires intense focus and attention to detail. Project managers who can successfully navigate this environment are likely to be able to be successful within any project milieu.

The aviation industry is also a highly technical field. Machines capable of traveling at over 500 mph at 7 to 8 miles in the air while carrying hundreds of passengers is quite a technological feat. Organizations that run aviation projects recognize that technological developments do not happen overnight and may take quite a bit of time and iterations to evolve into a functionally reliable product. For example, an aviation product development project is likely to employ systems that are part of a long-term technology and innovation roadmap. Such roadmaps feature the development of components, platforms, and systems from which multiple products may be developed. In addition to the long-term research, development, innovation, and technology development, successful aviation project teams also develop technical and engineering strategies for the implementation of technology.

Finally, it goes without saying that aviation projects, like all projects, exist to produce deliverables that satisfy client, regulatory, and stakeholder requirements. This requires the development, implementation, and continuous improvement of quality management systems (QMSs). Aviation project managers inform us that quality management practices in their project work are not the same as those employed in traditional mass production. They are highly focused on the effective management of the project lifecycle that includes significant phase reviews. The point of such reviews is not only to ensure that the project is on track but also to confirm that project quality systems are resulting in deliverables that meet requirements.

Aviation project managers therefore tell us quite a bit about the significant challenges faced within the aviation environment as well as the attention to detail required in any aviation project endeavor.

CHAPTER 1

Why a New Framework?

The field of project management is at a crossroads. Over the last 30 years, the Project Management Institute (PMI) has dominated the industry with its framework—the Guide to the Project Management Body of Knowledge (PMBOK). Recently, however, PMI shifted to a more conceptual standard that is more general in its approach compared to the process focus of earlier standards such as the sixth edition of the PMBOK. This has led other industry bodies to draft their own standards for project managers. Furthermore, European standards such as the International Project Management Association (IPMA) and PRINCE2 (Projects in Controlled Environments) have been observed to be increasing in market share.

This situation comes at a bad time for the aviation industry. The fact that projects within the aviation industry have unique constraints involving government regulation, industry requirements, and the constant need to focus on matters such as risk and safety that require significant guidelines and process support that exist only in embryonic form in current standards.

Support for typical categories of projects executed within the field of aviation is warranted by a unique standard for managing aviation projects such as:

Construction: This includes airports, hangars, repair facilities, towers for radar, and other navigational beacons. While such projects do not result in products that carry passengers, they do provide passenger services including the all-important guidance systems. Because of these, such projects are highly regulated and require close management beyond that found in a generic project management framework.

Maintenance, Repair, and Overhaul (MRO): Aircraft require strict maintenance schedules with unique regulatory requirements for how maintenance is carried out and documented.

Aircraft are extremely complex and, as such, maintenance events qualify as projects since the efforts tend to be temporary, unique, complex, and involve specialized resources. This is particularly true of a complete overhaul of aircraft and aircraft engines.

Aviation Systems: The design of complex system and software projects such as avionics as well as projects with other complex architectures and significant components require close management and unique requirements. The 737 MCAS system is one such example of an aviation systems project that has gone wrong.

Product Development: New aircraft design projects are notoriously lengthy and challenging and fraught with significant technical difficulties and unique requirements. Furthermore, once aircraft are designed and are transferred to manufacturing, customization projects typically ensue to prepare aircraft for stakeholders with specific requirements.

Changes in project management standards toward more generic and conceptual models have led to a gap in process guidance and methodologies for undertaking complex and challenging projects. This is a particular concern within the exacting and highly demanding aviation industry.

The opportunity, therefore, exists within the aviation industry to introduce a research-based aviation project management framework tailored to the demanding constraints of the aviation industry and one that addresses the significant risk, safety, and regulatory environment. An aviation-centric project management framework provides the possibility for training and certification revenues as well as growth of project management degree programs.

CHAPTER 2

The Aviation Project Management Framework Overview

When developing a project management framework tailored to the aviation industry, it is natural to first consider where to begin. A natural starting point is to analyze the activities that aviation project managers must undertake as they navigate aviation projects. Imagine for example a project manager faced with managing a project within the aviation industry for the first time. What would such a project manager do in this case to get started? In a generic project guided by processes from the Guide to the Project Management Body of Knowledge (PMBOK), it could be suggested that the first step in any project is to identify stakeholders and to charter the project. There is however implicit recognition by the PMBOK that there are unspecified activities carried out prior to the start of the project. These include confirming the strategic direction of the company so that any project that is selected is aligned with company strategy. There is also the general need to acknowledge enterprise environmental factors (the culture or way of doing things in the company), as well as organizational process assets. What follows these general activities is the selection of the project itself. The project selection decision is a function of the oversight and governance of the organization, which typically involves a program or project management organization (PMO).

With this guidance in mind, a project manager new to aviation projects would recognize that there is more work to be done prior to starting an aviation project. As an example, not only is an aviation project selected, the nature of the project itself suggests what form the project lifecycle should take. While many categories of projects will employ the traditional waterfall or plan driven lifecycle, some software-intensive projects are likely to be better supported by an iterative lifecycle. The aviation project manager and assigned team make this decision in conjunction with the PMO prior to the actual start of the project.

Stakeholders also take on more significance given that so many stakeholder groups exist within the aviation industry. Stakeholders drive requirements, and, in aviation projects, many layers of requirements exist. These include requirements from clients, requirements from those who use the client project deliverables—such as airline passengers, and requirements dictated by the safety and regulatory environment. Aviation project managers also operate within organizations that have their own internal standards and guidelines that resolve into project requirements. It is not realistic to produce many of these requirements from the scratch. Technologies employed in projects take time to mature and are not likely to be realized within the limited timeframe of a project. This infers that technologies and innovation should already be present in the form of components or platforms that may be employed in the project. Rather than starting a new technology development at the start of a new project, an aviation project manager and associated team will likely interact with the extended organization to obtain guidance on any components, technologies, or available platforms that may be employed in the project.

Many other concerns are faced by the aviation project manager. These concerns involve consideration of the risk appetite as well as safety concerns. The intensity of thought and management activity that an aviation project manager faces suggests the need for a lifecycle that provides process support for significant early pre-project activities.

The Aviation Project Management (AVPM Lifecycle)

Although aviation project management (AVPM) lifecycles vary depending on being iterative or plan driven, the basic steps in the lifecycle are the same. The simplest approach to envisioning the AVPM lifecycle is to consider a plan-driven lifecycle and applying a commonsense approach. The AVPM lifecycle is expressed in six phases as follows:

1. Pre-project
2. Start

3. Plan
4. Execute
5. Control
6. Close

The six phases of project activity are expressed somewhat differently in plan-driven versus iterative projects while retaining the key concepts and activities throughout. In the context of a plan-driven project, each of the lifecycle phases is executed one after another in the typical approach used in the waterfall method. Iterative project lifecycles however may be envisioned as employing the same lifecycle steps, but, instead of carrying out one phase after another in lockstep, they employ an iterative approach where the larger projects are broken into smaller "mini projects" as represented in Figure 2.1:

The iterative lifecycle uses the same phase names as the plan-driven lifecycle, but it does draw upon agile nomenclature within each phase. This allows for the seamless integration of iterative and agile methods to support aviation projects that are better served with an iterative lifecycle (Figure 2.2).

The Value Chain

Given the exacting nature of aviation projects, it is important to be systematic when cataloging essential aviation project activities. A useful way to approach this is by using a tool designed to identify and assess activities that are said to create value within an operation. One such model is the value chain.

While the value chain model was originally conceived as a tool for analyzing cost, effectiveness, and benchmarking against competing firms, the structure of the value chain is very useful for cataloging and inventorying essential activities. While it is true that the value chain traditionally modeled manufacturing organizations, there is no reason to conclude that the value chain model could not be employed to capture all value-added activities in projects.

The value chain model (see Figure 2.3) for operations outlines the end-to-end sequence of primary and supporting activities that lead to

The phases in the AVPM Plan-Driven Lifecycle

Pre-project	Start	Plan	Execute	Control	Close

Iterative Lifecycle (Agile & Hybrid)

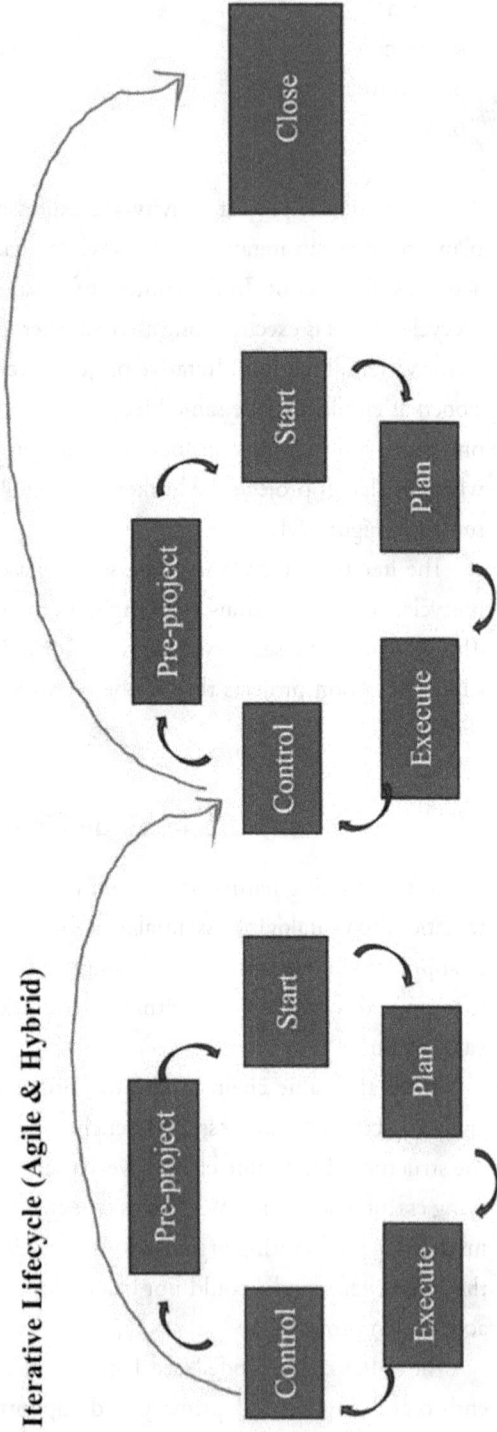

Figure 2.1 *Graphical depiction of Iterative Lifecycle breaking down larger projects into "mini projects"*

Integrating Agile into AVPM

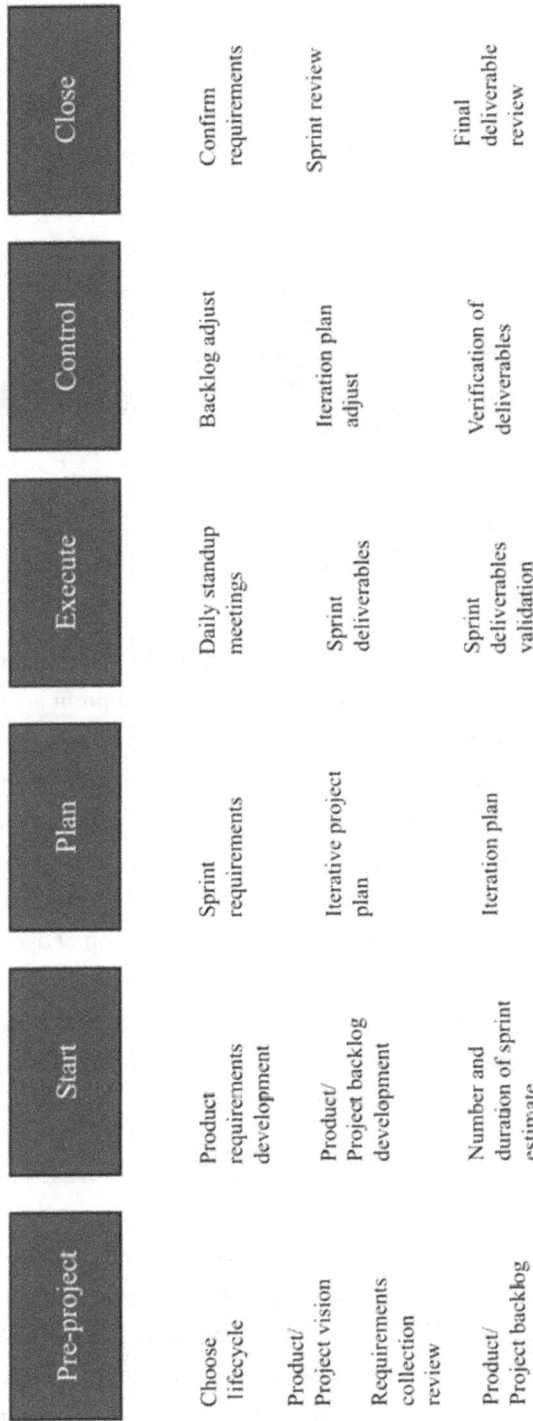

Pre-project	Start	Plan	Execute	Control	Close
Choose lifecycle	Product requirements development	Sprint requirements	Daily standup meetings	Backlog adjust	Confirm requirements
Product/ Project vision	Product/ Project backlog development	Iterative project plan	Sprint deliverables	Iteration plan adjust	Sprint review
Requirements collection review					
Product/ Project backlog estimate	Number and duration of sprint estimate	Iteration plan	Sprint deliverables validation	Verification of deliverables	Final deliverable review

Figure 2.2 Graphical depiction of AVPM Lifecycle Phases with Integrated Iterative and Agile Methods

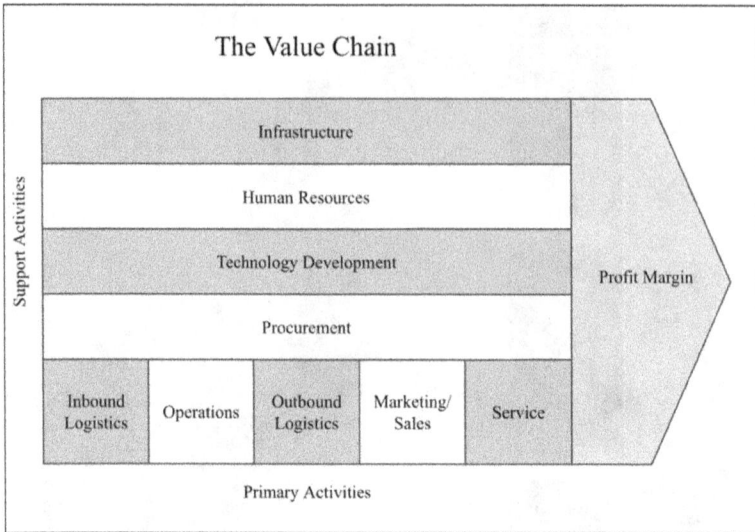

Figure 2.3 Graphical depiction of the Value Chain Model for Operations

a profitable operation. From inspection of the value chain model, it is observed that the primary activities that result in profit are those focused on the reception of components from the supply chain, the construction of product and service deliverables through the means of the operation, the delivery of such products and services, and, finally, the outreach and connection to the customer via sales, marketing, and service.

The remaining activities found within an organization support the flow of inputs from suppliers, the efficient execution of operational work, and deliveries. These support activities involve acquiring and managing people, developing suppliers, creating new technologies that ultimately find their place in products and services, and, finally, the underlying infrastructure upon which the organization relies.

The Project Value Chain

Like an ongoing operation, a project receives inputs, performs value-added work on the inputs to the process, and then provides the project deliverables to the client. The primary difference in such a value chain is that it models activities that are temporary and unique. If a project were modeled as a value chain, what would it look like? A comparison of project management processes from the PMBOK with those present in an operation results in the following example (see Figure 2.4).

Given that a project is temporary and highly focused on producing specific and tangible deliverables in the short term, the focus is on identifying and vetting requirements and converting requirements to in-depth plans associated with scope, schedule, and budget. Doing the work requires resources, and keeping the project on track involves significant risk management actions. Finally, the extent to which the deliverables meet the client requirements is a function of quality management. It could be said then that the specific activities associated with producing client deliverables and ensuring that they meet client requirements within the scope, schedule, and budget stipulation are primary activities.

As may be observed in the following diagram (Figure 2.5), unlike the operational value chain primary activities that emphasize the ongoing throughput of products and services, the project's primary activities support the creation of unique and one-time-only deliverables.

The generic PMBOK-centric project value chain model has the benefit of being tightly focused on the production of deliverables. The question arises, "Why isn't this model sufficient for use within the aviation project environment?" In fact, this value chain model could support any form of project.

However, a project value chain model tailored to the unique needs of the aviation industry would include primary and supporting activities that a generic model would miss.

Explaining the Need for the Aviation Project Value Chain

While there is no doubt that scope, schedule, and budget are key primary project activities, all three of the components of the traditional triple constraint are impacted by aviation industry constraints and unique needs.

To begin with, the schedule of an aviation project will naturally depend upon the lifecycle required by the project. Some aviation projects such as aviation software and systems projects will benefit from an iterative lifecycle. Others are best supported by plan-driven projects. The schedule will therefore vary between one that involves a single integrated plan versus one that involves multiple iterations or sprints.

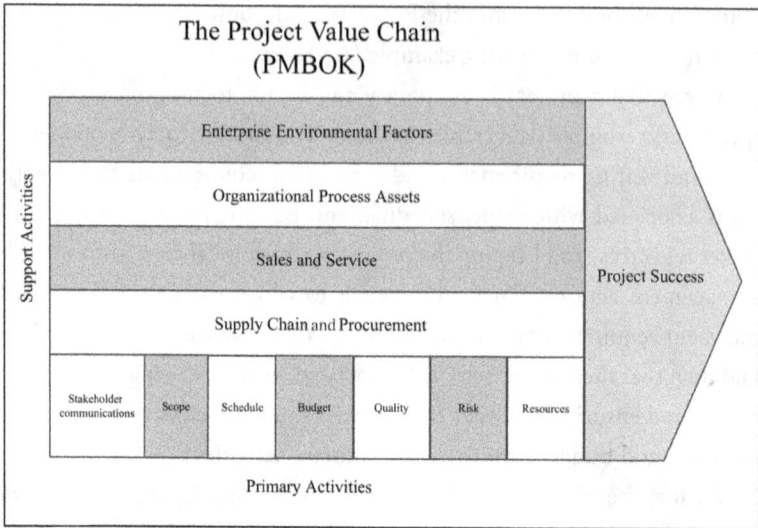

Figure 2.4 Graphical depiction of a Project Management Process compared with an Operational Value Chain (PMBOK-centric)

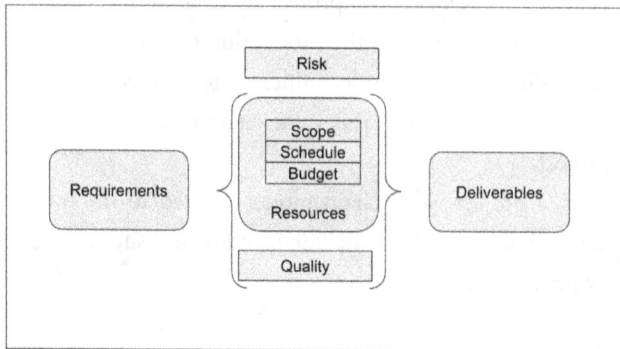

Figure 2.5 Graphical depiction of a Generic PMBOK-centric Project Value Chain Model emphasizing Primary Activities for Unique Deliverables

The lifecycle therefore informs the overall schedule management process. The importance of the lifecycle decision in aviation projects suggests the need for a specific lifecycle management practice that provides guidance on various lifecycle options as well as criteria for making lifecycle decisions.

The scope, schedule, and budget are also impacted by the project requirements. This is true of any project, but the vast number and range of requirements originating from the many stakeholder groups within this

The Aviation Project Value Chain

Support Activities	Innovation and Research Management						
	Supply Chain and Procurement Management						
	Aviation Safety and Compliance Management						
	Technical and Engineering Management						
	Aviation Quality Assurance Management						Project Success
	Aviation Regulatory and Certification Management						
	Environmental and Sustainability Management						
	Lifecycle Management	Requirements Management	Schedule Management	Stakeholder and Customer Relations	Risk and Safety Management	Financial Management	HR and Team Management

Primary Activities

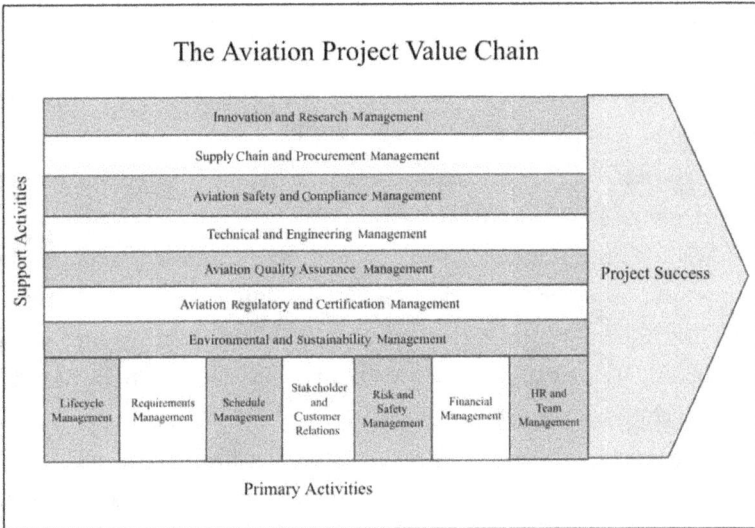

Figure 2.6 Graphical depiction of how Project Lifecycle Decisions and Requirements Impact Scope, Schedule, and Budget

industry require expertise in requirements elicitation as well as transforming requirements into scope elements that may be traced to the underlying needs of the client (Figure 2.6).

The project budget is also affected by project requirements as well as the project schedule. Yet, aviation projects are typically very expensive, requiring the additional focus on the financial component of the project rather than the singular focus of everyday projects on the project budget.

Primary Versus Supporting Activities

In the traditional operations view of the value chain, the primary activities are those associated with the throughput that generates the value or profit for the operation. Supporting activities provide the ecosystem—or policy, procedure, and longtime operational framework—to support the primary value-added activities. In the project value chain, the primary activities are those carried out within the project team itself. In the context of earlier versions of the PMBOK, these activities are outlined in a table of knowledge areas that, in addition to scope, schedule, and budget, include quality, risk, stakeholder, communication, and resource plans. In addition to such primary activities, project teams require supporting activities in which the project team draws upon the extended organization to successfully complete. In terms of the PMBOK, such supporting activities are not necessarily spelled out but are referred to generically as "Enterprise Environmental Factors" (EEF) as well as "Organizational Process Assets" (OPA) and Sales, Service, and Supply Chain development (see Figure 2.7).

Aviation operations do things that continue indefinitely and are not temporary like projects—yet they are complex, intensive, and comprehensive. Rather than refer to such supporting activities implicitly, it is useful to explicitly identify supporting activities that are essential to the project. These include developing supply chains and vendors, creating and continuously improving quality systems, navigating the aviation regulatory and certification environment, incorporating innovation and resources, and environmental and sustainability concerns. The AVPM primary and supporting elements are compared to the PMBOK in Figure 2.8.

Given the extensive activities pursued by the ongoing operation for the long term, and the need for the project team to interact with the extended organization during the project, the primary and supporting activities in the project value chain are clearly delineated in the AVPM framework. It is further clarified that the project team produces primary

The PMBOK:
Scope, Schedule, & and Budget Is the Essence

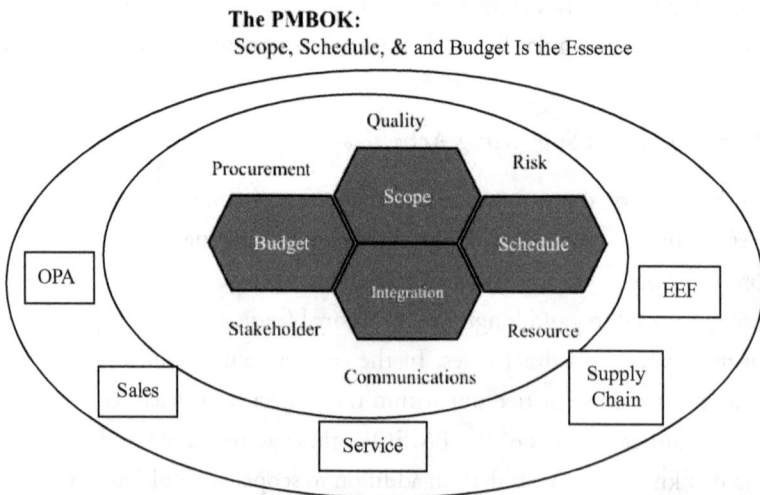

Figure 2.7 *Graphical depiction of PMBOK Supporting Activities (EEF, OPA, Sales, Service, Supply Chain)*

The AVPM:
Requirements, Lifecycle, Finance, and Schedule Is the Essence

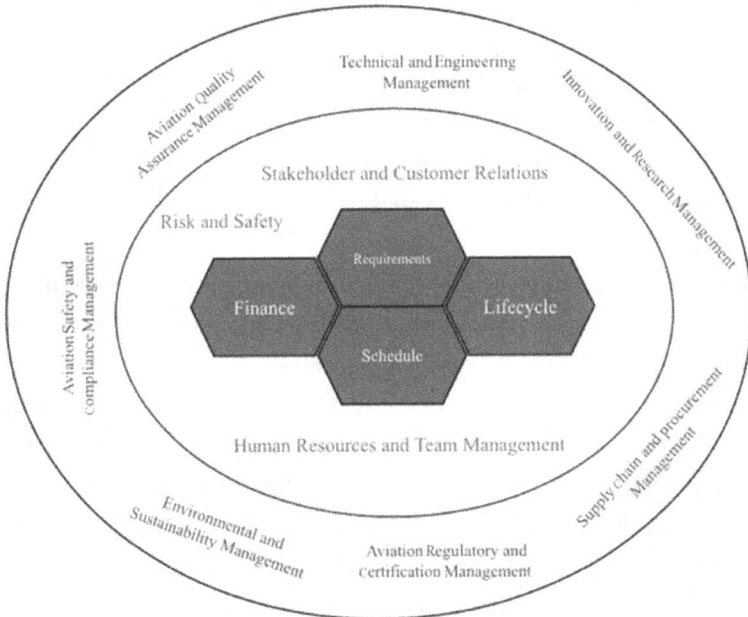

Figure 2.8 Graphical depiction of the Comparison between PMBOK Knowledge Areas and AVPM Primary and Supporting Practices

deliverables itself whereas the collaboration between the project team and the extended organization is managed through a series of checklists designed for this purpose.

Activities as Practices

The earlier versions of the PMBOK referred to groups of related activities carried out in phases of the project as "knowledge areas." The knowledge areas continued through the sixth edition of the PMBOK as well as the practice guide for project management processes. The knowledge areas are taken together as a group, and no distinction is made between primary and supporting activities. The knowledge areas are given as follows:

1. Project Integration Management
2. Project Scope Management

3. Project Schedule Management
4. Project Cost Management
5. Project Quality Management
6. Project Resource Management
7. Project Risk Management
8. Project Communication Management
9. Project Procurement Management
10. Project Stakeholder Management

Knowledge areas outline what is to be done throughout the lifecycle of the project. The knowledge areas include guidance and processes for essential project work. While important and useful for carrying out the work of the project, project managers do not only need to possess knowledge about critical activities but, instead, apply knowledge and continually develop and improve the processes employed in the project. It is for this reason that the AVPM framework has adopted the concept of "practices" versus knowledge areas to guide the work of aviation project managers.

While every organization manages practices in different ways, it is common for practices to be led by subject-matter experts who are able to define, implement, and improve processes surrounding a given practice. Such "practice leads" monitor and optimize processes associated with their respective practice, seek to incorporate knowledge associated with practices within the organization for the long term, and, finally, act as consultants for their practice within the organization. Practice leads in the AVPM would therefore act as a source of "expert judgment"—a concept applied throughout all processes outlined in the PMBOK and noted implicitly in the AVPM. Practices and their associated management are therefore critical to management and optimization of essential processes.

The Aviation Project Management Framework Practices

The AVPM features 14 practices—seven of them associated with the primary lane of the AVPM value chain and another seven relating to supporting activities of the AVPM value chain. Each practice is defined by a succinct outline that lists key elements to inform project managers about what is to be carried out throughout the project. The practice guides are reinforced by templates and checklists that direct the work to be completed within each phase of the lifecycle. The primary practices are supported by templates reflecting the deliverables to be developed by the project team. In contrast, the supporting practices feature checklists for each phase. This is because the working assumption is that supporting practices involve significant interaction and collection of deliverables from the extended organization. For this reason, checklists aid in ensuring that none of the deliverables from the extended organization are missing and that all are fully integrated by the project team. The 14 practices organized by primary and supporting activities are presented in Figure 2.9.

In AVPM projects, practice templates and checklists clarify specific activities and deliverables that are produced within each phase. It is of interest to note that unlike the PMBOK, some activity is required by each AVPM practice within each phase. By way of contrast, note that there are only two knowledge areas that come into play in project initiation—Integration Management with the project charter, and Stakeholder Management with the requirement to identify stakeholders. None of the other knowledge areas are applied within project initiation. On the

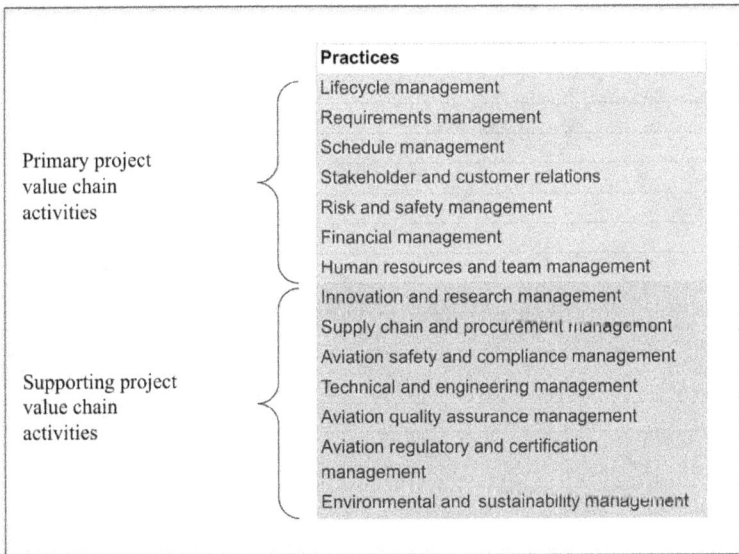

Figure 2.9 Graphical depiction of the 14 AVPM Practices Organized by Primary and Supporting Activities

other hand, is it realistic to assume that project managers take no action at all when it comes to the remaining eight knowledge areas? In practice, some activity, at least implicitly, occurs in all knowledge areas in every PMBOK process group. The AVPM makes each practice-related activity explicit in all phases. This helps ensure that no practice is missed and that all practice activities are documented throughout all project phases.

Finally, the practice guide succinctly sums up high-level guidance for each practice that unfolds into highly detailed templates and checklists that guide the hand of the project team within each phase.

This is a departure from the PMBOK in that PMBOK knowledge areas unfold as prescribed in each phase and have no foundational master document governing each knowledge area (see Figure 2.10).

Practice guides therefore outline the basic processes, activities, and deliverables, whereas the phase-specific practice templates and checklists support the details. The following overview of lifecycle phases explains the rationale of the lifecycle framework and points to the specific issues that each primary and supporting practice seeks to address.

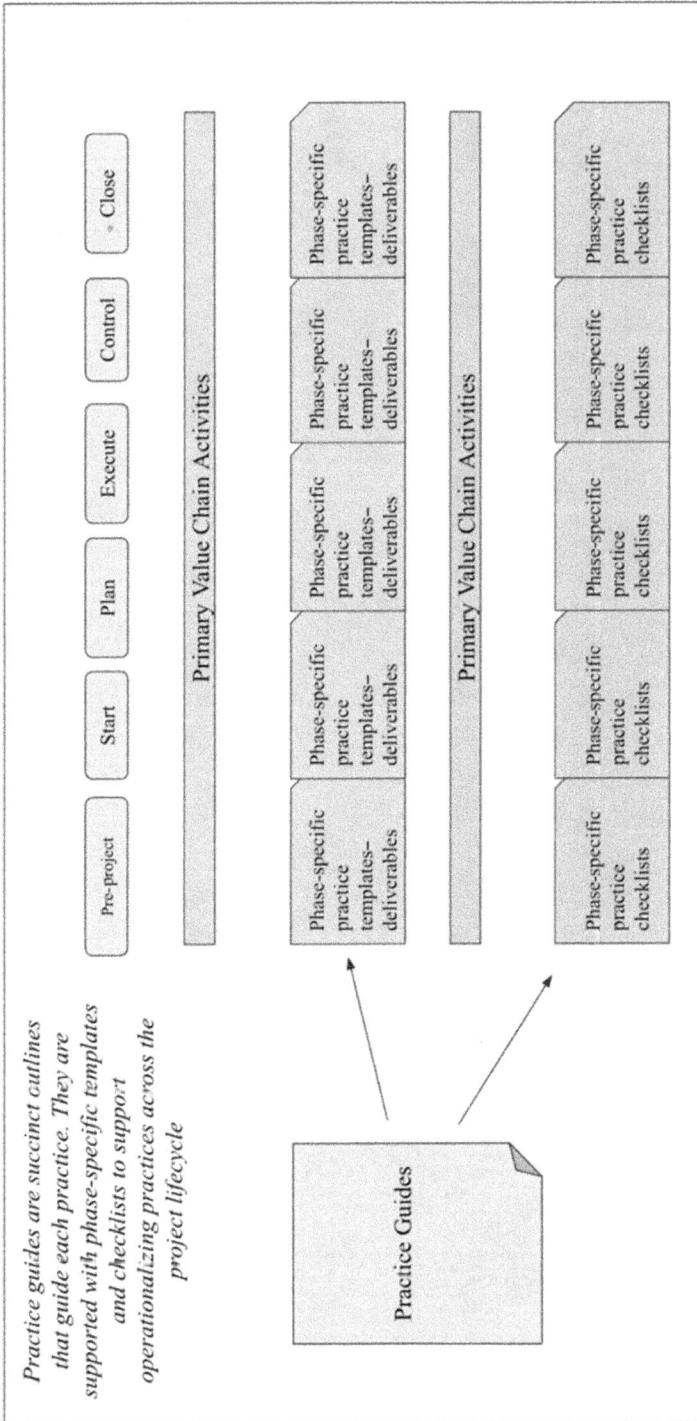

Figure 2.10 Graphical depiction of the AVPM Practice Guide Structure compared with PMBOK Knowledge Area Structure

CHAPTER 3

In What Order? Phases of a Project

There are 14 practices in the AVPM; while each of these unfolds in every phase, a question arises regarding where to start. That is, which practice activity should be carried out first, which should be last, and, finally, "Does it matter?" The answer to this question—like many in life—is "It depends." For example, the pre-project phase involves laying the groundwork for the project prior to its start. Much of this early work is strategic in nature as the early preparation involves the assessment of internal capabilities as well as alignment of the project with the long-term direction of the organization. Since there is no immediate need for detailed scope, schedule, and budget at this juncture, the project team and the organization may consider focusing first on what is deemed to be most important depending upon the nature of the project. Once the project starts, the practices could be thought of, by way of analogy, as a funnel that provides many elements, deliverables, and milestones that result in the project scope, schedule, and budget. The beginning of the project therefore shifts the focus from activities that are more operational in scope rather than strategic. When the project winds down in the close phase, the focus shifts once again to the long term as reports are filed, lessons learned are captured, and thought turns to determining how to incorporate what was learned in the project into the ongoing optimization of the practices. Again, the order in which each practice is employed is not strictly specified and is based on the needs of the project and the organization,

Figure 3.1 illustrates how the focus prior to the start of the project as well as at the end is more strategic in emphasis. Planning, executing, and control are more focused on operational matters. The strategic versus operational component of each phase may be used to inform the order in which each practice is applied.

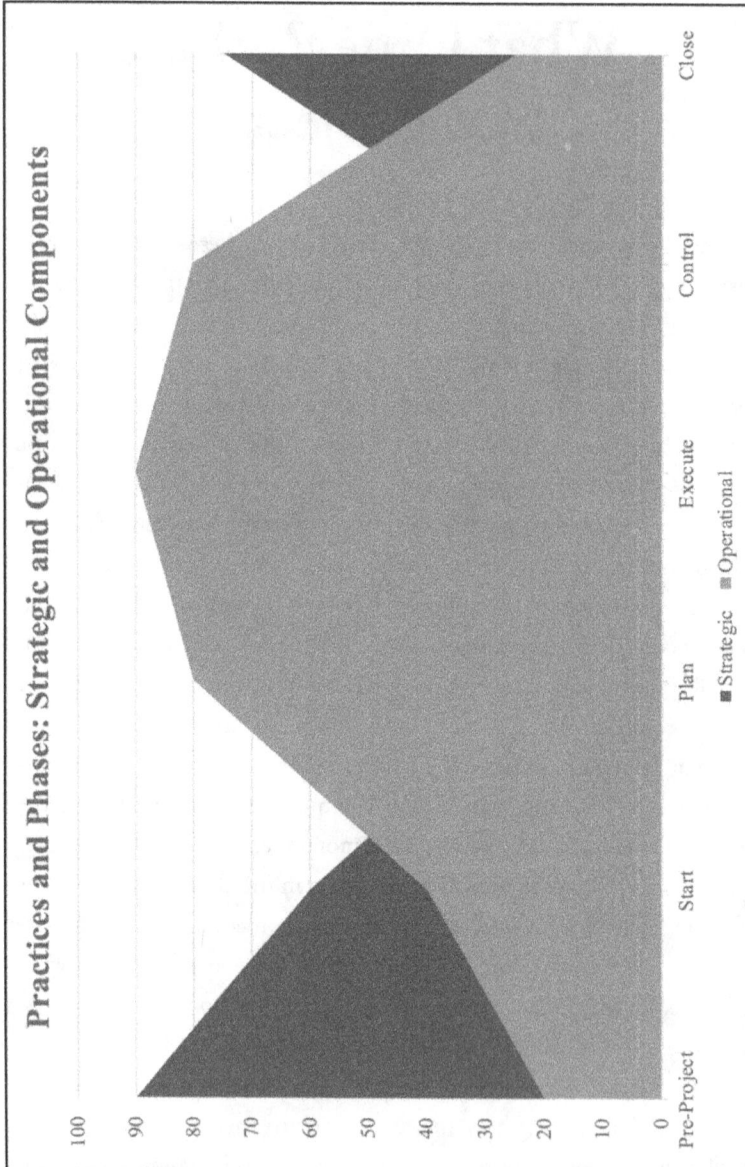

Figure 3.1 Graphical depiction of Strategic versus Operational Focus across AVPM Project Lifecycle Phases

This doesn't imply that all 14 practices no longer apply in the planning and executing phase. Rather, the practices could be viewed in terms of yielding additional requirements to be planned, executed, and controlled. This is illustrated in Figure 3.2 along with a suggested order of practice implementation based upon strategic versus operational focus.

There may be cases where specific practices may only be tangentially required for the work at hand. However, if this is determined to be the case, the practice guide and template should at a minimum be reviewed with any decisions on what activities are not carried out, noted, and logged. This does, on the other hand, raise the question of "under what circumstances would one consider not implementing a practice deliverable or checklist?" In some cases, the work associated with a specific practice may have already been completed—the practice template or checklist may be used to confirm this. In other cases, the scale of the project may be sufficiently small that some practices may not be necessary or only partially necessary. Resource constraints or the lack of process maturity may result in limited or partial implementation of a practice. Finally, regulatory or contractual constraints may mandate the full completion of a practice. Practices, in any case, are essential components of managing aviation projects so the implementation of each within each phase must be carefully considered.

The Pre-Project Phase

As referenced earlier in the example of the first-time aviation project manager, before a project starts there is much that an organization must consider and for which the organization must prepare.

Specifically, there are many questions that need to be answered, and these include the following along with elaboration:

1. *Should this project be selected?*
   Project selection techniques are described in detail in the PMBOK. The same techniques may be applied to aviation projects. However, the scale of aviation projects as well as the intensity and risk make project selection an even more important activity than what might be required in projects of lesser impact. See graphical depiction of Project Selection Practice Template (Figure 3.3).

Pre-Project	Start	Plan	Execute	Control	Close
Innovation	Innovation	Lifecycle	Lifecycle	Lifecycle	Requirements
Safety & Compliance	Safety & Compliance	Stakeholder	Stakeholder	Stakeholder	Regulatory & Certification
Regulatory & Certification	Regulatory & Certification	*Requirements*	*Requirements*	*Requirements*	Stakeholder
Environmental	Environmental	Schedule	Schedule	Schedule	Financial
Supply Chain & Procurement	Supply Chain & Procurement	HR & Team	HR & Team	HR & Team	HR & Team
Quality	Quality	Financial	Financial	Financial	Innovation
Technical & Engineering	Technical & Engineering	Risk & Safety	Risk & Safety	Risk & Safety	Safety & Compliance
Stakeholder and Customer	Stakeholder and Customer	Supply Chain & Procurement	Supply Chain & Procurement	Supply Chain & Procurement	Environmental
Requirements	Requirements				Supply Chain & Procurement
Lifecycle	Lifecycle				Quality
Financial	Financial				Technical & Engineering
Risk & Safety	Risk & Safety				Lifecycle
HR & Team	HR & Team				Risk & Safety
Schedule	Schedule				Schedule

Primary

Supporting

Scope, activities, milestones

→ *Requirements*

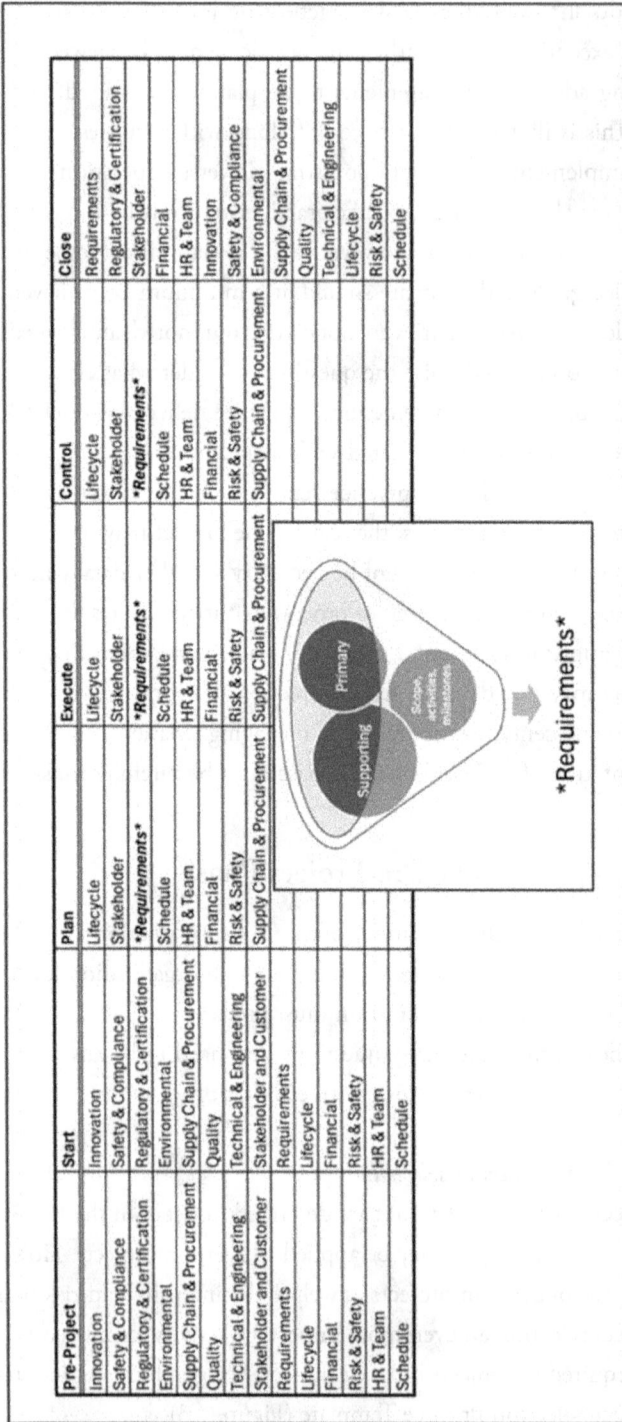

Figure 3.2 Graphical depiction of the Suggested Order of AVPM Practice Implementation by Phase, based on Strategic versus Operational Focus

Project Selection Guide

Document Title: [Title] I Project Name: [Project] I Document ID: [ID] I Prepared by: [Name] I Date: [Date] I Approval: [Name]

Project Candidates

Project A [Description]	Project B [Description]	Additional Projects

Strategic Evaluation	Feasibility Assessment
1. Strategic Alignment	1. Technical Feasibility
- Long-term goals	- Technology requirements
- Business offerings	- Infrastructure needs
2. Market Analysis	2. Economic Feasibility
- Customer demand	- Cost–analysis
- Value proposition	- Financial returns
3. Financial Assessment	3. Operational Feasibility
- Cost–benefit analysis	- Resource availability
- ROI evaluation	- Process requirements
4. Risk Profile	4. Schedule Feasibility
- Risk identification	- Timeline analysis
- Mitigation strategies	- Milestone planning
5. Competitive Position	5. Legal/Regulatory
- Market advantage	- Compliance requirements
- Industry positioning	- Required approvals

Scoring Scale: 1-5 for each criterion I Final selection based on cumulative evaluation

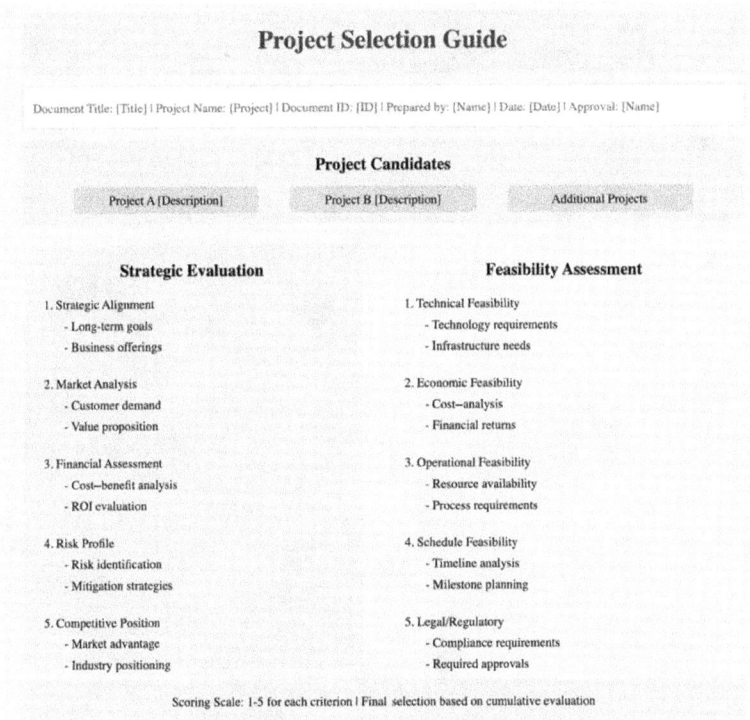

Figure 3.3 Graphical depiction of Project Selection Practice Template

2. *What kind of lifecycle will need to be chosen for the given project?*
   The type of project signals what lifecycle should be employed for managing the project. Most aviation product development and construction projects for example would likely be managed using a plan-driven lifecycle. This is due to the difficulty of breaking the project into iterative cycles where functionality and feature sets are evaluated by the client. Aviation software and systems projects on the other hand might be more likely to adopt an iterative lifecycle. MRO (Maintenance, Repair, and Overhaul) projects might fall somewhere in the middle depending upon the nature of the work as well as the respective software and systems components— particularly because software and systems projects lend themselves to an iterative approach. See graphical depiction of Lifecycle Selection Template (Figure 3.4).

Lifecycle Selection Template

Document Title: [Title] | Project Name: [Project] | Document ID: [ID] | Prepared by: [Name] | Date: [Date] | Approval: [Name]

Lifecycle Options

W ——— A ——— I ——— H
Waterfall   Agile   Iterative   Hybrid

Lifecycle Assumptions

1. Project Scope and Requirements
   - Well-defined and stable scope
   - Clear goals and deliverables

2. Team Composition
   - Team size and structure
   - Required skillsets

3. Stakeholder Involvement
   - Availability and engagement
   - Participation commitment

4. Time and Budget
   - Schedule constraints
   - Resource availability

5. Technical Requirements
   - Project complexity
   - Technical constraints

Selection Criteria

1. Project Complexity
   - Technical complexity level
   - Integration requirements

2. Stakeholder Engagement
   - Communication needs
   - Feedback frequency

3. Change Management
   - Flexibility requirements
   - Adaptation capability

4. Delivery Timeline
   - Schedule constraints
   - Milestone requirements

5. Governance
   - Control mechanisms
   - Reporting requirements

Note: Evaluate each lifecycle option against these criteria to determine the most suitable approach.

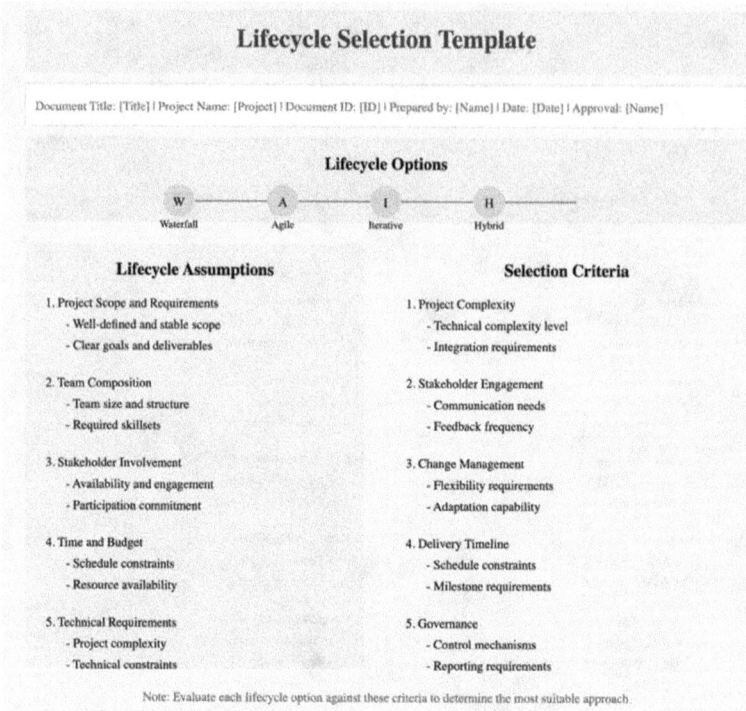

Figure 3.4 Graphical depiction of Lifecycle Selection Template

3. *What sources for the project requirements must be considered?*
   Aviation projects face a wide array of requirements including internal, external, clients, and significant stakeholder groups in between. While requirements are part of planning and required for developing the scope and schedule—the time right before the project actually begins is an important time to identify the requirements sources so that requirements are not left out and an appreciation for the overall scale of the requirements is developed. See graphical depiction of Requirements Sources Template (Figure 3.5).

4. *What is a reasonable ballpark estimate for budget and schedule?*
   Budgets and schedules are never complete until significant associated planning has taken place. Most project costs arise from the assignment of project resources. However, resources are not assigned until the project scope is developed and activities are defined and sequences. None of these activities take place prior to the start of

Sources of Requirements Document Template

Project: [Name] | Document ID: [ID] | Prepared by: [Name] | Date: [Date] | Approval: [Name]

Document Purpose

- Project Overview   • Requirements Scope   • Expected Outcomes

Direct Input

Internal Sources   **Sources of Requirements Collection**   External Sources

Primary Sources   **Requirements Framework**

1. Stakeholder Input   1. Categorization
   • Interviews   • Functional Requirements
   • Workshops   • Nonfunctional Requirements

2. Documentation   2. Regulatory Compliance
   • RFP Details   • Aviation Standards
   • Technical Specs   • Legal Requirements

3. Historical Data   3. Validation Process
   • Past Projects   • Priority Criteria
   • Lessons Learned   • Stakeholder Review

4. Market Analysis   4. Documentation
   • Industry Standards   • Requirements Baseline
   • Customer Needs   • Supporting Appendices

Approval: Prepared by [Name] | Reviewed by [Name] | Approved by [Name]

Figure 3.5 Graphical depiction of Requirements Sources Template

the project—so the best that can be done is to perform a high-level "ballpark" or Rough Order of Magnitude (ROM) estimate. While a ROM budget misses significant detail, it does provide an idea of the scale of the project. This is important information to consider prior to the start of the project.

For example, if it is determined that the project is only a $10,000 project rather than a $1,000,000 project, this provides guidance for how the organization should prepare accordingly for the overall scale of the project, financing, and cash flow. See graphical depiction of ROM Budget Estimate Template (Figure 3.6) and graphical depiction of ROM Schedule Estimate Template (Figure 3.7).

ROM Budget Estimate Framework

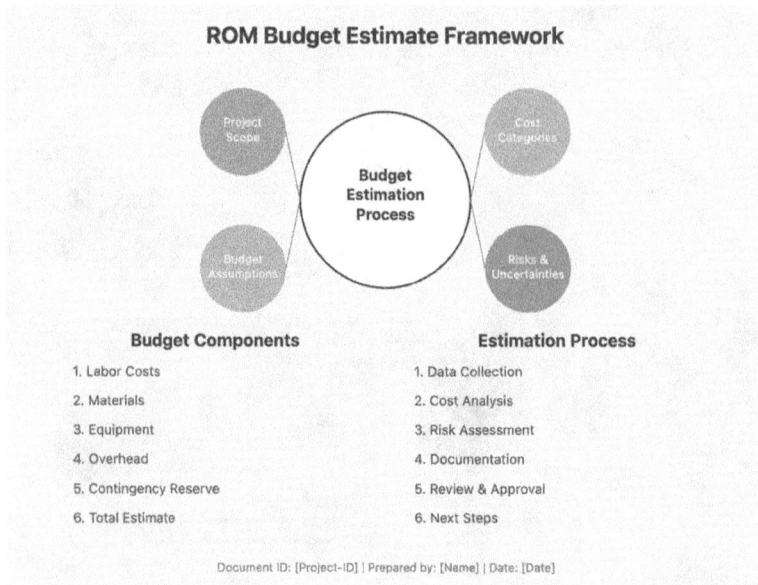

Budget Components	Estimation Process
1. Labor Costs	1. Data Collection
2. Materials	2. Cost Analysis
3. Equipment	3. Risk Assessment
4. Overhead	4. Documentation
5. Contingency Reserve	5. Review & Approval
6. Total Estimate	6. Next Steps

Document ID: [Project-ID] | Prepared by: [Name] | Date: [Date]

Figure 3.6 Graphical depiction of ROM Budget Estimate Template

5. *What does the landscape of project stakeholders look like?*
   Prior to the start of a project, there is no need to identify and assess stakeholders. However, once the project begins, the project team will need to be aware of where to look for stakeholders who are relevant to the project. This is the stakeholder landscape—and defining this prior to the beginning of the project lays the foundation for effective stakeholder identification and assessment. See graphical depiction of Stakeholder Landscape Analysis Template (Figure 3.8).

6. *What innovations could be applied (or be expected to emerge) from this project?*
   The development and commercialization of innovation take time and tend to evolve in the background as projects come and go. Innovation is likely to involve components, technological platforms, processes, and new approaches to doing things. Prior to beginning a project, a crucial step is to consider what innovations are available and sufficiently mature that they may be of benefit to the project. The maturity of any given innovation is a serious concern within

ROM High-level Schedule Estimate

Project: [Name] | Document ID: [ID] | Prepared by: [Name] | Date: [Date] | Approval: [Name]

Project Overview

• Project Scope   • Key Objectives   • Deliverables

Phase Gates

Project Start

Schedule Estimation Framework

Project End

Timeline Components   **Estimation Framework**

1. Key Milestones   1. Assumptions
   • Phase Completions   • Resource Planning
   • Critical Points   • Availability

2. Dependencies   2. Risk Assessment
   • Task Relations   • Schedule Risks
   • External Factors   • Contingencies

3. Duration Estimates   3. Confidence Levels
   • Phase Lengths   • Estimate Accuracy
   • Overall Timeline   • Uncertainty Factors

4. Constraints   4. Review Process
   • Time Limitations   • Stakeholder Input
   • Resource Bounds   • Revision History

Approval: Prepared by [Name] | Reviewed by [Name] | Approved by [Name]

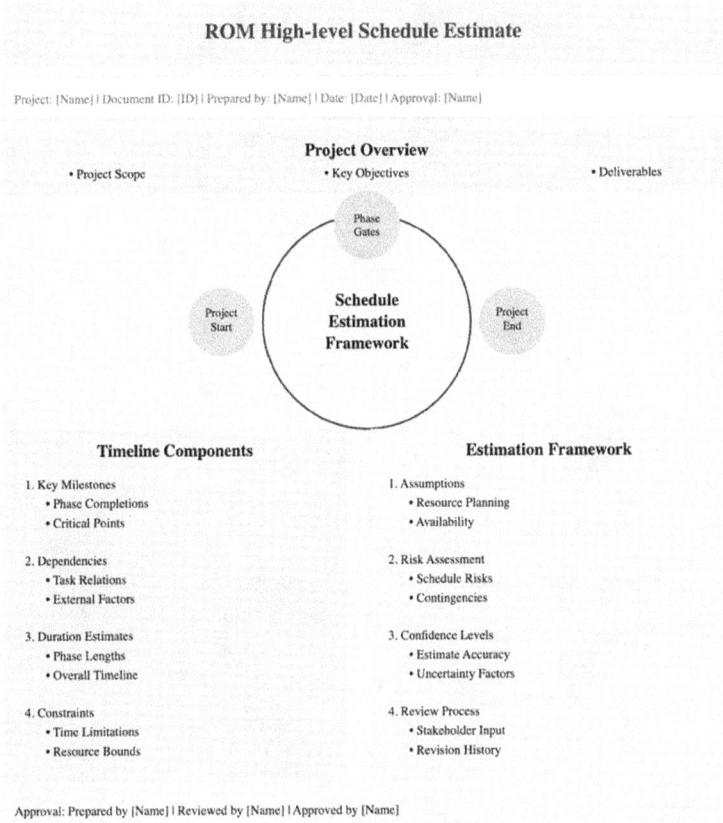

Figure 3.7 Graphical depiction of ROM Schedule Estimate Template

the aviation industry. Projects that produce deliverables with unproven technologies could raise safety and risk concerns, and this is why innovations are to be evaluated conservatively.

In addition to considering innovations to employ within the project, it is important to recognize that some innovations emerge from the project itself. The focus on innovation therefore involves both the application of innovation and the capture of innovations that may be forthcoming from a project. Finally, in addition to commercializing innovation, the protection of innovation and the organization is also a concern. It would be desirable to patent innovations applied to aviation projects. Furthermore, it is also important to seek to avoid infringing on existing patents from other

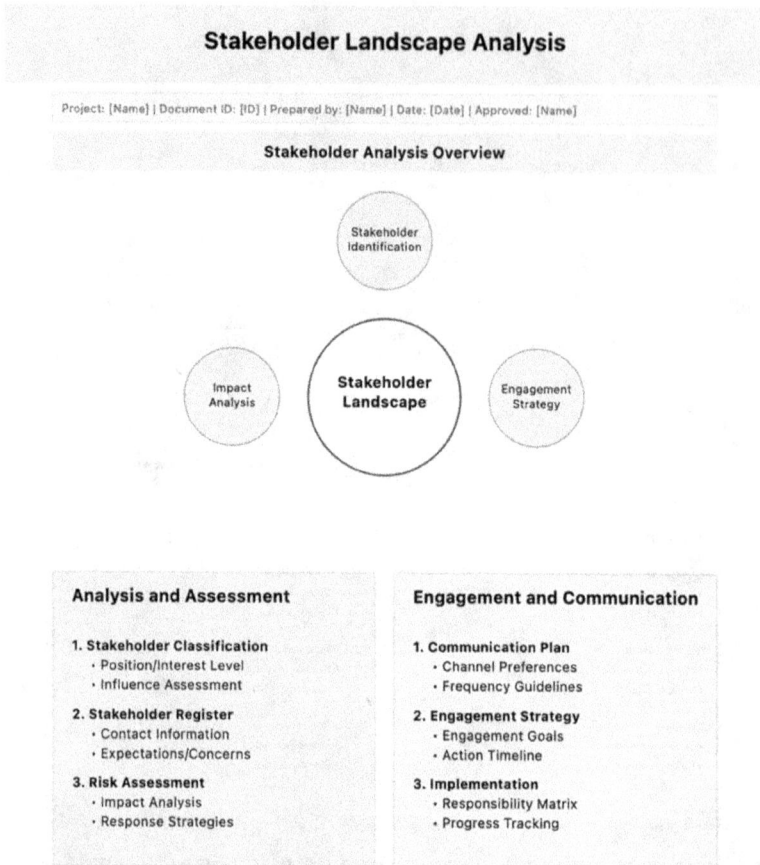

Figure 3.8 *Graphical depiction of Stakeholder Landscape Analysis Template*

organizations as innovation is developed and applied. See graphical depiction of Technology Needs Deliverables checklist (Figure 3.9).

7. *What is the overall risk level involved in the project, and is our risk appetite compatible?*

Projects within the aviation industry are fraught with risks, and, prior to making the decision to accept and begin work on the project, the project team must consider whether the organization is able to handle the risks associated with the project. While in-depth risk identification and assessment is not done until after the project begins, at minimum, the project team must characterize the level of risk at a high level and consider whether such risks align with the

Technology Needs Deliverable

Document ID | Project Name | Prepared by | Date

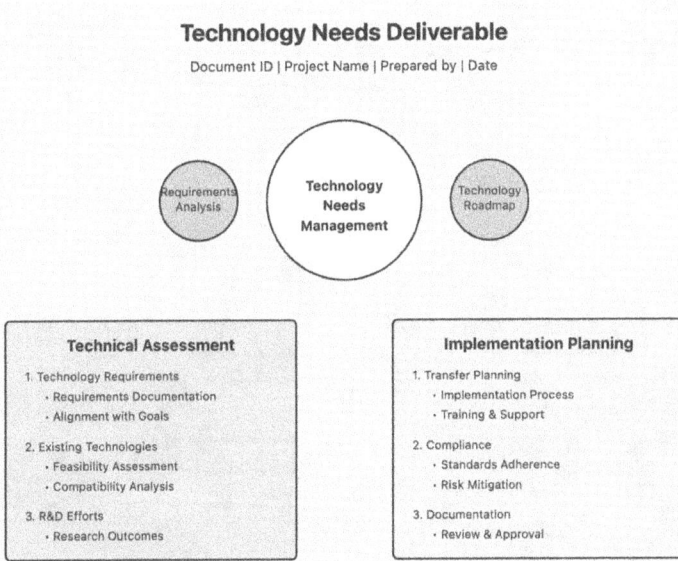

Technical Assessment

1. Technology Requirements
   - Requirements Documentation
   - Alignment with Goals

2. Existing Technologies
   - Feasibility Assessment
   - Compatibility Analysis

3. R&D Efforts
   - Research Outcomes

Implementation Planning

1. Transfer Planning
   - Implementation Process
   - Training & Support

2. Compliance
   - Standards Adherence
   - Risk Mitigation

3. Documentation
   - Review & Approval

Figure 3.9 Graphical depiction Technology Needs Deliverables Checklist

risk appetite of the larger organization. See graphical depiction of Historical Data and Risk Appetite Analysis Template (Figure 3.10).

8. *Should we make or buy critical components? And, if the answer is "buy," what does the supplier landscape look like?*

Project deliverables involve significant hardware and software components. It is an important step prior to the beginning of the project to perform a high-level assessment of what critical components will be required. Upon consideration of key components, the next step is to consider their source. If the required components are currently available, which suppliers are best able to support the delivery of such components at the appropriate time and costs— with acceptable quality? In the case of many available suppliers, the supplier landscape is captured so that the list of possible suppliers is ready for a possible Request for Proposal (RFP). The possibility also exists that required components could be developed in-house. The decision to use a supplier versus developing components in-house is referred to as a "make-or-buy" decision. It may be tempting to

Historical Data and Risk Appetite Analysis

Historical
Data

**Risk
Management**

Risk
Appetite

Historical Analysis

1. Data Collection Process

2. Safety Incidents Review

3. Industry Standards

4. Previous Projects

5. Lessons Learned

Risk Assessment

1. Risk Level Evaluation

2. Appetite Definition

3. Response Strategy

4. Communication Plan

5. Stakeholder Engagement

Low Risk   Medium Risk   High Risk

Document ID: [ID] | Prepared by: [Name] | Date: [Date] | Approved by: [Name]

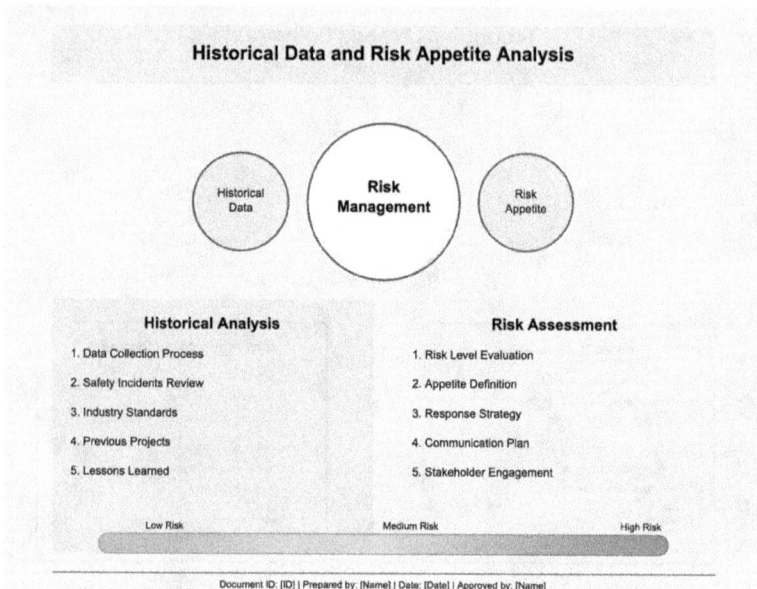

*Figure 3.10 Graphical depiction of Historical Data and Risk Appetite
Analysis Template*

consider in-house development to attempt to save money or to employ internal intellectual property in an important component. Internal development decisions should not be taken lightly as internal
development inevitably tends to take more time and money than
initially considered. Furthermore, the landscape of suppliers who
produce the required components likely sell to many others and, in
doing so, may employ various cost reduction efforts and integrate
an array of technical requirements from many different clients.
Given this likely scenario, the benefits of using outside sources may
outweigh the cost of purchase. Also, the complete package of cost
and benefits will likely be difficult to beat when developed for the
first time internally. See graphical depiction of Make/Buy/Supplier
Landscape Checklist (Figure 3.11).

9. *What is the current landscape of safety standards?*
Safety standards govern both the deliverables of the project and the
oversight of the work environment used to produce project deliverables. Standards change over time, and, as well, different categories

Make/Buy/Supplier Landscape Framework

Project Requirements

Market Analysis

Make/Buy Decision Framework

Cost Analysis

Risk Assessment

Internal Manufacturing

1. Production Capacity
2. Technical Expertise
3. Quality Control
4. Lead Time Analysis
5. Resource Allocation
6. Cost Structure

Supplier Engagement

1. Supplier Qualification
2. Contract Management
3. Supplier Performance
4. Supply Chain Risk
5. Legal Compliance
6. Strategic Alignment

Document ID: [Project-ID] | Prepared by: [Name] | Date: [Date]

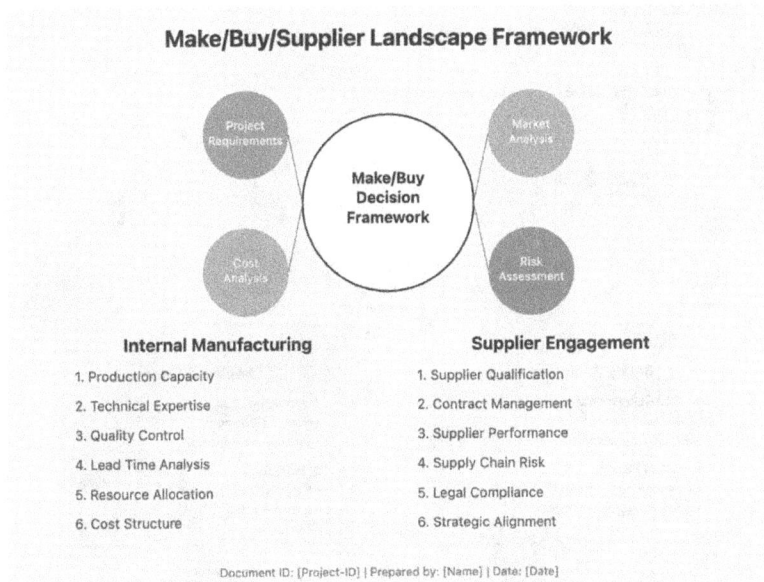

Figure 3.11 Graphical depiction of Make/Buy/Supplier Landscape Checklist

of projects may be impacted by safety standards more than others. Safety is a critical matter in aviation projects, so evaluating the landscape of safety standards prior to the start of the project is essential. It is for this reason that the risk and safety management practice is given consideration in the pre-project phase of the AVPM lifecycle. See graphical depiction of Safety Standards Landscape Checklist (Figure 3.12).

10. *Do we understand our talent needs for this project?*
   Project planning includes the assignment of resources to activities to produce the deliverables outlined in the project scope. Before the project starts and project scope is fully elaborated, an important step is to consider the specialized skills that might be required in the project. This avoids the mistake of assuming that the existing resource base is fully capable of delivering the project. It may not be, so a deep consideration of talent needs is a priority prior to the start of the project. See graphical depiction of Talent Needs Assessment Template (Figure 3.13).

Safety Standards Landscape

Project Name | Document ID | Prepared by | Date | Approval

Safety Management

Safety Standards Framework

Regulatory Framework

Compliance Monitoring

Safety Requirements

1. SMS Components
• Risk Management
• Safety Assurance

2. Human Factors
• Training Requirements
• Competency Assessment

Implementation

1. Documentation
• Record Keeping
• Emergency Response

2. Monitoring
• Safety Audits
• Data Analysis

Approved: Prepared by [Name] | Reviewed by [Name] | Approved by [Name]

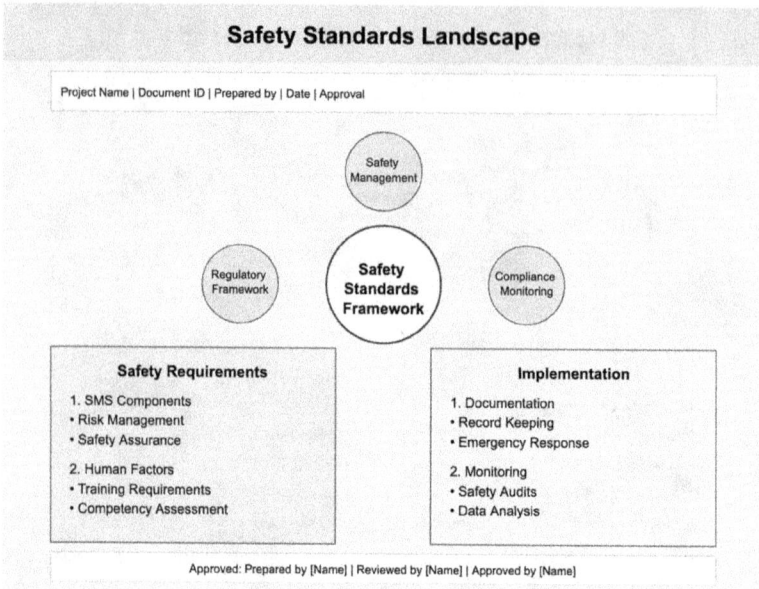

Figure 3.12 Graphical depiction of Safety Standards Landscape Checklist

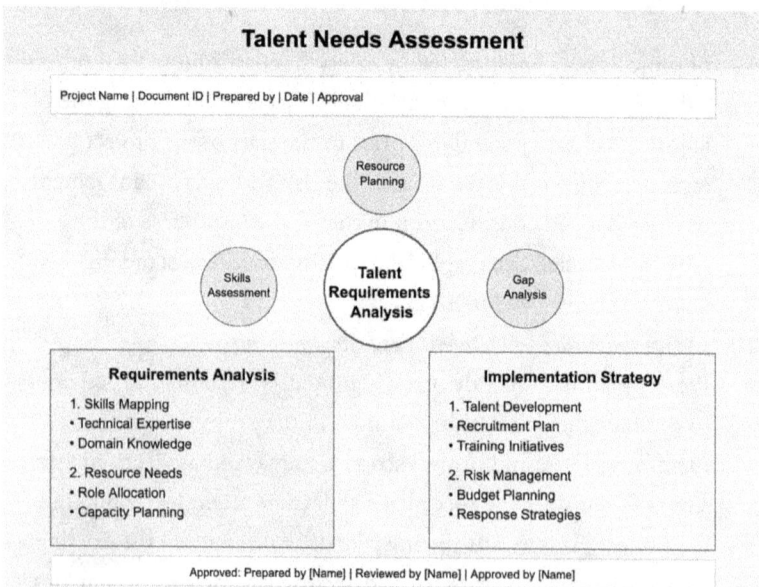

Talent Needs Assessment

Project Name | Document ID | Prepared by | Date | Approval

Resource Planning

Talent Requirements Analysis

Skills Assessment

Gap Analysis

Requirements Analysis

1. Skills Mapping
• Technical Expertise
• Domain Knowledge

2. Resource Needs
• Role Allocation
• Capacity Planning

Implementation Strategy

1. Talent Development
• Recruitment Plan
• Training Initiatives

2. Risk Management
• Budget Planning
• Response Strategies

Approved: Prepared by [Name] | Reviewed by [Name] | Approved by [Name]

Figure 3.13 Graphical depiction of Talent Needs Assessment Template

11. *What technology needs will we face in the upcoming project?*
Technologies in various forms will be required for any aviation project. Technologies that are very new could be classified as innovations and addressed within the innovation practice. Prior to the beginning of a project, it pays for the project team to consider what technologies are required for the project—as well as from where such technologies will be acquired. Specialized technologies may also be employed as part of the development process itself. Examples include special processes for handling or developing carbon fiber components or, in other cases, the use of 3D printers and unique production tools. The use of technologies often involves significant costs and specialized skill sets. These are reasons why technology needs are a concern for the aviation project prior to its beginning. See graphical depiction of Technology Assessment Management Checklist (Figure 3.14).

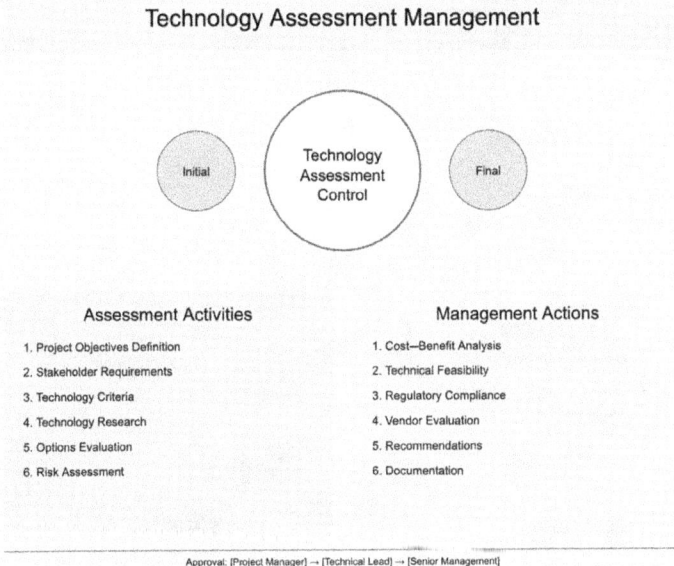

Technology Assessment Management

| Initial | Technology Assessment Control | Final |

Assessment Activities	Management Actions
1. Project Objectives Definition	1. Cost–Benefit Analysis
2. Stakeholder Requirements	2. Technical Feasibility
3. Technology Criteria	3. Regulatory Compliance
4. Technology Research	4. Vendor Evaluation
5. Options Evaluation	5. Recommendations
6. Risk Assessment	6. Documentation

Approval: [Project Manager] → [Technical Lead] → [Senior Management]

Figure 3.14 Graphical depiction of Technology Assessment Management Checklist

12. *How will quality be managed within the project?*
    Quality in aviation projects involves the focus on meeting the
    requirements of the client. Prior to the beginning of the project,
    the requirements are not yet known. However, what is important
    for managing quality prior to the start of the project is the con-
    sideration of the QMSs. By definition, projects are temporary and
    unique, so the QMS used by the project team may require some
    adaptation depending upon any new challenges associated with the
    project. This is one of the many concerns that lead to pre-project
    consideration of quality management. See graphical depiction of
    Quality Management Strategy Checklist (Figure 3.15).

13. *What regulatory concerns will be faced within the project?*
    The aviation industry is heavily regulated and requires detailed
    logs and reports to provide audit trails for auditing and certifica-
    tion purposes. The nature of what is being delivered will trigger
    relevant regulatory concerns. For example, a project that adds new
    hardware to an existing aircraft will involve the Federal Aviation

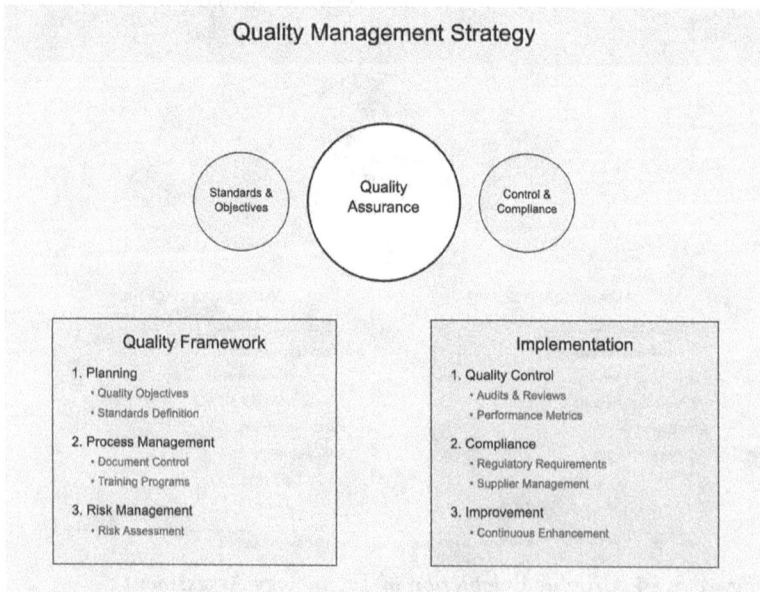

Figure 3.15 Graphical depiction of Quality Management Strategy Checklist

Administration (FAA). Furthermore, a project that involves avionics and radio technology will likely involve not only the FAA but the Federal Communication Commission (FCC). Often relevant approvals and certification takes time, effort, and specific milestones that will need to be included in the project schedule. For this reason, prior to the start of the project, the project team will seek to understand exactly what regulatory concerns will be faced by the project so that adequate preparation will ensue. See graphical depiction of Regulatory Landscape Checklist (Figure 3.16).

14. *What is the environmental impact of the project expected to be?*
Often aviation projects will take place within a highly industrial context. The project team as well as the company sponsoring the project will set the expectation that any work carried out will not negatively impact the environment. The deliverables of the project may also be of interest when it comes to factors such as fuel efficiency and emissions. Furthermore, the overall lifecycle of project deliverables from commissioning, to use, and to eventual decommissioning and disposal have environmental impact that should be

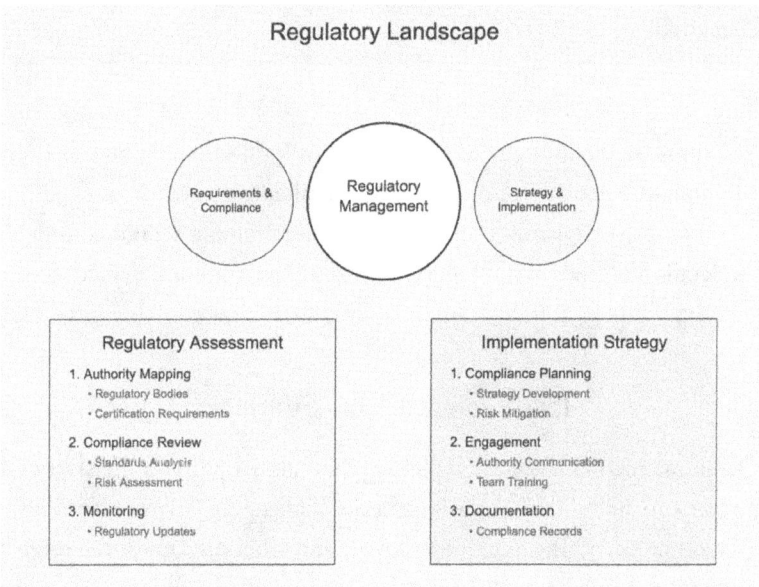

Figure 3.16 Graphical depiction of Regulatory Landscape Checklist

Environmental Impact Analysis Framework

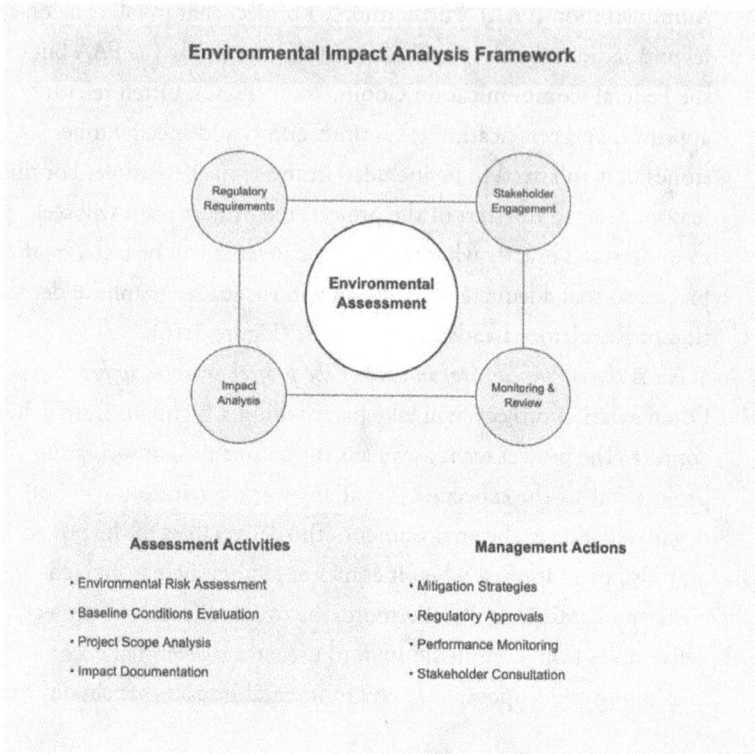

Figure 3.17 Graphical depiction of Environmental Impact Analysis Checklist

considered before the project begins. All projects could benefit from a pre-project environmental impact evaluation—but the scale and intensity of aviation projects lead to an even more serious consideration on the part of the project team. See graphical depiction of Environmental Impact Analysis Checklist (Figure 3.17).

Pre-Project Phase Summary

Questions such as these are typical of those asked prior to the start of a project and are more essential within the challenging environment of the aviation industry. The practice templates and Checklists guide the project manager through each of these questions so that the foundation of the project may be solidly established prior to the start of the project. On the face of it, this seems like quite a bit of work that is proposed to be done before the project even begins. While this may be true, it is also likely to be the case that many of these early activities get neglected, missed, or poorly documented. Spelling out each practice in detail ensures that this never happens. Furthermore, the unfolding of each practice in templates and checklists ensures a solid documentation foundation of the project. Finally, because all practices are templated, the burden on the project team is much less than the case of having to think of each practice and document each from scratch. The list of practices, templates, and checklists for the pre-project phase of the lifecycle are outlined in Figure 3.18.

The Start Phase

Once the groundwork for the project has been established, the project starts with kickoff activities tied to the AVPM practices. The following list outlines the key activities of the start phase of the AVPM lifecycle. It can be observed that there are 14 high-level activities in the start phase that correspond to each of the 14 practices.

1. *Begin the lifecycle selected in the pre-project phase*
   Once the project has been selected and the appropriate lifecycle determined, it is now the time to initiate the lifecycle and document assumptions and strategy for how the project lifecycle will be managed.

   Management practices are likely to differ based on the nature of the selected lifecycle and project deliverables. Nevertheless, it is important to document the assumptions associated with lifecycle management. See graphical depiction of Lifecycle Management Initiation Template (Figure 3.19).

2. *Collect requirements and statement of work*
   At the start of the project, the requirements collection process begins in earnest. In many cases, requirements will emerge naturally from a contractual statement of work or SOW. On the other hand, in spite of the details contained in the SOW, it is likely that significant discussion will be needed with the client to clarify details of the requirements. Furthermore, even with an SOW, there will

Practices	Pre-project
Practice Guide for Lifecycle Management in Aviation Project Management	Lifecycle Selection Template
AVPMPG-LM-1.000	AVPMP-LM-1.1
Practice Guide for Lifecycle Management in Aviation Project Management	Project Selection Template
AVPMPG-LM-1.000	AVPMP-LM-1.1.2
Practice Guide for Requirements Management in Aviation Project Management	Sources of Requirements Document Template
AVPMPG-RM-1.000	AVPMP-RM-1.1
Practice Guide for Schedule Management in Aviation Project Management	ROM High-Level Schedule Estimate Template
AVPMPG-SM-1.000	AVPMP-SM-1.1
Practice Guide for Stakeholder and Customer Relations Management in Aviation Project Management	Stakeholder Landscape Analysis Template
AVPMPG-ST-1.000	AVPMP-ST-1.1
Practice Guide for Risk and Safety Management in Aviation Project Management	Historical Data/Risk Level & Appetite Analysis Template
AVPMPG-RS-1.000	AVPMP-RS-1.1
Practice Guide for Financial Management in Aviation Project Management	Rough Order of Magnitude Budget Template
AVPMPG-FM-1.000	AVPMP-FM-1.1
Practice Guide for Human Resource and Team Management in Aviation Project Management	Talent Needs Assessment Template
AVPMPG-HR-1.000	AVPMP-HR-1.1
Practice Guide for Innovation and Research Management in Aviation Project Management	I&R Technology Needs Checklist
AVPMPGS-IR-1.000	AVPMS-IR-1.1
Practice Guide for Supply Chain and Procurement Management in Aviation Project Management	Make/Buy/Supplier Landscape Deliverable Checklist
AVPMPGS-SC-1.000	AVPMS-SC-1.1
Practice Guide for Aviation Safety Management in Aviation Project Management	Safety Standards Landscape Deliverable Checklist
AVPMPGS-AS-1.000	AVPMS-AS-1.1
Practice Guide for Technology and Engineering Management in Aviation Project Management	Technology Assessment Deliverable Checklist
AVPMPGS-TE-1.000	AVPMS-TE-1.1
Practice Guide for Aviation Quality Management in Aviation Project Management	Quality Management Strategy Deliverable Checklist
AVPMPGS-AQ-1.000	AVPMS-AQ-1.1
Practice Guide for Aviation Regulation Compliance and Certification Management in Aviation Project Management	Regulatory Landscape Deliverable Checklist
AVPMPGS-AR-1.000	AVPMS-AR-1.1
Practice Guide for Environmental and Sustainability Management in Aviation Project Management	Environmental Impact Analysis Checklist
AVPMPGS-ES-1.000	AVPMS-ES-1.1

Practices	Iterative Pre-Project
Practice Guide for Lifecycle Management in Aviation Project Management	Project Selection Deliverable Template for Iterative Lifecycle
AVPMIT-LM-1.1	
Practice Guide for Lifecycle Management in Aviation Project Management	
Practice Guide for Requirements Management in Aviation Project Management	Source/RFP Deliverable Template
AVPMIT-RM-1.1	
Practice Guide for Requirements Management in Aviation Project Management	Backlog Estimate Deliverable Template
AVPMIT-RM-1.1.2	

Figure 3.18 Pre-project phase lifecycle practices, templates, and checklists

Lifecycle Management Initiation Template

Project: [Name] I Project Manager: [Name] I Lifecycle Methodology: [Type] I Date: [Start Date]

Project Overview
• Project Description: [Objectives and Expected Outcomes]
• Lifecycle Methodology Rationale: [Suitability Explanation]

Planning Components	Management Systems
1. Initial Project Scope • Key Deliverables • Project Boundaries	1. Stakeholder Engagement • Key Stakeholders • Engagement Plan
2. Resource Allocation • Resource Needs • Acquisition Plan	2. Compliance/Regulations • Requirements • Compliance Plan
3. Risk Management • Risk Identification • Response Strategies	3. Communication Plan • Framework • Channels
4. Quality Management • Quality Standards • Management Activities	4. Transition Planning • Next Steps • Plan Phase Activities
5. Documentation • Recordkeeping • Milestone Tracking	

CONFIRM

Approval: [Name/Position] I Date: [Approval Date]   Lifecycle Alignment Confirmed

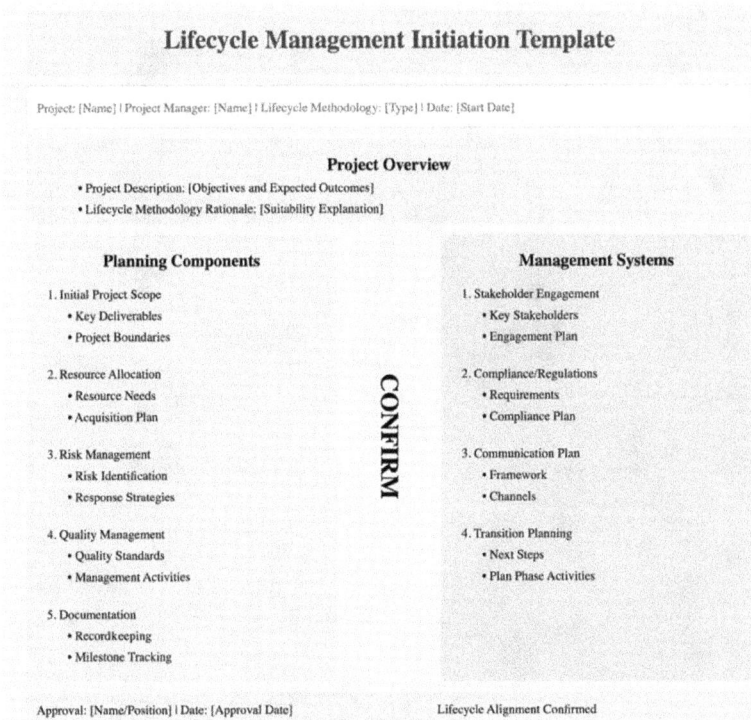

Figure 3.19 Graphical depiction of Lifecycle Management Initiation Template

be other sources of requirements to be elicited from both internal and external stakeholders. The requirements elicited in the start phase of the project go on to inform the project deliverables that are outlined in detail in the plan phase. See graphical depiction of Requirements Collection Template (Figure 3.20).

3. *Develop the schedule management plan*
Schedules represent a clear roadmap for the sequence of activities to be completed in the project. The term "roadmap" is nomenclature that fits well with schedule management. As an example, when applied to travel, the roadmap provides a sequence of directions. At the same time, it is understood that traffic might get in the way, weather may derail a particular route, and, finally, detours arise along the route. Likewise, the schedule provides direction even though it is understood that some activities might be

Requirements Collection and SOW Document Template

Project: [Name] | Document ID: [ID] | Prepared by: [Name] | Date: [Date] | Approval: [Name]

Document Purpose
• Requirements Scope   • Collection Methods   • Expected Deliverables

Non Functional

Functional Reqs

Requirements Collection Framework

Safety Reqs

Requirements Details

1. Functional Requirements
   • System Functions
   • User Interactions

2. Nonfunctional Requirements
   • Performance Criteria
   • Security Standards

3. Safety Requirements
   • Regulatory Compliance
   • Safety Measures

4. Validation Process
   • Stakeholder Review
   • Traceability Matrix

Statement of Work

1. Project Scope
   • Work Breakdown
   • Deliverables List

2. Project Timeline
   • Key Milestones
   • Schedule Details

3. Change Management
   • Control Process
   • Documentation

4. Supporting Documents
   • Detailed Requirements
   • Compliance Records

Approval: Prepared by [Name] | Reviewed by [Name] | Approved by [Name]

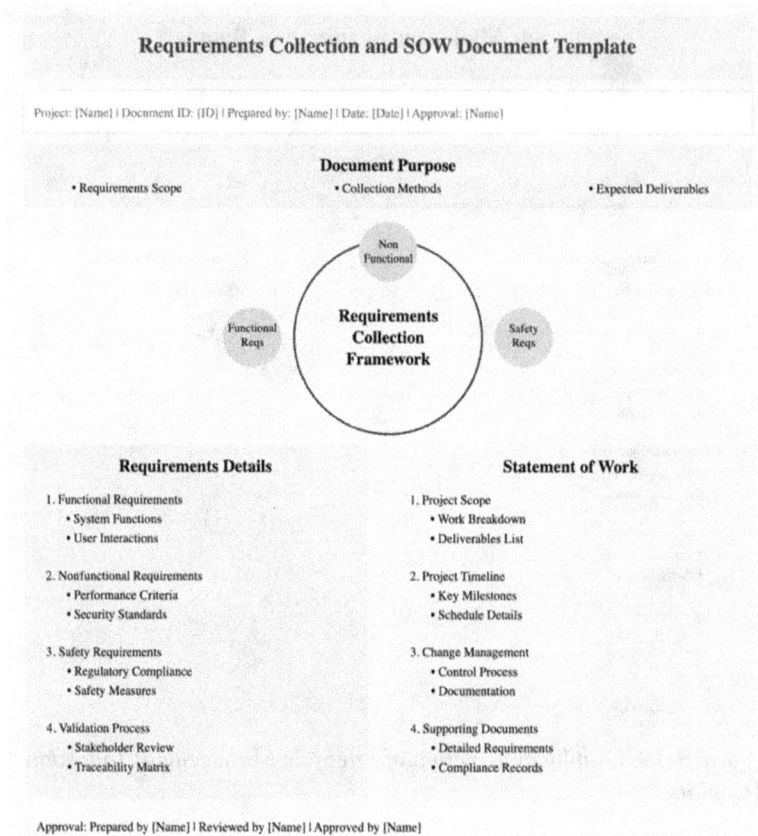

Figure 3.20 Graphical depiction of Requirements Collection Template

delayed, altered due to requirements changes, or halted in place due to emergent problems. The complexity of keeping the project schedule on track despite possible distractions makes the schedule management plan an essential component of starting the project. See graphical depiction of Schedule Management Process Template (Figure 3.21).

4. *Identify project stakeholders*

The identification of the stakeholder landscape in the pre-project phase dovetails well into stakeholder identification in the start phase of the project. At this phase, it is understood from where stakeholders will likely be found. In the aviation industry,

Project Schedule Management Plan

Project: [Name] I Document ID: [ID] I Prepared by: [Name] I Date: [Date] I Approval: [Name]

Schedule Management Overview
• Approach   • Methodology   • Tools

Monitor
Control

Develop
Plan

**Schedule
Management
Process**

Manage
Change

Development Framework   **Management Controls**

1. Schedule Baseline   1. Risk Management
   • Development Steps   • Risk Assessment
   • Approval Process   • Mitigation Plans

2. Estimating Method   2. Change Control
   • Duration Guidelines   • Change Process
   • Resource Planning   • Impact Analysis

3. Task Management   3. Communication
   • Dependencies   • Reporting Format
   • Sequencing   • Update Frequency

4. Performance Metrics   4. Roles
   • KPIs   • Responsibilities
   • Variance Tracking   • Accountabilities

Approval: Prepared by [Name] I Reviewed by [Name] I Approved by [Name]

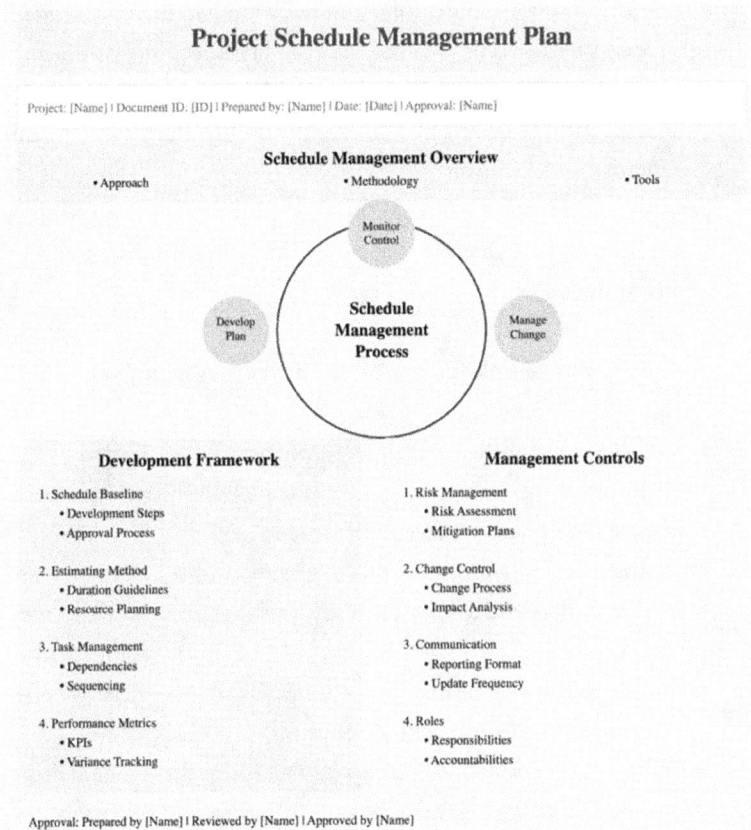

Figure 3.21 Graphical depiction of Schedule Management Process Template

stakeholders are many, and the stakeholders that fail to be identified could be the ones that pose problems for the project as it unfolds. One approach to stakeholder identification in aviation projects is to think in terms of primary and secondary stakeholders.

Primary Stakeholders are likely to include the following:

Airlines and Air Carriers: These are directly impacted by any changes in aviation infrastructure or regulations. They are concerned about operational efficiency, cost-effectiveness, and passenger satisfaction.

Airport Operators and Authorities: They manage and operate airports, ensuring safety, security, and efficient operations.

Passengers: The ultimate users of aviation services and their needs and concerns relate to convenience, affordability, safety, and comfort.

Government Agencies (e.g., FAA, FCC, TSA): They regulate and oversee various aspects of aviation, including safety, security, and environmental impact.

Investors and Financiers: Those who provide funding for aviation projects are interested in project viability and return on investment.

Secondary Stakeholders on the other hand are likely to include:

Local Communities: Residents living near airports or affected by flight paths are concerned about noise pollution, environmental impact, and potential economic benefits.

Businesses and Economic Development Organizations: They may benefit from increased aviation activity, such as tourism, trade, and job creation.

Environmental Groups: They focus on minimizing the negative environmental impact of aviation projects.

Aviation Industry Suppliers and Service Providers: These include companies providing fuel, maintenance, catering, and other services to the aviation industry.

Employees in the Aviation Sector: Pilots, cabin crew, ground staff, and so on, whose livelihoods are directly tied to the aviation industry.

The given primary and secondary stakeholder groups are examples of the stakeholder landscape as developed in the pre-project phase. There may be more groups and specific stakeholders to consider. The effort to identify relevant stakeholders takes place in the start phase and relies on brainstorming techniques to uncover so that a comprehensive listing is prepared. See graphical depiction of Stakeholder Identification Matrix Template (Figure 3.22).

5. *Roadmap evaluation*

Innovations developed by the organization over time are characterized by a roadmap that captures its evolution and future trajectory. Innovations can play an important role in aviation projects, but,

Stakeholder Identification Matrix

Project: [Name] | Document ID: [ID] | Prepared by: [Name] | Date: [Date] | Approved: [Name]

Matrix Analysis Overview

Category Mapping

Stakeholder Analysis

Stakeholder Matrix

Impact Assessment

Identification and Analysis

1. Internal Stakeholders
- Project Team Members
- Department Leaders

2. External Stakeholders
- Customers/Suppliers
- Regulatory Bodies

3. Stakeholder Register
- Contact Information
- Role Classifications

Matrix Components

1. Position Analysis
- Interest Levels
- Influence Mapping

2. Engagement Planning
- Communication Needs
- Engagement Strategy

3. Impact Evaluation
- Project Impact Level
- Response Strategies

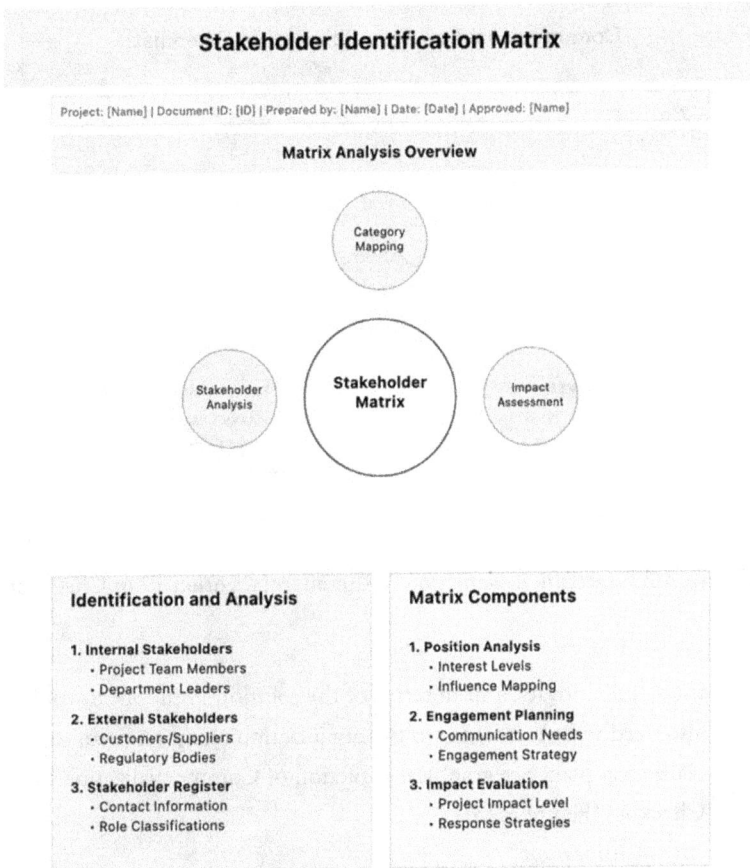

Figure 3.22 Graphical depiction of Stakeholder Identification Matrix Template

prior to implementation, it is critical to evaluate the roadmap to determine any elements that might fit in any given project. Given the risks involved in aviation projects, an important first step is to evaluate roadmap components for maturity. Also, the use of novel technologies in a project has implications that could ripple through some, if not all, aviation project management practices. For example, new technologies are likely to need regulatory review prior to use. Also, the project will need to determine if the project team and extended organization is capable of implementing the new technology. Finally, and perhaps most important, is the relevance of the innovation under consideration to be applied in the project. Not only

Commercialization Plan Deliverable Checklist

Project Name: [Project Title] | Document ID: [Unique ID] | Prepared by: [Name] | Date: [Date] | Approval: [Approver]

Market Analysis

Product Strategy

Sales & Distribution

Market Entry Strategy

Market Assessment
1. Market Analysis & Trends
2. Customer Segmentation
3. Product Positioning
4. Brand Development
5. Risk Management

Implementation Strategy
1. Go-to-Market Strategy
2. Marketing & Promotion
3. Sales Forecasting
4. Partnership Development
5. Regulatory Compliance

Figure 3.23 Graphical depiction of Commercialization Plan Checklist

must the innovation fit in terms of the solution itself, but it would also need to be factored into the organization's long-term commercialization plan. See graphical depiction of Commercialization Plan Checklist (Figure 3.23).

6. *Risk identification*

Risks are identified at the start of the project, and the effort is nontrivial. One of the most important challenges involves the complexity and interdependency of risks in the aviation environment. It is often easier to imagine the impact of a risk rather than to capture those small initial triggers that may cascade into a series of consequences that lead to a disaster. Often it is the risks that fail to be identified that end up causing problems in projects, and, in projects where human lives are at stake, it is even more important to find as many risks as possible. One of the primary tools for risk identification is structured brainstorming using prompts such as a Risk Breakdown Structure (RBS). Tools such as this include specific categories for focused brainstorming. The risk and safety issues report associated with the risk and safety management practice in the start phase of the project guides this activity and requires risk

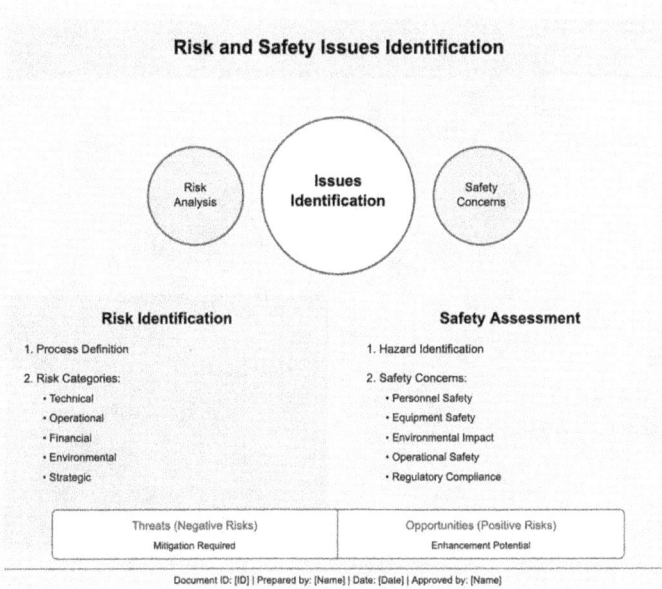

Risk and Safety Issues Identification

Risk Analysis — **Issues Identification** — **Safety Concerns**

Risk Identification

1. Process Definition

2. Risk Categories:
 • Technical
 • Operational
 • Financial
 • Environmental
 • Strategic

Safety Assessment

1. Hazard Identification

2. Safety Concerns:
 • Personnel Safety
 • Equipment Safety
 • Environmental Impact
 • Operational Safety
 • Regulatory Compliance

Threats (Negative Risks)	Opportunities (Positive Risks)
Mitigation Required	Enhancement Potential

Document ID: [ID] | Prepared by: [Name] | Date: [Date] | Approved by: [Name]

Figure 3.24 Graphical depiction of Risk and Safety Issues Identification Template

identification documentation. See graphical depiction of Risk and Safety Issues Identification Template (Figure 3.24).

7. *Approved suppliers*

Every project will employ outside suppliers to one degree or another. Once the supplier landscape is assessed in the pre-project phase, the next step involves reviewing approved suppliers and confirming the level of readiness to engage in the project. Also, the approved supplier's deliverables in the start phase provide general housekeeping for onboarding the supplier for the project and outlining how the engagement will be managed. See graphical depiction of Approved Supplier's Framework Checklist (Figure 3.25).

8. *Top-down refined estimate*

A ROM budget estimate provides a general idea of the overall anticipated budget level but provides little additional detail. The next step in developing a budget estimate is to provide a top-down characterization of the budget. While a top-down approach might approach "wishful thinking" as it seeks to constrain the budget by

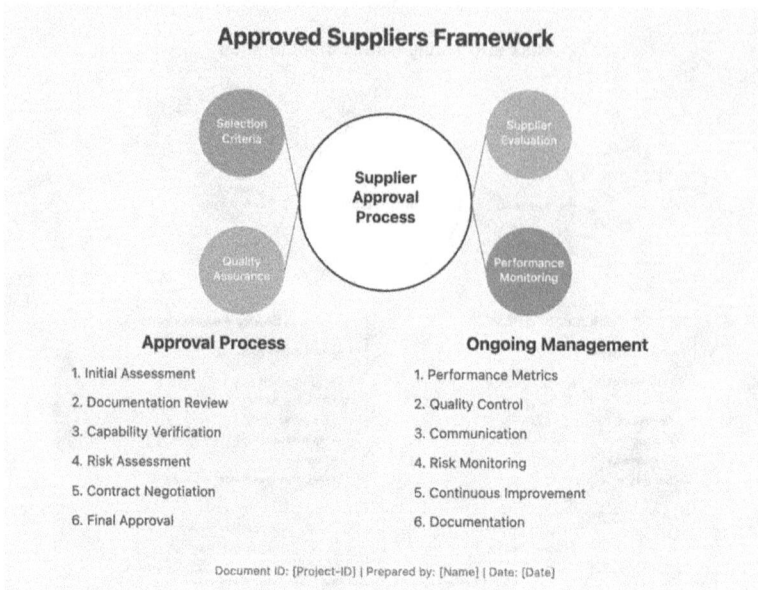

Figure 3.25 Graphical depiction of Approved Supplier's Framework Checklist

beginning with a top-level number and allocating it across important project budget categories, it is at least a start to the budgeting process. As the project unfolds, more details on deliverables, activities, and resources become available, thereby leading to a more detailed bottom-up budget development and analysis. Yet, given the time and effort required to produce a comprehensive bottom-up budget, a top-down refined estimate is an important initial start. See graphical depiction of Top-Down Budget Estimate Template (Figure 3.26).

9. *Safety and compliance framework*

Several important questions arise at the start of the project with respect to safety and compliance. One of the main outcomes of this activity in the start phase of an AVPM project is to assess the regulatory environment associated with safety and compliance so that appropriate policies and management systems may be put in place for the duration of the project lifecycle. The Safety and Compliance Framework Deliverables Checklist provides guidance to project

Top-Down Budget Framework

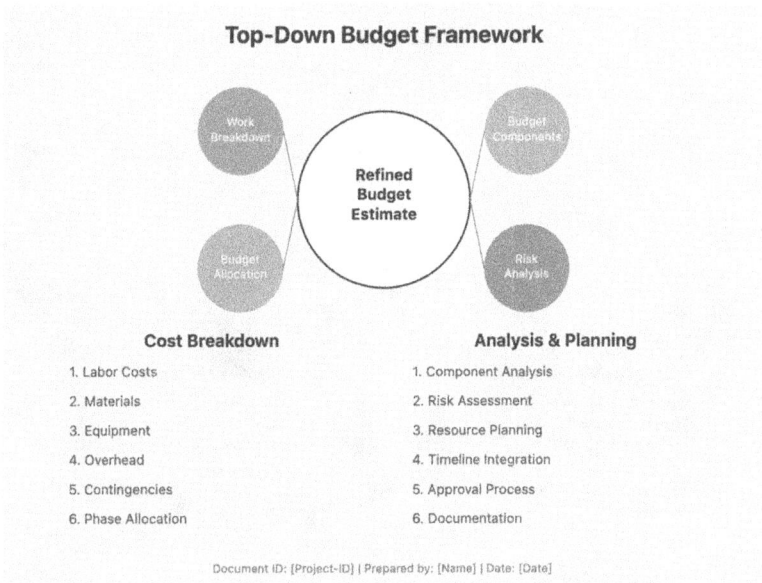

Cost Breakdown	Analysis & Planning
1. Labor Costs	1. Component Analysis
2. Materials	2. Risk Assessment
3. Equipment	3. Resource Planning
4. Overhead	4. Timeline Integration
5. Contingencies	5. Approval Process
6. Phase Allocation	6. Documentation

Document ID: [Project-ID] | Prepared by: [Name] | Date: [Date]

Figure 3.26 Graphical depiction of Top-Down Budget Estimate Template

managers to successfully establish policies systems. See graphical depiction of Safety and Compliance Checklist (Figure 3.27).

10. *Talent landscape/source*

With the talent needs assessment carried out in the pre-project phase of the AVPM lifecycle in hand, the next step with respect to resource planning is to identify from where such project resources may be sourced. Internal resources are evaluated to consider employing them in the project, but many external sources may be considered. These may include partners, suppliers, contractors, and even recruiters. An important exercise is to not only identify such sources but also consider the relevant strengths, weaknesses, and costs of each across the landscape of available talent and resources. See graphical depiction of Talent Landscape Management Template (Figure 3.28).

11. *Commercialization plan*

Should innovations be sufficiently mature to be viable within the project, the next consideration is the commercialization of the

Safety and Compliance Framework

Project Name | Document ID | Prepared by | Date | Approval

Risk Management

Policy Development

Safety and Compliance System

Continuous Improvement

Implementation	Culture and Engagement
1. Safety Management • Training Programs • Emergency Response 2. Reporting System • Incident Reporting • Documentation	1. Safety Culture • Communication • Accountability 2. Stakeholder Focus • Engagement • Feedback Systems

Approved: Prepared by [Name] | Reviewed by [Name] | Approved by [Name]

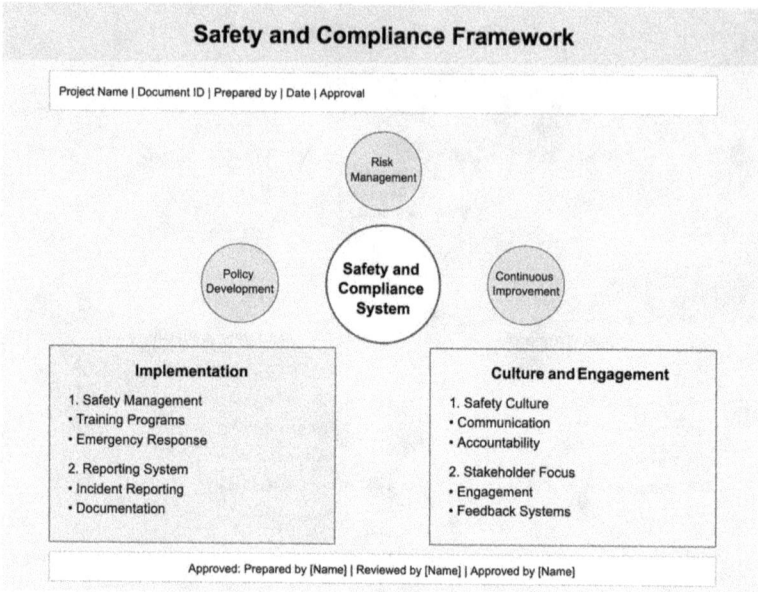

Figure 3.27 Graphical depiction of Safety and Compliance Checklist

innovation. This could be a piece of new technology, a process, a new method, or anything new and useful to be included as either a deliverable or a means for producing the deliverable. If an innovation is deemed ready to deploy, the organization and project team will need to consider how to protect it, profit from it, and market it as a means of distinguishing unique company capabilities. All of these considerations relate to the commercialization plan in the start phase. See graphical depiction of Commercialization Plan Checklist (Figure 3.29).

12. *Quality systems/assurance*

The requirements in aviation projects can be substantial, and it is the quality management practice that ensures that requirements are met. This requires the development and implementation of a QMS, a quality policy, metrics, and associated plans. The start phase of the lifecycle is the point in the process where such plans and systems are developed as guided by the associated supporting checklist. See graphical depiction of Quality Systems and Assurance Checklist (Figure 3.30).

Talent Landscape Management

Talent Management

Internal Sources

External Sources

Source Analysis

1. Talent Pool Assessment
   - Availability Analysis
   - Skill Mapping

2. Cost Analysis
   - Budget Impact
   - Resource Allocation

3. Risk Assessment
   - Mitigation Strategies

Management Actions

1. Acquisition Strategy
   - Recruitment Planning
   - Source Selection

2. Implementation
   - Resource Onboarding
   - Team Integration

3. Monitoring
   - Performance Tracking

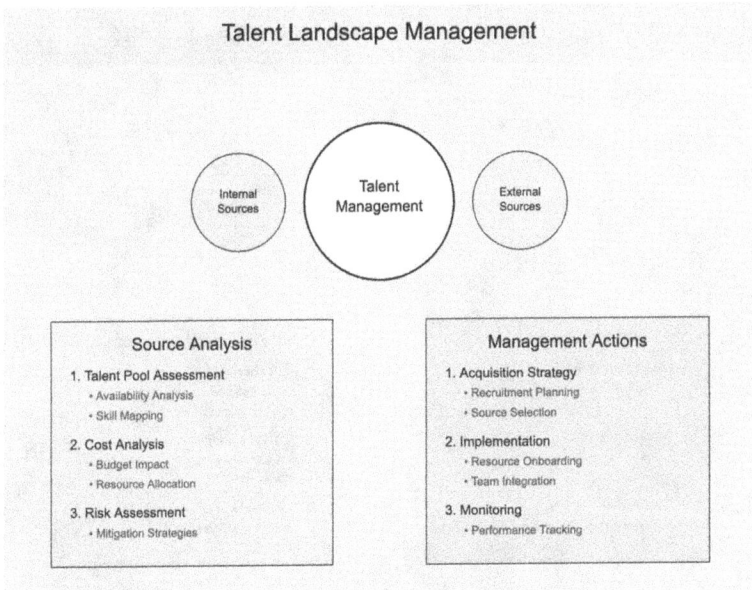

Figure 3.28 Graphical depiction of Talent Landscape Management Template

Commercialization Plan Deliverable Checklist

Project Name: [Project Title] | Document ID: [Unique ID] | Prepared by: [Name] | Date: [Date] | Approval: [Approver]

Product Strategy

Market Analysis

Sales & Distribution

Market Entry Strategy

Market Assessment

1. Market Analysis & Trends
2. Customer Segmentation
3. Product Positioning
4. Brand Development
5. Risk Management

Implementation Strategy

1. Go-to-Market Strategy
2. Marketing & Promotion
3. Sales Forecasting
4. Partnership Development
5. Regulatory Compliance

Figure 3.29 Graphical depiction of Commercialization Plan Checklist

Quality Systems and Assurance

Quality
Systems

Policy &
Planning

Measurement &
Improvement

System Framework

1. QMS Foundation
   • System Structure
   • Policy Development

2. Documentation
   • Quality Standards
   • Process Controls

3. Resource Management
   • Training & Competency

Assurance Activities

1. Performance Monitoring
   • Quality Metrics
   • Risk Assessment

2. Supplier Management
   • Vendor Assessment
   • Quality Controls

3. Continuous Improvement
   • System Enhancement

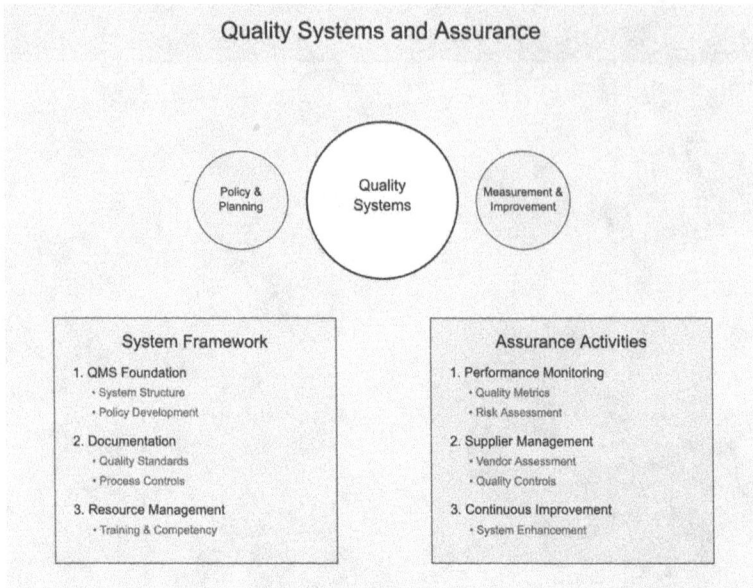

Figure 3.30 *Graphical depiction of Quality Systems and Assurance Checklist*

13. *Certification plan*

    Certification is something that occurs toward the end of the project as deliverables are documented and submitted for review and inspection. The focus on certification within the start phase however is on developing the strategy and plan for achieving required certification. Certification activities within the start phase are focused on reviewing requirements, setting objectives, and making plans to achieve stated objectives. See graphical depiction of Certification Plan Checklist (Figure 3.31).

14. *Environmental and sustainability policy*

    The first step in the development of environmental and sustainability policy is to attain a solid grasp of any specific regulatory requirements. Whereas an organization may seek to establish leadership with some environmental goals, at minimum, those environmental requirements outlined by the legal framework are the first that must be met. Following this, the development of environmental and

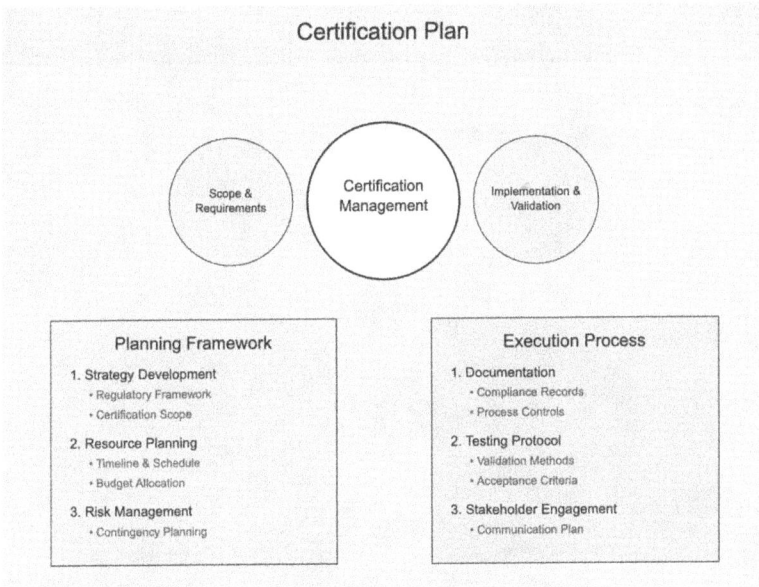

Figure 3.31 Graphical depiction of Certification Plan Checklist

sustainability policy emerges from requirements from the body of stakeholders associated with the project. See graphical depiction of Environmental and Sustainability Policy Checklist (Figure 3.32).

Start Phase Practices Summary

The complete list of templates and checklists for supporting activities within the start phase is given below (Figure 3.33). As is the case of the pre-project phase comprehensive document list, all documents that pertain to the supporting activities are color-coded according to the position of those activities within the project value chain as well as lifecycle category. Furthermore, each document is numbered for ease of reference.

The Plan Phase

Once the identification of both the pre-project and the start phase preliminary activities, deliverables, and documentation is complete, it is time to begin planning the project in earnest. There is a fork in the road when

Environmental and Sustainability Policy Framework

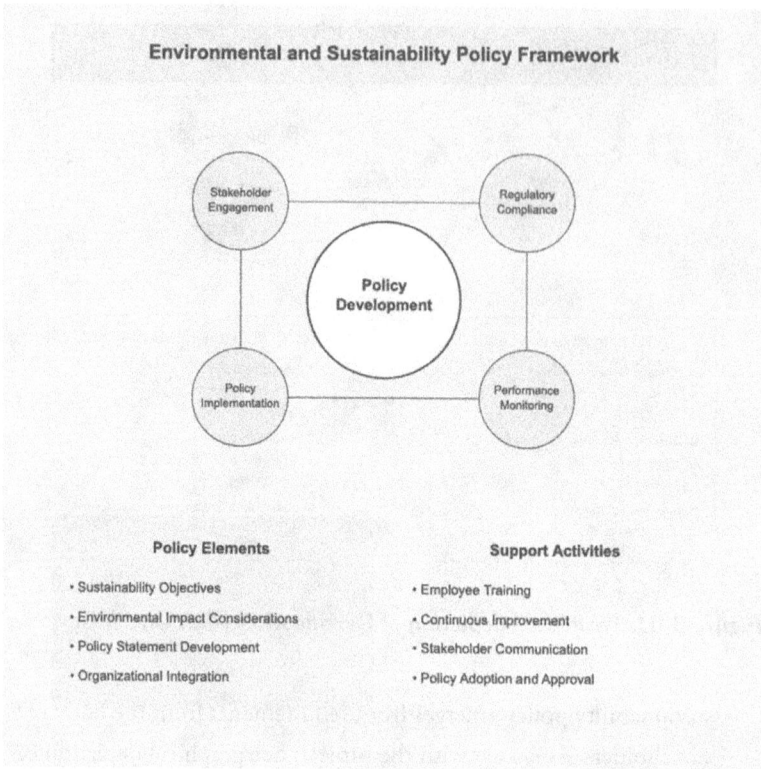

Policy Elements

- Sustainability Objectives
- Environmental Impact Considerations
- Policy Statement Development
- Organizational Integration

Support Activities

- Employee Training
- Continuous Improvement
- Stakeholder Communication
- Policy Adoption and Approval

Figure 3.32 Graphical depiction of Environmental and Sustainability Policy Checklist

it comes to planning, and the fork is the decision linked to the choice of project lifecycle. Plan-driven project plans focus on planning the entire project, whereas iterative projects employ specialized techniques for planning one increment or sprint at a time rather than the complete project.

1. *Lifecycle plan*

   The project lifecycle is selected in the pre-project phase and initiated in the start phase. The plan phase develops the lifecycle management plan and, in doing so, describes important aspects of the lifecycle, such as how the lifecycle is to be managed, relevant management roles and responsibilities, as well as important lifecycle monitoring and control milestones. The lifecycle differs from the schedule in that it outlines the overall governance of all

Practices	Start
Practice Guide for Lifecycle Management in Aviation Project Management	Lifecycle Management Initiation Template
AVPMPG-LM-1.000	AVPMP-LM-1.2
Practice Guide for Lifecycle Management in Aviation Project Management	
AVPMPG-LM-1.000	
Practice Guide for Requirements Management in Aviation Project Management	Requirements Collection and Statement of Work Template
AVPMPG-RM-1.000	AVPMP-RM-1.2
Practice Guide for Schedule Management in Aviation Project Management	Project Schedule Management Plan Template
AVPMPG-SM-1.000	AVPMP-SM-1.2
Practice Guide for Stakeholder and Customer Relations Management in Aviation Project Management	Stakeholder Identification Matrix Template
AVPMPG-ST-1.000	AVPMP-ST-1.2
Practice Guide for Risk and Safety Management in Aviation Project Management	Risk and Safety Issues Identification Report Template
AVPMPG-RS-1.000	AVPMP-RS-1.2
Practice Guide for Financial Management in Aviation Project Management	Top Down Refined Budget Estimate Template
AVPMPG-FM-1.000	AVPMP-FM-1.2
Practice Guide for Human Resource and Team Management in Aviation Project Management	Talent Landscape/Source Template
AVPMPG-HR-1.000	AVPMP-HR-1.2
Practice Guide for Innovation and Research Management in Aviation Project Management	I&R Commercialization Plan Deliverable Checklist
AVPMPGS-IR-1.000	AVPMS-IR-1.2
Practice Guide for Supply Chain and Procurement Management in Aviation Project Management	Approved Suppliers Deliverable Checklist
AVPMPGS-SC-1.000	AVPMS-SC-1.2
Practice Guide for Aviation Safety Management in Aviation Project Management	Safety and Compliance Framework Deliverable Checklist
AVPMPGS-AS-1.000	AVPMS-AS-1.2
Practice Guide for Technology and Engineering Management in Aviation Project Management	Commercialization Plan Deliverable Checklist
AVPMPGS-TE-1.000	AVPMS-TE-1.2
Practice Guide for Aviation Quality Management in Aviation Project Management	Quality Systems and Assurance Deliverable Checklist
AVPMPGS-AQ-1.000	AVPMS-AQ-1.2
Practice Guide for Aviation Regulation Compliance and Certification Management in Aviation Project Management	Certification Plan Deliverable Checklist
AVPMPGS-AR-1.000	AVPMS-AR-1.2
Practice Guide for Environmental and Sustainability Management in Aviation Project Management	Environmental and Sustainability Policy Checklist
AVPMPGS-ES-1.000	AVPMS-ES-1.2

Practices	Iterative Start
Practice Guide for Lifecycle Management in Aviation Project Management	Sprint Number and Duration Framework Template
	AVPMIT-LM-1.2
Practice Guide for Lifecycle Management in Aviation Project Management	
Practice Guide for Requirements Management in Aviation Project Management	Product Requirements Deliverable Template
	AVPMIT-RM-1.2
Practice Guide for Requirements Management in Aviation Project Management	Product Backlog Deliverable Template
	AVPMIT-RM-1.2.2

Figure 3.33 Summarizes start phase lifecycle practices, templates, and checklists

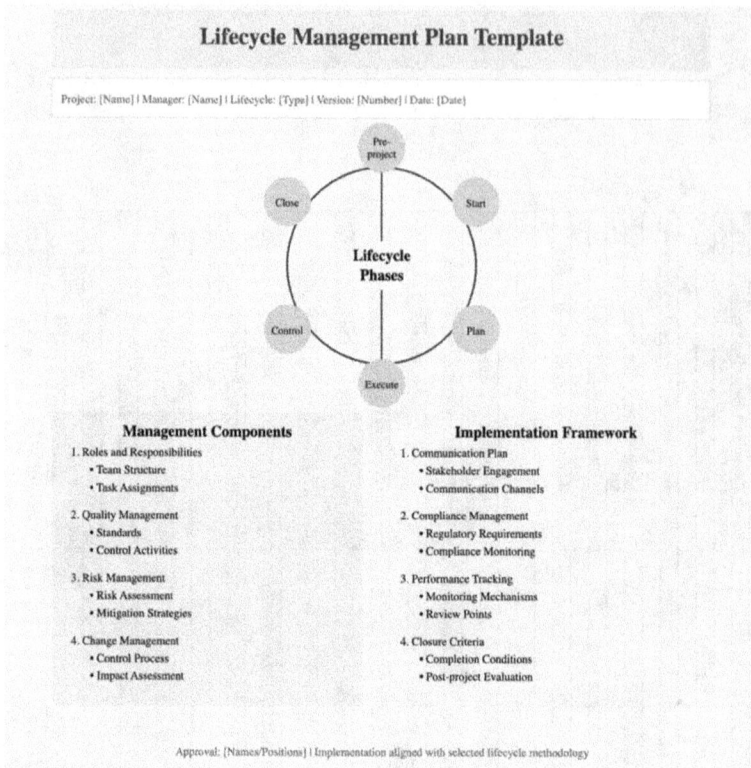

Figure 3.34 Graphical depiction of Lifecycle Management Plan Template

project phases, including the relevant business decisions that need to be made. See graphical depiction of Lifecycle Management Plan Template (Figure 3.34).

2. *Stakeholder assessment*

Stakeholders are sources of requirements in aviation projects—but they also variously act as supporters or detractors of the project. Once stakeholders have been identified in the start phase of the project, the next step is to assess stakeholders in terms of power and interest. In the aviation world, there are many powerful and interested stakeholders, particularly in the regulatory and client domain. The high-power/high-interest stakeholders could make the difference between success and failure. The assessment of stakeholders as outlined by the stakeholder management deliverables in the plan

Stakeholder Assessment Report

Project: [Name] | Document ID: [ID] | Prepared by: [Name] | Date: [Date] | Approved: [Name]

Assessment Process Overview

Stakeholder
Prioritization

Impact
Analysis

**Stakeholder
Assessment**

Engagement
Planning

Analysis and Evaluation

1. Stakeholder Analysis
 · Position/Interest Level
 · Influence/Power Rating

2. Assessment Criteria
 · Expectations/Concerns
 · Impact Assessment

3. Risk Evaluation
 · Risk Identification
 · Mitigation Strategies

Engagement Strategy

1. Communication Plan
 · Channel Selection
 · Frequency Planning

2. Engagement Activities
 · Consultation Methods
 · Feedback Mechanisms

3. Implementation
 · Action Timeline
 · Success Metrics

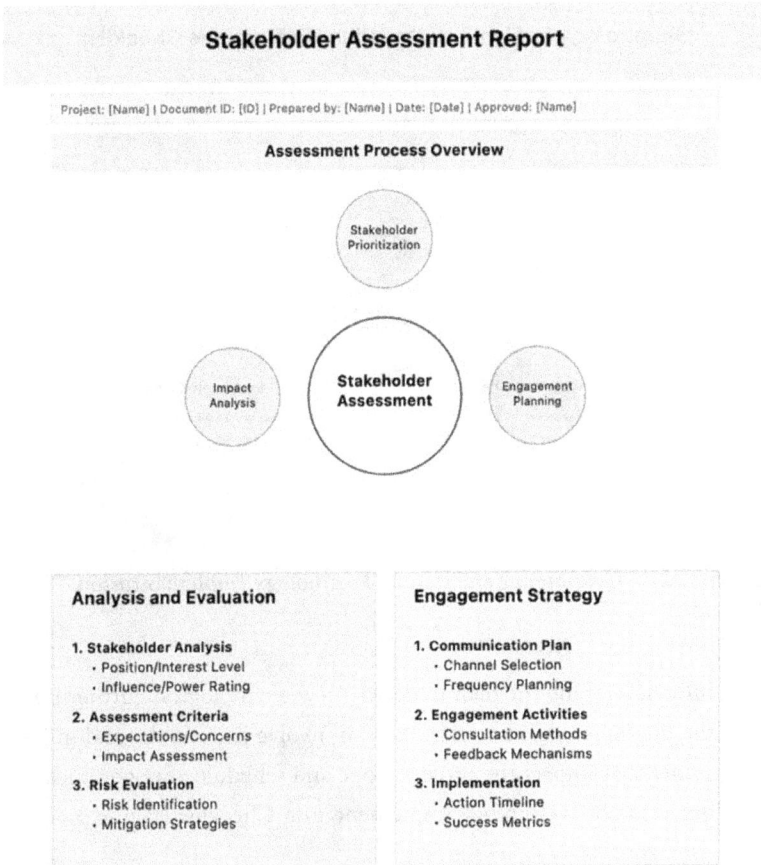

Figure 3.35 Graphical depiction of Stakeholder Assessment Report Template

phase is an activity that cannot be ignored. See graphical depiction of Stakeholder Assessment Report Template (Figure 3.35).

3. *Technology implementation plan*

The deployment of innovation is organized through the technology implementation plan deliverable. This deliverable aids in answering the following questions: "Why was the technology selected?" "Is the technology ready?" "Who will implement it?" By definition, innovation involves something new—and anything new is likely to require training, new processes and procedures, and new quality standards. The technology plan implementation checklist aids in

Technology Implementation Plan Deliverables Checklist

Project Name: [Project Title] | Document ID: [Unique ID] | Prepared by: [Name] | Date: [Date] | Approval: [Approver]

Resource Management

Solution Planning

Quality Assurance

Technology Implementation Control

Planning & Requirements

1. Technology Requirements
2. Selection Criteria
3. Solution Recommendations
4. Implementation Timeline
5. Risk Assessment

Execution & Control

1. Resource Allocation
2. Training & Support
3. Testing Procedures
4. Communication Plan
5. Documentation

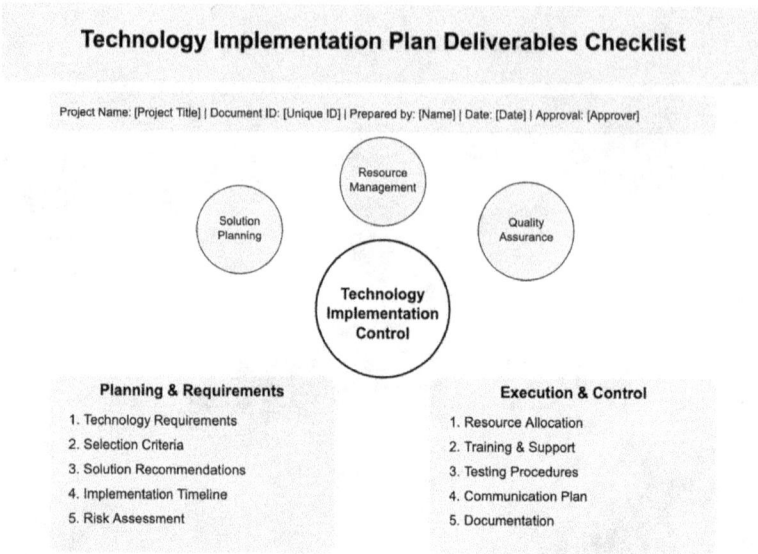

Figure 3.36 Graphical depiction of Technology Implementation Checklist

fully developing the plan to deploy new technologies. Furthermore, the implementation plan is likely to involve deliverables and milestones that impact the project scope and schedule. See graphical depiction of Technology Implementation Checklist (Figure 3.36).

4. *Risk register and safety issue log*
   The management of risk and safety in the plan phase is focused on the risk register and the safety log development. Risks are ranked by probability, impact, and, in some cases, "ability to detect" in the risk register. Each risk is accompanied by a description and a risk owner, and it also may include some notes about the risk response strategy. The safety log captures all safety issues that have been identified and captures them in the log so that they may be monitored throughout the project. See graphical depiction of Risk Register and Safety Issue Log Template (Figure 3.37).

5. *Supplier selection*
   Now that the supplier landscape and the approved suppliers are determined in the pre-project and start phases, it is now the time to select suppliers that will be used in the project. Typically, this will require a process rather than a single selection step. The process

Risk Register and Safety Issue Log

Figure 3.37 Graphical depiction of Risk Register and Safety Issue Log Template

often requires activities such as reaching out to approved suppliers for additional information, issuing RFPs and evaluating supplier responses, and finally awarding the business to a selected supplier. In some projects, it may be decided to "make" (in-house) rather than "buy," and this could change the complexion of the supplier selection process. However, suppliers are likely to still be needed for support, including the delivery of components or other work to support the in-house development. See graphical depiction of Supplier Selection Checklist (Figure 3.38).

6. *Regulatory and compliance plan*
   Regulatory matters are carefully considered within the plan phase of the project. The regulatory and compliance plan is developed by first reconfirming the required standards to be met, what aspects of the project are affected by regulatory matters, and exactly how such compliance will be achieved. All of this, including the resources and schedule for compliance, is addressed within the plan phase. See graphical depiction of Compliance Plan Checklist (Figure 3.39).

Supplier Selection Process

Project Requirements

Proposal Evaluation

Supplier
Selection
Framework

RFI/RFP Process

Contract Preparation

Selection Process Steps	Documentation & Communication
1. Market Research	1. Proposal Documentation
2. Prequalification	2. Evaluation Records
3. RFI Distribution	3. Selection Decisions
4. Response Analysis	4. Contract Documents
5. Site Visits/Audits	5. Supplier Notifications
6. Final Selection	6. Process Records

Document ID: [Project-ID] | Prepared by: [Name] | Date: [Date]

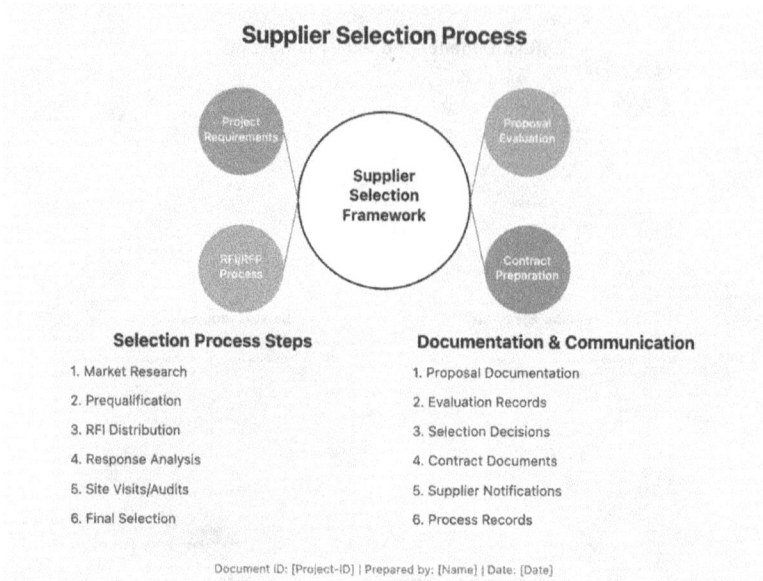

Figure 3.38 Graphical depiction of Supplier Selection Checklist

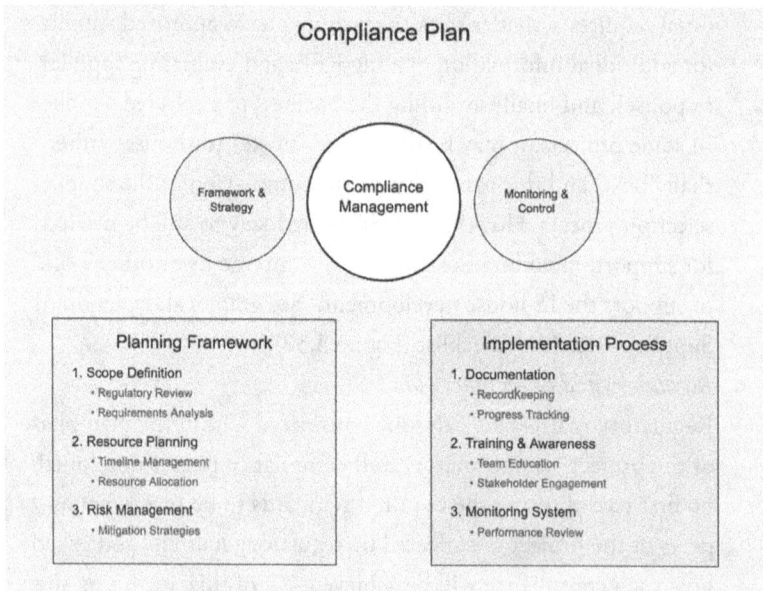

Compliance Plan

Framework & Strategy

Compliance Management

Monitoring & Control

Planning Framework	Implementation Process
1. Scope Definition	1. Documentation
• Regulatory Review	• RecordKeeping
• Requirements Analysis	• Progress Tracking
2. Resource Planning	2. Training & Awareness
• Timeline Management	• Team Education
• Resource Allocation	• Stakeholder Engagement
3. Risk Management	3. Monitoring System
• Mitigation Strategies	• Performance Review

Figure 3.39 Graphical depiction of Compliance Plan Checklist

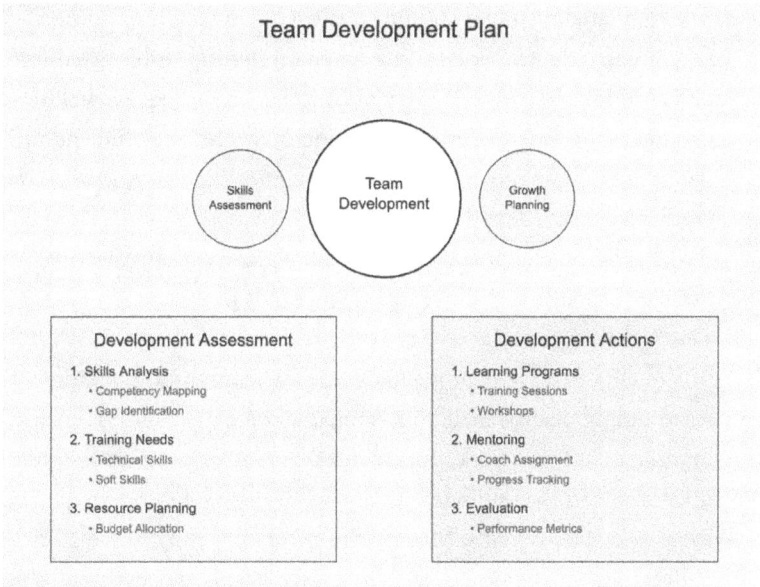

Team Development Plan

Development Assessment	Development Actions
1. Skills Analysis • Competency Mapping • Gap Identification 2. Training Needs • Technical Skills • Soft Skills 3. Resource Planning • Budget Allocation	1. Learning Programs • Training Sessions • Workshops 2. Mentoring • Coach Assignment • Progress Tracking 3. Evaluation • Performance Metrics

Figure 3.40 Graphical depiction of Team Development Plan Template

7. *Team development plan*

   It is well established that aviation projects are challenging. Strong and productive teams are required to produce the deliverables that satisfy the client requirements. The resources selected for the project team may require some skills assessment, training, and teambuilding to achieve maximum effectiveness. The activities associated with team development are included in the Human Resource and Team Management Practice Template in the plan phase of the project lifecycle. See graphical depiction of Team Development Plan Template (Figure 3.40).

8. *Engineering strategy*

   The engineering strategy is confirmed in the technology and engineering checklist employed in the plan phase of the project. This activity aids in establishing the optimal approach for implementing the technical work within the project. One of the key elements of the checklist involves architectural decision-making. Architecture is one of the more important technological decisions in the project.

The right architecture will support the requirements and possibly future-proof the technology implementation for possible extension and additional features. By way of contrast, an inadequate architecture may constrain the implementation of key features and end up hamstringing the project. Finally, the engineering strategy checklist confirms objectives and confirms how the technical work is broken down and implemented. See graphical depiction of Engineering Strategy Management Checklist (Figure 3.41).

9. *Quality management plan*

The quality management plan answers many important questions surrounding quality, including standards to be used, overall quality management framework, documentation requirements and specific measures, and how supplier quality will be assured. Modern quality theory involves systems. Manage the system correctly, and quality deliverables will be produced. Ultimately, quality management is complicated by the need to satisfy requirements from an array of stakeholders. The quality management plan ensures that the project

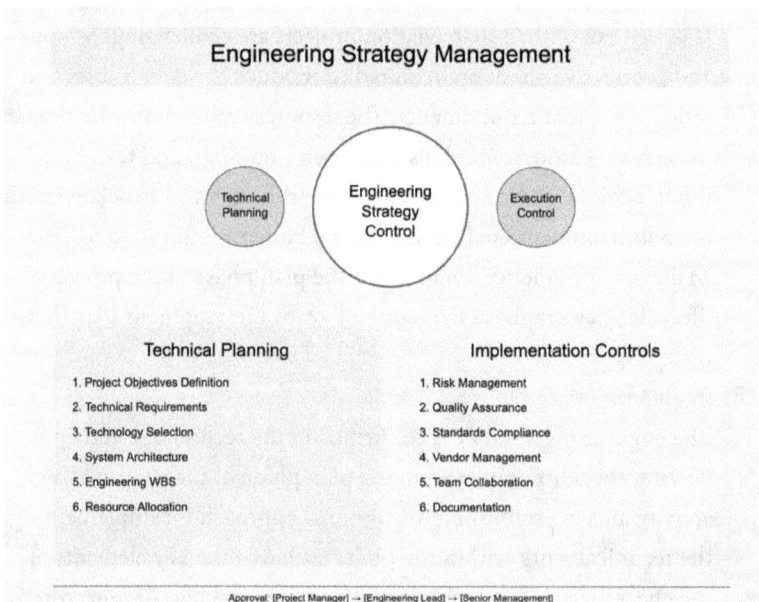

Engineering Strategy Management

Technical Planning

Engineering Strategy Control

Execution Control

Technical Planning	Implementation Controls
1. Project Objectives Definition	1. Risk Management
2. Technical Requirements	2. Quality Assurance
3. Technology Selection	3. Standards Compliance
4. System Architecture	4. Vendor Management
5. Engineering WBS	5. Team Collaboration
6. Resource Allocation	6. Documentation

Approval: [Project Manager] → [Engineering Lead] → [Senior Management]

Figure 3.41 Graphical depiction of Engineering Strategy Management Checklist

Quality Management Plan

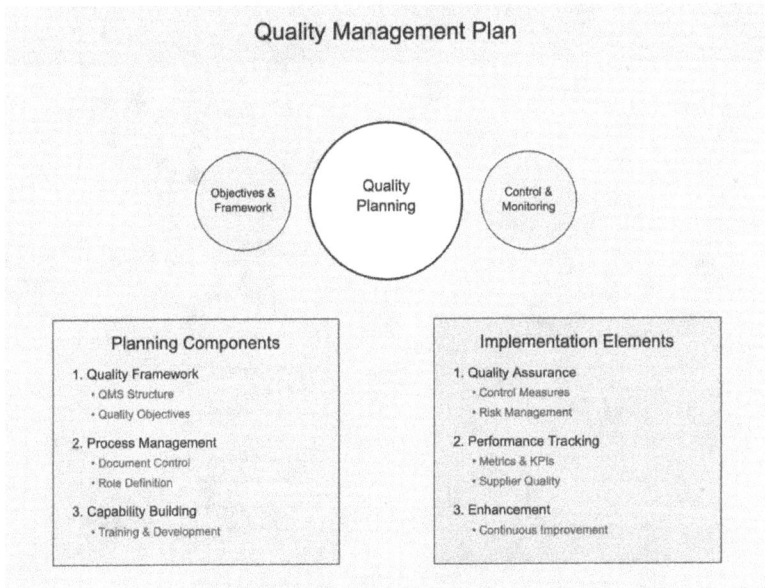

Planning Components	Implementation Elements
1. Quality Framework	1. Quality Assurance
• QMS Structure	• Control Measures
• Quality Objectives	• Risk Management
2. Process Management	2. Performance Tracking
• Document Control	• Metrics & KPIs
• Role Definition	• Supplier Quality
3. Capability Building	3. Enhancement
• Training & Development	• Continuous Improvement

Figure 3.42 Graphical depiction of Quality Management Plan Checklist

produces features and deliverables that match what was originally requested and documented. See graphical depiction of Quality Management Plan Checklist (Figure 3.42).

10. *Compliance plan*

The compliance plan resolves key concerns such as what compliance the project will face, how the project intends to achieve it, and, finally, what is likely to stand in the way of successfully achieving full compliance for all deliverables. The compliance plan also captures any important deliverables and milestones as well as the resources required to achieve them. Resources may need training, and, as well, those working on compliance deliverables will have reporting requirements. The compliance plan deliverable in the plan phase is the means for successfully achieving compliance. See graphical depiction of Compliance Plan Checklist (Figure 3.43).

11. *Environmental and sustainability plan*

Many environmental practices are addressed within the regulatory environment and, therefore, as required by law. However, the company sponsoring the aviation project may have internal policies that

Compliance Plan

Framework & Strategy

Compliance Management

Monitoring & Control

Planning Framework

1. Scope Definition
   • Regulatory Review
   • Requirements Analysis

2. Resource Planning
   • Timeline Management
   • Resource Allocation

3. Risk Management
   • Mitigation Strategies

Implementation Process

1. Documentation
   • Recordkeeping
   • Progress Tracking

2. Training & Awareness
   • Team Education
   • Stakeholder Engagement

3. Monitoring System
   • Performance Review

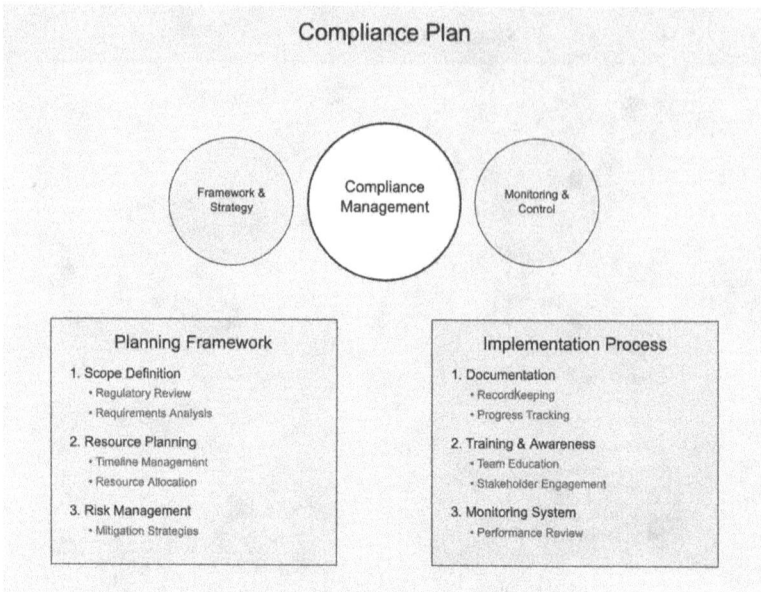

Figure 3.43 Graphical depiction of Compliance Plan Checklist

must be incorporated within the project. Sustainability concerns also typically emerge internally in company policy, but they are often promoted to the public as a means for demonstrating corporate social responsibility. See graphical depiction of Environmental and Sustainability Checklist (Figure 3.44).

12. *Scope*

    Scope is fully elaborated in the plan phase of the project. In the plan-driven lifecycle, the scope elaboration takes as its input the scope statement, SOW, and requirements from the layers of aviation industry stakeholders. Furthermore, elements of scope also emerge from practices that lead to specific deliverables unique to the aviation industry. Practices often lead to more work to do in aviation projects, yet such additional scope satisfies requirements that in the absence of documented practices might be overlooked. In the case of the iterative lifecycle, scope is envisioned as the product backlog and is further elaborated in terms of the sprint backlog for each of the iterations. See graphical depiction of Scope Development Template (Figure 3.45).

Environmental and Sustainability Plan Framework

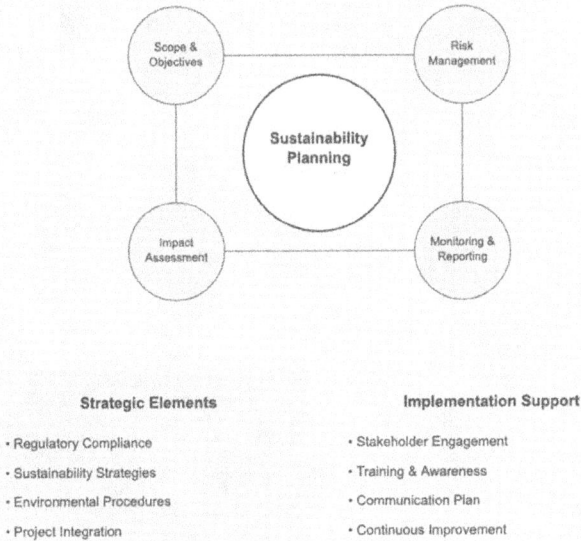

Strategic Elements

- Regulatory Compliance
- Sustainability Strategies
- Environmental Procedures
- Project Integration

Implementation Support

- Stakeholder Engagement
- Training & Awareness
- Communication Plan
- Continuous Improvement

Figure 3.44 Graphical depiction of Environmental and Sustainability Checklist

13. *Develop schedule*

As is the case of projects outside the aviation industry, the schedule is developed within the plan phase of the project lifecycle. The development of the schedule begins with the identification of activities required to produce each of the project scope deliverables. After this step, the activities are sequenced in order, and, once the order is established, resources are assigned to each activity. See graphical depiction of Schedule Development Template (Figure 3.46).

14. *Project budget baseline/time phase*

A project budget consists of many different elements such as fixed and variable costs and direct and indirect costs. In practice, the bulk of the project budget is developed by the assignment of resources to activities. Costs are "attached" to resources, and, once resources are

Scope Development Based on Requirements

Project: [Name] I Document ID: [ID] I Prepared by: [Name] I Date: [Date] I Approval: [Name]

Scope Definition Purpose

• Project Background   • Requirements Summary   • Expected Outcomes

Validate
Content

Define
Scope

**Scope
Development
Process**

Baseline
Scope

Scope Elements

1. Project Boundaries
   • Inclusions
   • Exclusions

2. Deliverables
   • Work Breakdown
   • Requirements Mapping

3. Assumptions
   • Project Conditions
   • Dependencies

4. Constraints
   • Resource Limits
   • Time Boundaries

Management Process

1. Validation Process
   • Stakeholder Review
   • Approval Steps

2. Change Management
   • Control Process
   • Documentation

3. Baseline Management
   • Establishment
   • Updates

4. Supporting Documents
   • WBS Details
   • Feedback Records

Approval: Prepared by [Name] I Reviewed by [Name] I Approved by [Name]

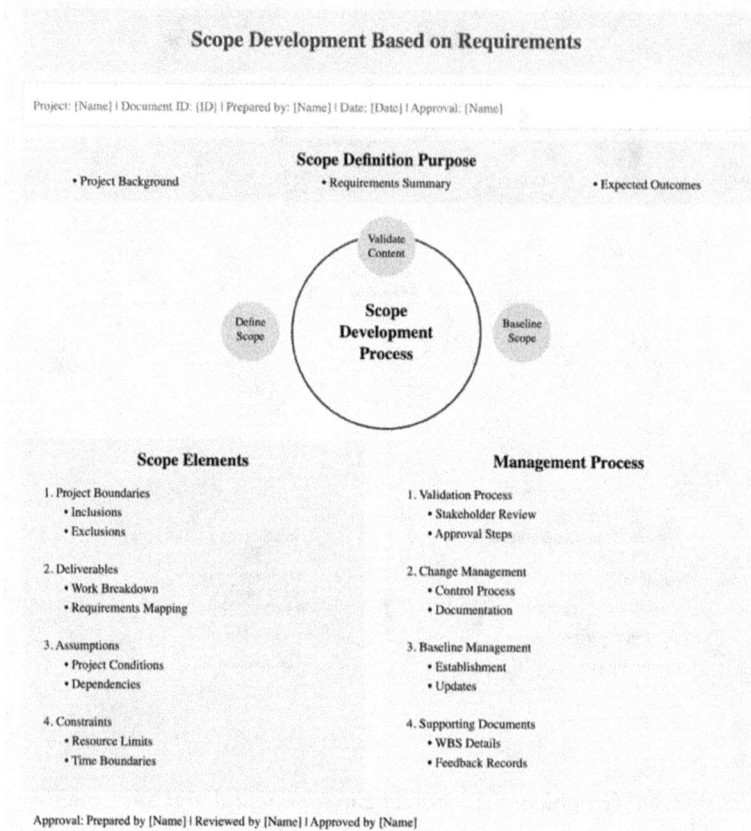

Figure 3.45 Graphical depiction of Scope Development Template

assigned to activities, the costs naturally follow automatically. Other costs beyond resources do exist, but it is also common practice to allocate other costs such as overhead to resources as a percentage of salary. Furthermore, capital resources assigned to specific scheduled activities also automatically bring in costs to the project budget. This is often done by allocating a percentage of depreciation or leasing costs to activities that employ the resource. Once the costs per period are tabulated, the cumulative cost is developed so that a baseline budget "S-Curve" is created. This becomes the budget baseline or project budget commitment that remains unchanged unless or until changes to the project are reviewed and approved via

Project Schedule Development

Project: [Name] | Document ID: [ID] | Prepared by: [Name] | Date: [Date] | Approval: [Name]

Schedule Development Overview

• Project Scope   • Key Objectives   • Major Milestones

Resource Allocation

Task Planning

Schedule Development Process

Timeline Analysis

Schedule Components	Management Elements
1. Baseline Schedule	1. Schedule Controls
• Phase Timelines	• Change Process
• Key Dates	• Reporting System
2. Critical Path	2. Compression Options
• Key Activities	• Fast-tracking
• Dependencies	• Task Crashing
3. Resource Planning	3. Constraints
• Team Allocation	• Time Limitations
• Equipment Needs	• Resource Bounds
4. Contingency Plans	4. Documentation
• Buffer Time	• Progress Reports
• Risk Mitigation	• Change Records

Approval: Prepared by [Name] | Reviewed by [Name] | Approved by [Name]

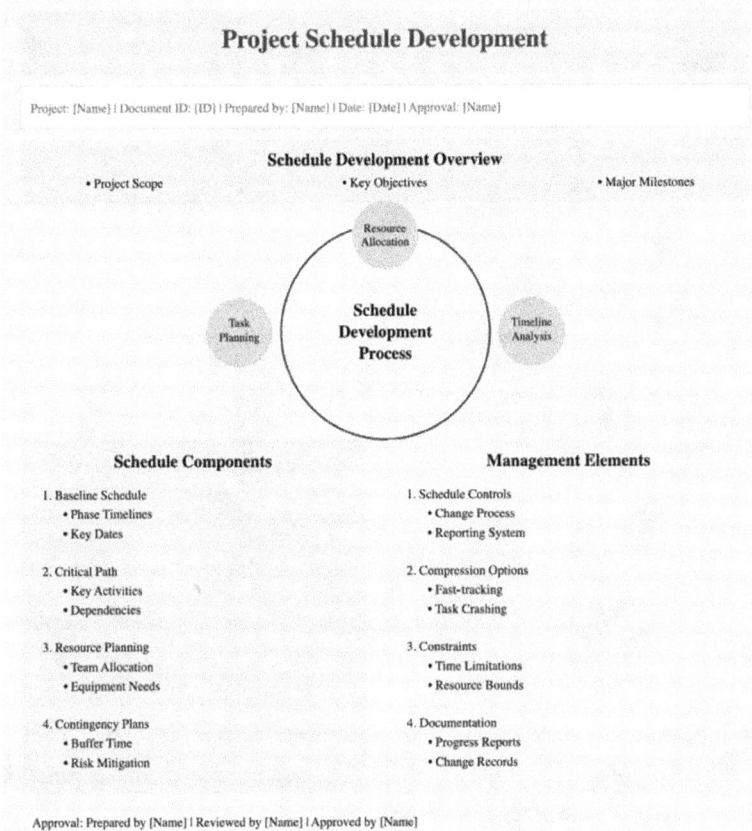

Figure 3.46 Graphical depiction of Schedule Development Template

project-integrated change-control mechanisms. See graphical depiction of Project Budget Baseline Template (Figure 3.47).

Plan Phase Summary

The templates for plan-driven and iterative lifecycles as well as the primary and supporting practices are summarized in Figure 3.48.

The Execute Phase

The AVPM, like other frameworks, focuses on planning before "doing." The "Execute phase" is where the "doing" is carried out within the AVPM

Project Budget Baseline Framework

Budget
Categories

Time
Periods

**Time-Phased
Budget
Baseline**

Resource
Allocation

Contingency
Management

Budget Structure

1. Labor Allocations
2. Material Costs
3. Equipment Expenses
4. Overhead Costs
5. Phase Distribution
6. Total Baseline

Time Management

1. Period Planning
2. Resource Scheduling
3. Cost Distribution
4. Milestone Tracking
5. Budget Control
6. Review Process

Document ID: [Project-ID] | Prepared by: [Name] | Date: [Date]

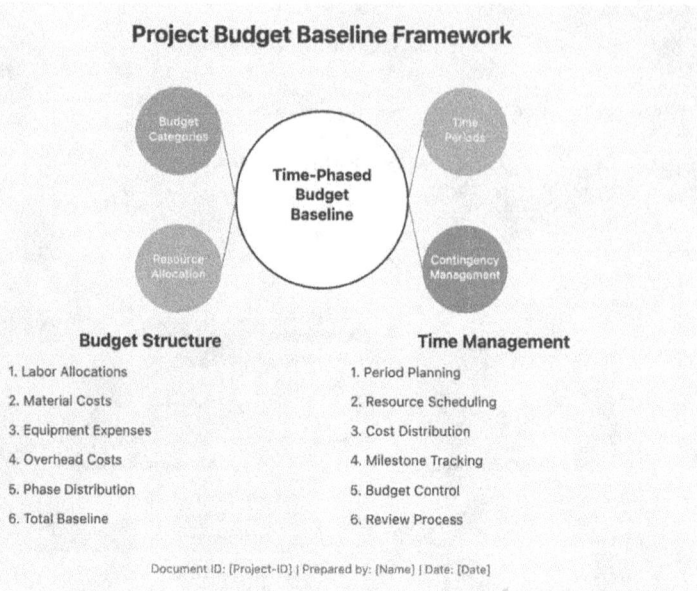

Figure 3.47 Graphical depiction of Project Budget Baseline Template

and the practices supporting project execution focus on reporting what is being accomplished within this phase. The essence of each of the practice progress reports are given as follows:

1. *Lifecycle Execution Report Template*
   During the execution phase, stakeholders seek to understand how the project lifecycle is unfolding. The lifecycle of the project is the governance mechanism to oversee the stages of the project. The interest in information about the lifecycle progress is comprehensive and involves seeking details about project status, risks, and metrics in order to accurately gauge whether the project is producing that which it was intended to deliver as well as achieving it within the array of constraints faced by the project. See graphical depiction of Lifecycle Execution Report Template (Figure 3.49).

2. *Requirements Validation Report Template*
   Validation is a check to confirm that the specification for the project deliverables is in alignment with what the client requested. During execution, it is crucial to reconfirm that this is the case. The

Practices	Plan
Practice Guide for Lifecycle Management in Aviation Project Management	Lifecycle Management Plan Template
AVPMPG-LM-1.000	AVPMP-LM-1.3
Practice Guide for Lifecycle Management in Aviation Project Management	
AVPMPG-LM-1.000	
Practice Guide for Requirements Management in Aviation Project Management	Scope Development Based on Requirements Document Template
AVPMPG-RM-1.000	AVPMP-RM-1.3
Practice Guide for Schedule Management in Aviation Project Management	Project Schedule Development Template
AVPMPG-SM-1.000	AVPMP-SM-1.3
Practice Guide for Stakeholder and Customer Relations Management in Aviation Project Management	Stakeholder Assessment Report Template
AVPMPG-ST-1.000	AVPMP-ST-1.3
Practice Guide for Risk and Safety Management in Aviation Project Management	Risk Register and Safety Issue Log Template
AVPMPG-RS-1.000	AVPMP-RS-1.3
Practice Guide for Financial Management in Aviation Project Management	Project Budget Baseline/Time-Phased Deliverable Template
AVPMPG-FM-1.000	AVPMP-FM-1.3
Practice Guide for Human Resource and Team Management in Aviation Project Management	Team Development Plan Template
AVPMPG-HR-1.000	AVPMP-HR-1.3
Practice Guide for Innovation and Research Management in Aviation Project Management	Technology Implementation Plan Deliverables Checklist
AVPMPGS-IR-1.000	AVPMS-IR-1.3
Practice Guide for Supply Chain and Procurement Management in Aviation Project Management	Supplier Selection Deliverable Checklist
AVPMPGS-SC-1.000	AVPMS-SC-1.3
Practice Guide for Aviation Safety Management in Aviation Project Management	Safety and Compliance Plan Deliverable Checklist
AVPMPGS-AS-1.000	AVPMS-AS-1.3
Practice Guide for Technology and Engineering Management in Aviation Project Management	Engineering Strategy Deliverable Checklist
AVPMPGS-TE-1.000	AVPMS-TE-1.3
Practice Guide for Aviation Quality Management in Aviation Project Management	Quality Management Plan Deliverable Checklist
AVPMPGS-AQ-1.000	AVPMS-AQ-1.3
Practice Guide for Aviation Regulation Compliance and Certification Management in Aviation Project Management	Compliance Plan Deliverable Checklist
AVPMPGS-AR-1.000	AVPMS-AR-1.3
Practice Guide for Environmental and Sustainability Management in Aviation Project Management	Environmental and Sustainability Plan Checklist
AVPMPGS-ES-1.000	AVPMS-ES-1.3

Practices	Iterative Plan
Practice Guide for Lifecycle Management in Aviation Project Management	Iteration Plan Deliverable Template
	AVPMIT-LM-1.3
Practice Guide for Lifecycle Management in Aviation Project Management	Iterative Project Plan Template
Practice Guide for Requirements Management in Aviation Project Management	Sprint Requirements Deliverable Template
Practice Guide for Requirements Management in Aviation Project Management	AVPMIT-RM-1.3

Figure 3.48 Summarizes plan phase primary and supporting practices templates for both plan-driven and iterative lifecycles

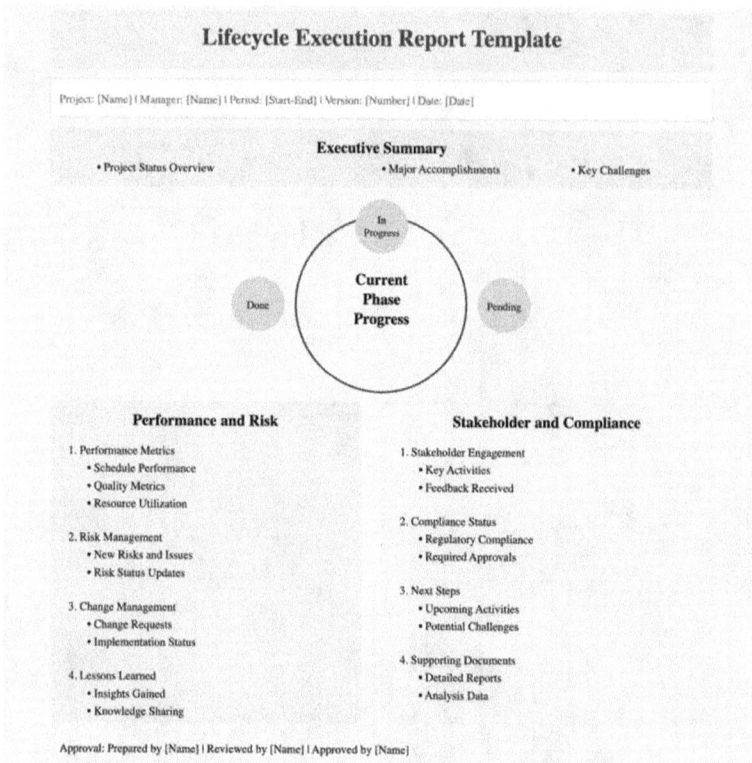

Figure 3.49 Graphical depiction of Lifecycle Execution Report Template

requirements validation report provides such a confirmation and, as well, describes the accompanying validation methodology used to confirm such alignment. See graphical depiction of Requirements Validation Report Template (Figure 3.50).

3. *Project Schedule Management Template*

As project execution proceeds, it is necessary to confirm the progress to plan. The Schedule Management Plan Template provides prompts to focus the attention of the aviation project manager on an array of aspects, such as project schedule progress, changes, risks, as well as any other matters relating to the status of the schedule. See graphical depiction of Project Schedule Management Template (Figure 3.51).

Requirements Validation Report Template

Project: [Name] | Document ID: [ID] | Prepared by: [Name] | Date: [Date] | Approval: [Name]

Validation Overview

• Objectives   • Methodology   • Expected Results

Test Results

Review Status

Validation Assessment Status

Issue Tracking

Validation Activities

1. Requirements Review
   • Validation Methods
   • Evidence Collection

2. Results Analysis
   • Findings Summary
   • Gap Assessment

3. Issue Management
   • Impact Analysis
   • Resolution Plans

4. Documentation
   • Activity Records
   • Evidence Files

Outcome Management

1. Stakeholder Input
   • Feedback Collection
   • Action Items

2. Results Review
   • Validation Status
   • Recommendations

3. Next Steps
   • Implementation Plan
   • Timeline Updates

4. Supporting Data
   • Detailed Results
   • Issue Logs

Approval: Prepared by [Name] | Reviewed by [Name] | Approved by [Name]

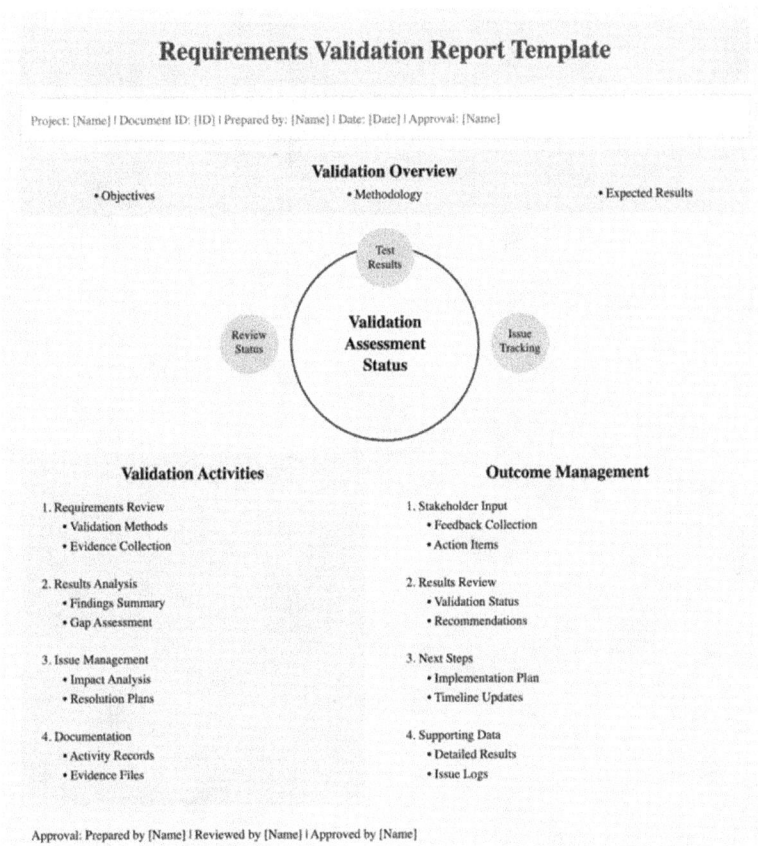

Figure 3.50 Graphical depiction of Requirements Validation Report Template

4. *Stakeholder engagement report*

Throughout the execution phase of the project, stakeholders are being engaged by the project team. Stakeholder reporting thereby involves providing updates on stakeholder engagement activities as well as describing the results of efforts to garner support from engaged stakeholders. Stakeholders are many in the world of aviation, and this makes the stakeholder engagement report a crucial aspect of the project execution phase. See graphical depiction of Stakeholder Engagement Management Template (Figure 3.52).

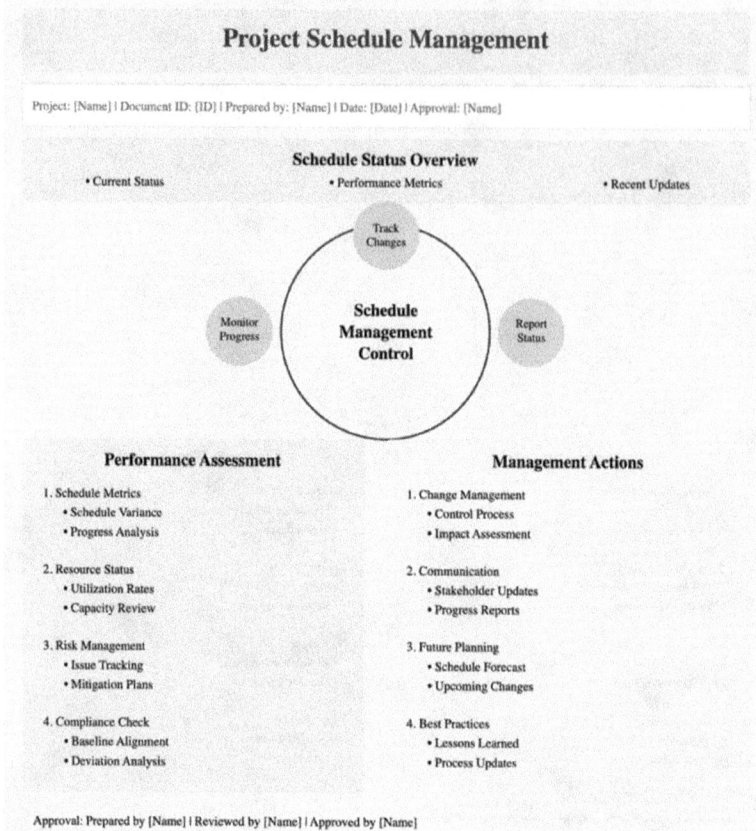

Project Schedule Management

Project: [Name] | Document ID: [ID] | Prepared by: [Name] | Date: [Date] | Approval: [Name]

Schedule Status Overview
• Current Status   • Performance Metrics   • Recent Updates

Track Changes

Schedule Management Control

Monitor Progress

Report Status

Performance Assessment

1. Schedule Metrics
   • Schedule Variance
   • Progress Analysis

2. Resource Status
   • Utilization Rates
   • Capacity Review

3. Risk Management
   • Issue Tracking
   • Mitigation Plans

4. Compliance Check
   • Baseline Alignment
   • Deviation Analysis

Management Actions

1. Change Management
   • Control Process
   • Impact Assessment

2. Communication
   • Stakeholder Updates
   • Progress Reports

3. Future Planning
   • Schedule Forecast
   • Upcoming Changes

4. Best Practices
   • Lessons Learned
   • Process Updates

Approval: Prepared by [Name] | Reviewed by [Name] | Approved by [Name]

Figure 3.51 Graphical depiction of Project Schedule Management Template

5. *Risk and safety issue response report*

   Risk and safety issues are identified in the planning phase of the project. During execution, it is important to step back and ask what, if any, safety issues were observed. Furthermore, any responses must be recorded. Finally, any new risks and safety concerns that have arisen during the execution phase are logged in along with corresponding updated response plans. See graphical depiction of Risk and Safety Issue Response Template (Figure 3.53).

6. *Budget progress report*

   Budget versus actual reporting is a mainstay of project management. The budget status provides information on the financial

Stakeholder Engagement Management

Project: [Name] | Document ID: [ID] | Prepared by: [Name] | Date: [Date] | Approved: [Name]

Status Overview

Feedback Analysis

Stakeholder Management Control

Progress Updates

Performance Assessment
1. Engagement Metrics
2. Satisfaction Analysis
3. Communication Effectiveness
4. Issue Resolution Tracking

Management Actions
1. Engagement Planning
2. Stakeholder Communication
3. Issue Resolution
4. Plan Updates

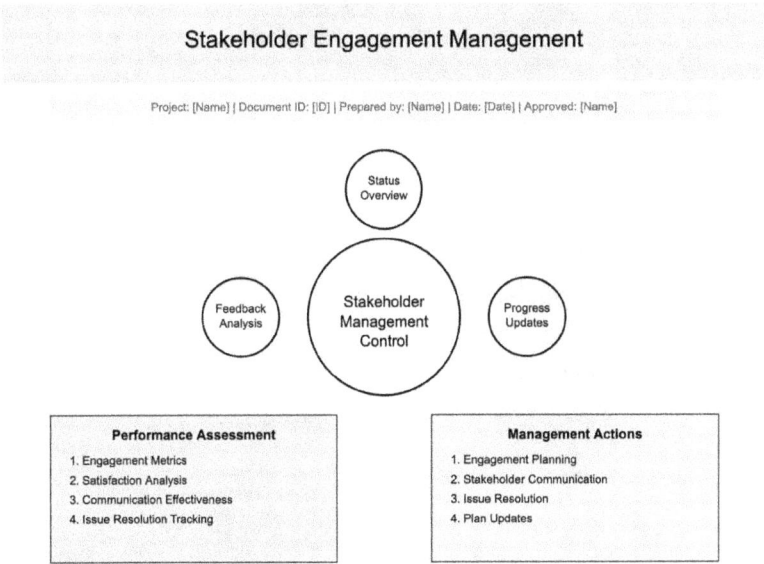

Figure 3.52 Graphical depiction of Stakeholder Engagement Management Template

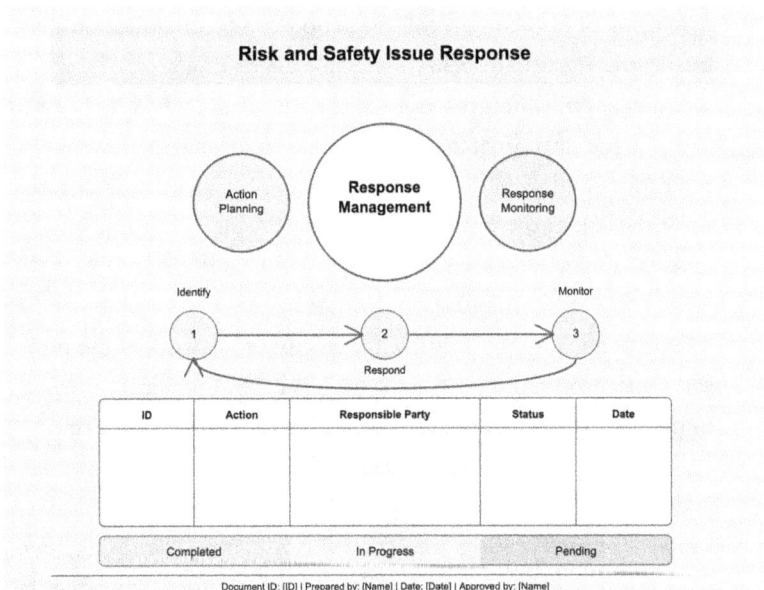

Risk and Safety Issue Response

Action Planning

Response Management

Response Monitoring

Identify

Monitor

1

2

3

Respond

ID	Action	Responsible Party	Status	Date

Completed	In Progress	Pending

Document ID: [ID] | Prepared by: [Name] | Date: [Date] | Approved by: [Name]

Figure 3.53 Graphical depiction of Risk and Safety Issue Response Template

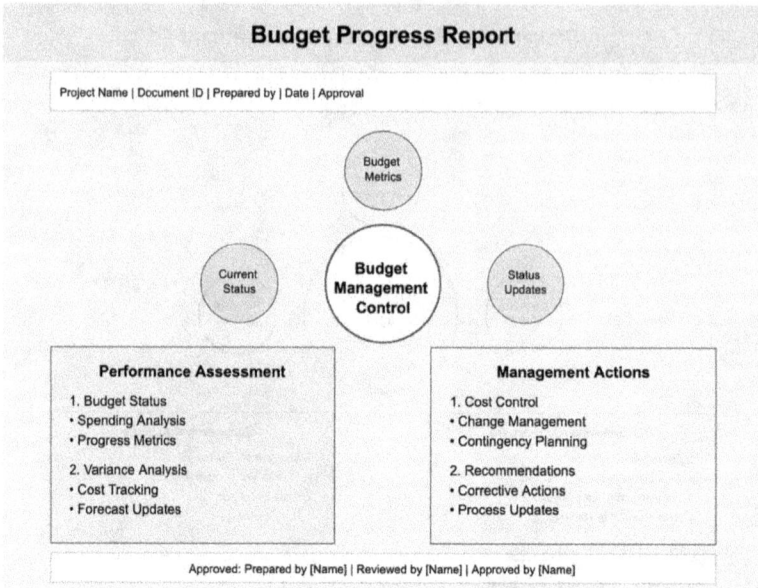

Budget Progress Report

Project Name | Document ID | Prepared by | Date | Approval

Budget
Metrics

Current
Status

**Budget
Management
Control**

Status
Updates

Performance Assessment

1. Budget Status
• Spending Analysis
• Progress Metrics

2. Variance Analysis
• Cost Tracking
• Forecast Updates

Management Actions

1. Cost Control
• Change Management
• Contingency Planning

2. Recommendations
• Corrective Actions
• Process Updates

Approved: Prepared by [Name] | Reviewed by [Name] | Approved by [Name]

Figure 3.54 Graphical depiction of Budget Progress Report Template

management of the project. It may also provide an indication that the project is ahead or behind schedule depending on the level of spending. While budget status looks backward as it revisits planned versus actual spending, it also provides data for making forecast projections and scenarios for where the project spending will end up at the end of the project. See graphical depiction of Budget Progress Report Template (Figure 3.54).

7. *Team Performance Monitoring Template*

The project team is responsible for executing the work of the project. During execution, project managers have a significant interest in the performance of the team as well as the progress the team has made since its inception. Data collected from the observation and reporting of the team could lead to possible actions, additional support, or intervention. The Team Performance Monitoring Template provides prompts and associated guidance for monitoring the performance of the project team. See graphical depiction of Team Performance Monitoring Template (Figure 3.55).

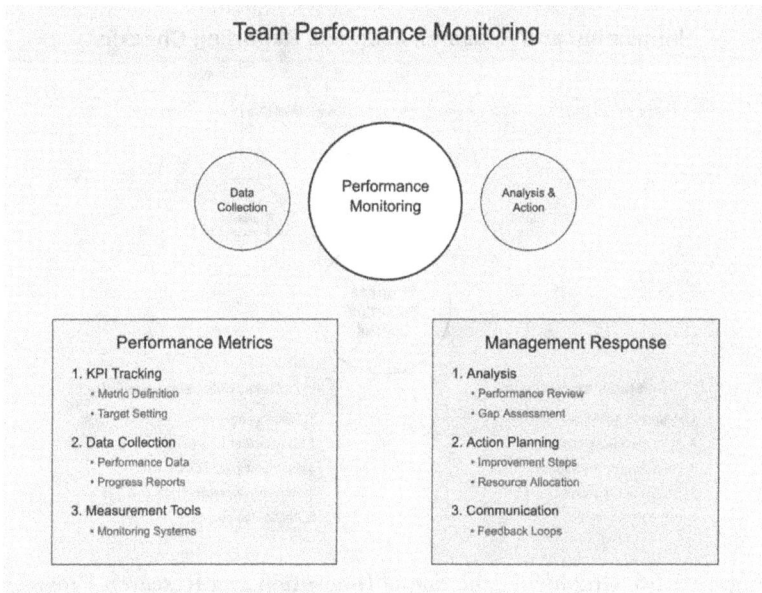

Figure 3.55 Graphical depiction of Team Performance Monitoring Template

8. *Innovation and Research Progress Reporting Checklist*

   Implementing innovation is a complex endeavor and requires the cooperation of resources from the extended organization, external partners, and integration into existing known technologies and platforms. The execution phase is where "the rubber meets the road"—that is, this phase encompasses implementing novel technologies, processes, or techniques. A comprehensive checklist is used to confirm that the innovation implementation is proceeding according to plan and that all resources and partners are fully engaged and meeting expectations. See graphical depiction of Innovation and Research Progress Reporting Checklist (Figure 3.56).

9. *Procurement Deliverables Checklist*

   Components and services that are supplied from external partners are received, tested, and integrated in the execution phase. The Procurement Deliverables Checklist ensures that orders, shipments, receivables, and payments to suppliers are in order so that the project may proceed smoothly. Furthermore, the performance of each supplier is

Innovation and Research Progress Reporting Checklist

Project Name: [Project Title] | Document ID: [Unique ID] | Prepared by: [Name] | Date: [Date] | Approval: [Approver]

Performance Evaluation

Progress Monitoring

Stakeholder Communication

Progress Reporting Control

Status Assessment

1. Research Activities
2. Innovation Development
3. Implementation Progress
4. Resource Utilization
5. KPI Achievement

Stakeholder Management

1. Risk Management
2. Stakeholder Engagement
3. Partnership Updates
4. Review Preparation
5. Action Planning

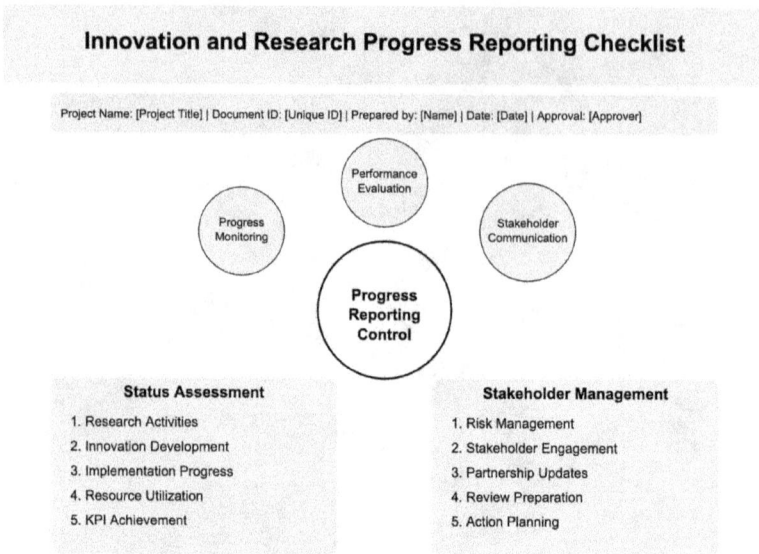

Figure 3.56 Graphical depiction of Innovation and Research Progress Reporting Checklist

monitored and recorded, and appropriate actions are taken. See graphical depiction of Procurement Deliverables Checklist (Figure 3.57).

10. *Safety and Compliance Reports Deliverables Checklist*

As the work of the project is carried out, the effectiveness of the safety and compliance plan is assessed by confirming the produced results. This is done by evaluating the number of accidents, safety incidents and concerns, and emergencies, as well as reporting on them. The reports include any responses to safety issues. By doing so, the project team also confirms compliance with appropriate safety standards. See graphical depiction of Safety and Compliance Reports Checklist (Figure 3.58).

11. *Technology Implementation Plan Deliverables Checklist*

As technology is implemented in the execution of the project, the project team confirms via checklist that the requirements are clear, the criterion for employing the technology is sound, the implementation is resourced, and, finally, the effort is well documented. Technology implementation—particularly implementing new technologies—can be a process of discovery in which new issues

Procurement Deliverables Framework

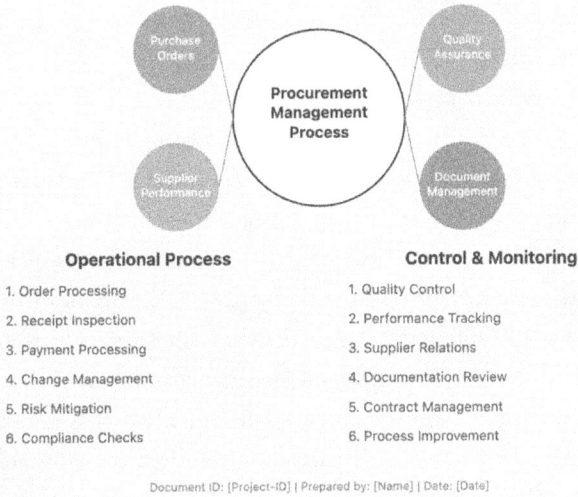

Purchase Orders

Quality Assurance

Procurement
Management
Process

Supplier
Performance

Document
Management

Operational Process	Control & Monitoring
1. Order Processing	1. Quality Control
2. Receipt Inspection	2. Performance Tracking
3. Payment Processing	3. Supplier Relations
4. Change Management	4. Documentation Review
5. Risk Mitigation	5. Contract Management
6. Compliance Checks	6. Process Improvement

Document ID: [Project-ID] | Prepared by: [Name] | Date: [Date]

Figure 3.57 Graphical depiction of Procurement Deliverables Checklist

Safety and Compliance Reports

Project Name | Document ID | Prepared by | Date | Approval

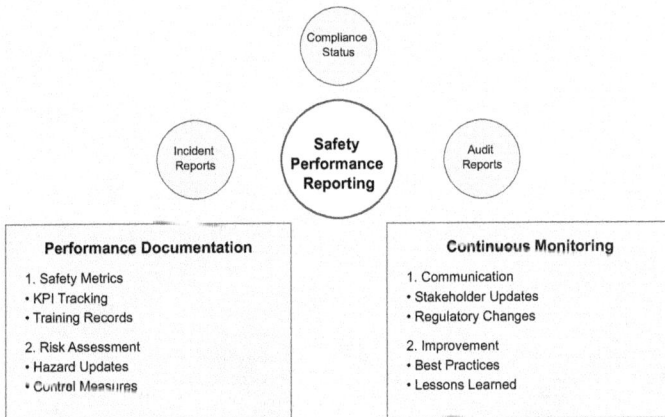

Compliance
Status

Incident
Reports

Safety
Performance
Reporting

Audit
Reports

Performance Documentation	Continuous Monitoring
1. Safety Metrics	1. Communication
• KPI Tracking	• Stakeholder Updates
• Training Records	• Regulatory Changes
2. Risk Assessment	2. Improvement
• Hazard Updates	• Best Practices
• Control Measures	• Lessons Learned

Approved: Prepared by [Name] | Reviewed by [Name] | Approved by [Name]

Figure 3.58 Graphical depiction of Safety and Compliance Reports Checklist

and characteristics of the technology unfold as implementation work is performed. The checklist aids in capturing such issues. See graphical depiction of Technology Implementation Management Checklist (Figure 3.59).

12. *Quality Control Reports Deliverables Checklist*

In the execution phase, the key concerns relating to quality involve confirming that the QMS is working. The checklist supports this by focusing attention on trends, nonconformance, compliance to standards and requirements, and client feedback. Checklists are noted as an important quality tool by ASQ (The American Society for Quality). While quality planning establishes systems and firmly establishes relevant standards and requirements, frequent checks during execution confirm that the plan is proceeding as intended. See graphical depiction of Quality Control Reports Deliverables Checklist (Figure 3.60).

13. *Compliance Management Deliverables Checklist*

The Compliance Management Deliverables Checklist aids the team in confirming that the team is on track to comply with

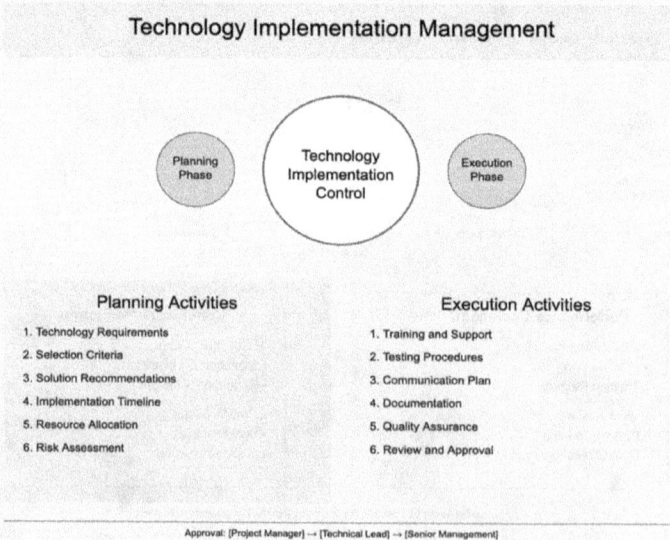

Figure 3.59 Graphical depiction of Technology Implementation Management Checklist

Quality Control Reports

Inspection & Testing

Quality Reporting

Analysis & Actions

Quality Monitoring

1. Control Measures
   • Inspection Results
   • Testing Outcomes

2. Performance Review
   • Supplier Evaluation
   • Customer Feedback

3. Compliance Check
   • Regulatory Standards

Response Actions

1. Nonconformance
   • Issue Identification
   • Corrective Actions

2. Trend Analysis
   • Quality Patterns
   • Risk Assessment

3. Recommendations
   • Improvement Plans

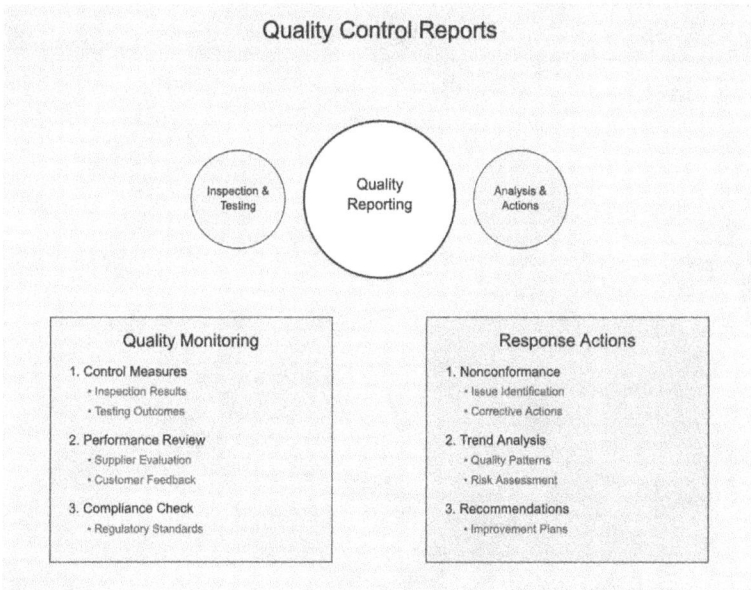

Figure 3.60 Graphical depiction of Quality Control Reports Checklist

appropriate regulatory standards. To support this, the checklist requires the project team to make note of any regulatory changes, noncompliance concerns, and documentation. The Compliance Management Deliverables Checklist also captures any interaction and engagement with relevant regulatory bodies. See graphical depiction of Compliance Management Deliverables Checklist (Figure 3.61).

14. *Environmental/Sustainability Reports Checklist*

The Environmental/Sustainability Reports Checklist address two major elements relating to the environment: (a) to ensure that the project follows all environmental regulations and (b) tracking the result of any sustainability initiatives mandated to be incorporated by the project. Finally, it is essential for the project to establish a track record of environmental responsibility. For this reason, the checklist in the execute phase confirms that all relevant documentation is in place. See graphical depiction of Environment and Sustainability Report Checklist (Figure 6.62).

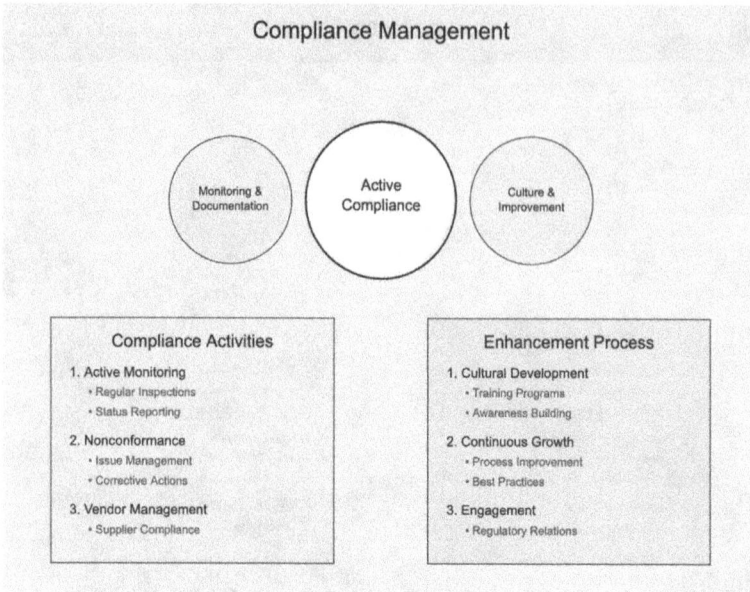

Figure 3.61 Graphical depiction of Compliance Management Deliverables Checklist

Execute Phase Summary

The templates for plan-driven and iterative lifecycles as well as the primary and supporting practices for the execute phase are summarized in Figure 3.63.

The Control Phase

1. *Lifecycle Control Report Template*

   In the Lifecycle Control Report Template, key control activities include: (1) schedule control, assessing timeline impact and milestone achievements; (2) quality control, evaluating metrics, audits, and inspections; (3) risk control, implementing measures to mitigate risks; (4) issue resolution, addressing significant issues; (5) change control, managing change requests and decisions; (6) compliance monitoring, ensuring regulatory adherence; and (7) stakeholder engagement, maintaining communication and managing expectations. These control measures are reviewed and updated through

Environmental/Sustainability Reports Framework

Compliance
Status

Impact
Monitoring

**Report
Development**

Documentation
& Evidence

Review &
Approval

Current Status

- Mitigation Measures
- Sustainability Initiatives
- Challenges Identified
- Solutions Implemented

Future Planning

- Short-term Goals
- Long-term Targets
- Planned Initiatives
- Continuous Improvement

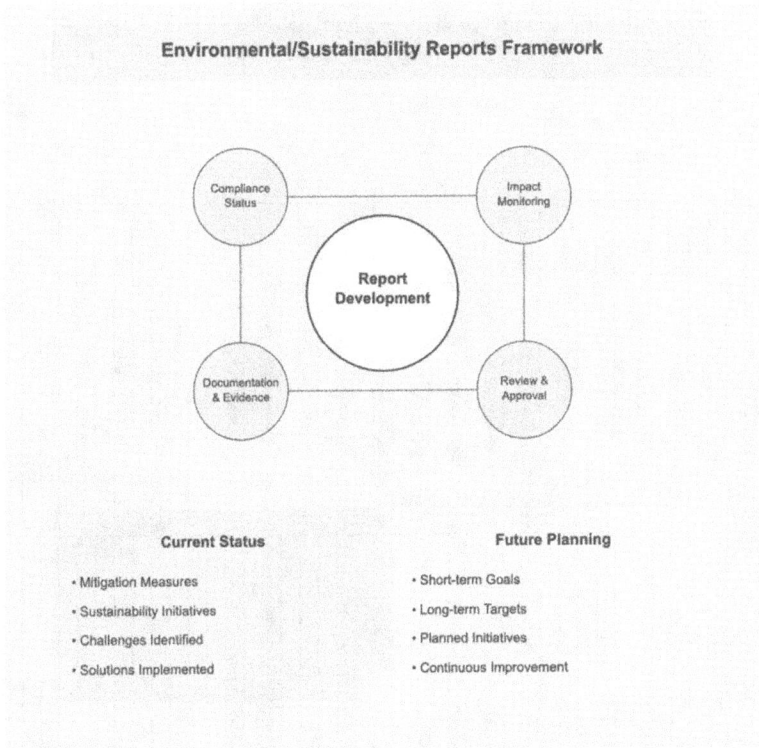

Figure 3.62 Graphical depiction of Environment and Sustainability Report Checklist

regular lifecycle phase reviews, performance reviews, and stakeholder feedback. See graphical depiction of Lifecycle Control Report Template (Figure 3.64).

2. *Requirements Measurement and Verification Report Template*
In the Requirements Measurement and Verification Report Template document, key control measures include measurement and verification activities, such as metrics analysis, testing, reviews, and audits, to assess compliance with requirements. The document outlines phase-specific activities for implementing requirements management practice, including requirements summary, compliance and deviation analysis, corrective actions, and stakeholder feedback and engagement. It also emphasizes the importance of documentation, including detailed measurement results, deviation

Practices	Execute
Practice Guide for Lifecycle Management in Aviation Project Management	Lifecycle Execution Report Template
AVPMPG-LM-1.000	AVPMP-LM-1.4
Practice Guide for Lifecycle Management in Aviation Project Management	
AVPMPG-LM-1.000	
Practice Guide for Requirements Management in Aviation Project Management	Requirements Validation Report Template
AVPMPG-RM-1.000	AVPMP-RM-1.4
Practice Guide for Schedule Management in Aviation Project Management	Project Schedule Management Template
AVPMPG-SM-1.000	AVPMP-SM-1.4
Practice Guide for Stakeholder and Customer Relations Management in Aviation Project Management	Stakeholder Engagement Report Template
AVPMPG-ST-1.000	AVPMP-ST-1.4
Practice Guide for Risk and Safety Management in Aviation Project Management	Risk and Safety Issue Response Report Template
AVPMPG-RS-1.000	AVPMP-RS-1.4
Practice Guide for Financial Management in Aviation Project Management	Budget Progress Report Template
AVPMPG-FM-1.000	AVPMP-FM-1.4
Practice Guide for Human Resource and Team Management in Aviation Project Management	Team Performance Monitoring Template
AVPMPG-HR-1.000	AVPMP-HR-1.4
Practice Guide for Innovation and Research Management in Aviation Project Management	Innovation and Research Progress Reporting Checklist
AVPMPGS-IR-1.000	AVPMS-IR-1.4
Practice Guide for Supply Chain and Procurement Management in Aviation Project Management	Procurement Deliverable Checklist
AVPMPGS-SC-1.000	AVPMS-SC-1.4
Practice Guide for Aviation Safety Management in Aviation Project Management	Safety and Compliance Reports Deliverable Checklist
AVPMPGS-AS-1.000	AVPMS-AS-1.4
Practice Guide for Technology and Engineering Management in Aviation Project Management	Technology Implementation Plan Deliverables Checklist
AVPMPGS-TE-1.000	AVPMS-TE-1.4
Practice Guide for Aviation Quality Management in Aviation Project Management	Quality Control Reports Deliverable Checklist
AVPMPGS-AQ-1.000	AVPMS-AQ-1.4
Practice Guide for Aviation Regulation Compliance and Certification Management in Aviation Project Management	Compliance Management Deliverable Checklist
AVPMPGS-AR-1.000	AVPMS-AR-1.4
Practice Guide for Environmental and Sustainability Management in Aviation Project Management	Environmental/Sustainability Reports Checklist
AVPMPGS-ES-1.000	AVPMS-ES-1.4

Practices	Iterative Execute
Practice Guide for Lifecycle Management in Aviation Project Management	Daily Standup Meeting Template
	AVPMIT-LM-1.4
Practice Guide for Lifecycle Management in Aviation Project Management	Sprint Plan Deliverable Template
	AVPMIT-LM-1.4.2
Practice Guide for Requirements Management in Aviation Project Management	Validation Deliverable Template
Practice Guide for Requirements Management in Aviation Project Management	AVPMIT-RM-1.4

Figure 3.63 Summarizes execute phase primary and supporting practices templates for both plan-driven and iterative lifecycles

Lifecycle Control Report Template

Project: [Name] | Manager: [Name] | Period: [Start-End] | Version: [Number] | Date: [Date]

Executive Summary

• Control Activities   • Key Achievements   • Major Adjustments

Control Actions

Control Status Review

Phase Review   Future Plans

Performance Controls

1. Schedule Control
   • Timeline Management
   • Milestone Tracking

2. Quality Control
   • Quality Metrics
   • Audit Outcomes

3. Risk Management
   • Control Measures
   • Issue Resolution

4. Change Control
   • Change Requests
   • Impact Analysis

Management Overview

1. Compliance Update
   • Regulatory Status
   • Corrective Actions

2. Stakeholder Update
   • Feedback Analysis
   • Engagement Activities

3. Lessons Learned
   • Control Insights
   • Knowledge Integration

4. Future Planning
   • Upcoming Controls
   • Improvement Plans

Approval: Prepared by [Name] | Reviewed by [Name] | Approved by [Name]

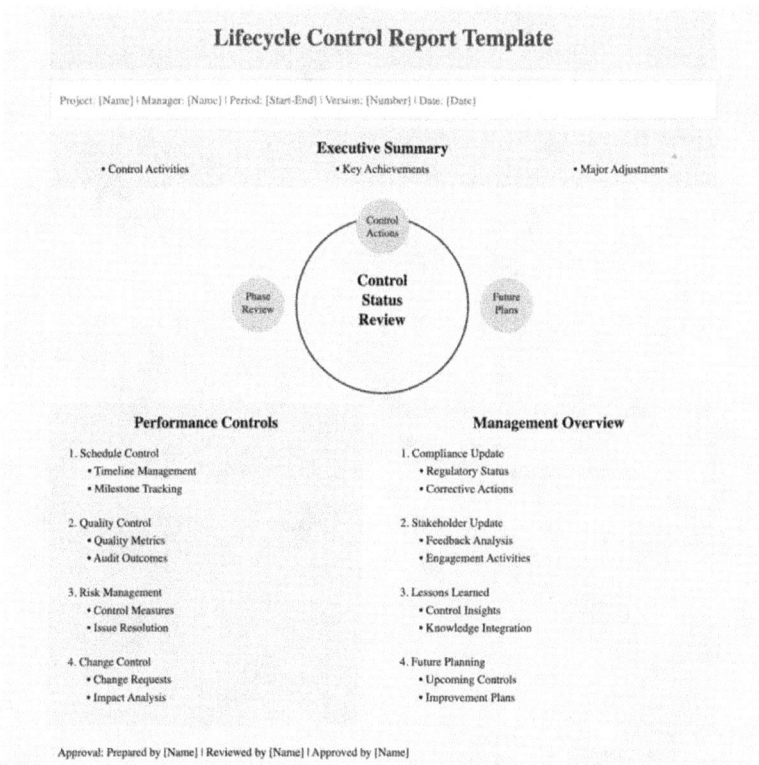

Figure 3.64 Graphical depiction of Lifecycle Control Report Template

and noncompliance logs, and stakeholder feedback documentation. Additionally, the framework ensures ongoing assessment of project deliverables against defined requirements, identification of areas needing attention, and implementation of corrective actions to address noncompliance or deviations. See graphical depiction of Requirements Measurement and Verification Report Template (Figure 3.65).

3. *Schedule Variance and Adjustments/Change-Control Reports Template*
   The Schedule Variance and Adjustments/Change-Control Reports Template provides guidance on managing variances and adjustments through a structured Change-Control Process. Key control measures include identifying and summarizing schedule variances, documenting and evaluating change requests, and approving changes through a defined process involving stakeholders.

Requirements Measurement and Verification Report

Project: [Name] | Document ID: [ID] | Prepared by: [Name] | Date: [Date] | Approval: [Name]

Process Overview

• Objectives   • Methodology   • Metrics

Verify
Compliance

Measure
Results

**Measurement
and
Verification**

Report
Status

Measurement Analysis

1. Activity Assessment
   • Verification Methods
   • Metrics Collection

2. Compliance Review
   • Requirements Status
   • Deviation Analysis

3. Performance Tracking
   • Metrics Analysis
   • Progress Monitoring

4. Documentation
   • Measurement Records
   • Verification Evidence

Results Management

1. Compliance Status
   • Met Requirements
   • Noncompliance Areas

2. Corrective Actions
   • Action Items
   • Implementation Plans

3. Stakeholder Input
   • Feedback Analysis
   • Engagement Results

4. Next Steps
   • Follow-up Activities
   • Process Updates

Approval: Prepared by [Name] | Reviewed by [Name] | Approved by [Name]

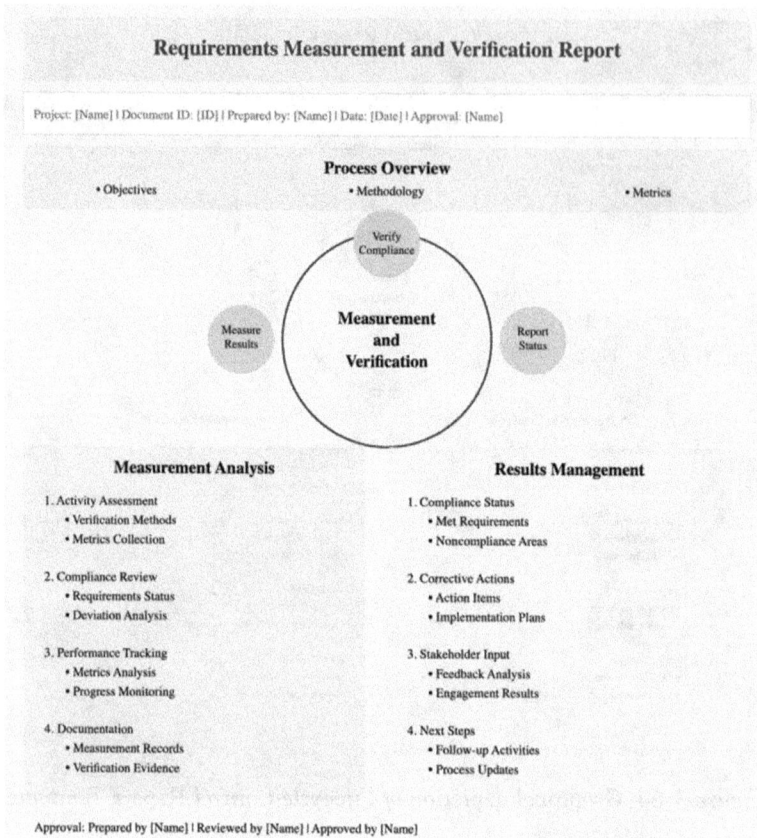

Figure 3.65 Graphical depiction of Requirements Measurement and Verification Report Template

The framework ensures that changes are assessed for impact on project schedule, budget, and scope and prioritized based on urgency, feasibility, and alignment with objectives. Implementation of approved changes is monitored, and communication is maintained with stakeholders. Additionally, a change-control log tracks request status and outcomes, and lessons learned are documented to improve future change-control processes and project planning. See graphical depiction of Project Schedule Management Template (Figure 3.66).

Project Schedule Management

Project: [Name] | Document ID: [ID] | Prepared by: [Name] | Date: [Date] | Approval: [Name]

Schedule Status Overview

• Current Status   • Performance Metrics   • Recent Updates

Track
Changes

Monitor
Progress

**Schedule
Management
Control**

Report
Status

Performance Assessment   **Management Actions**

1. Schedule Metrics   1. Change Management
   • Schedule Variance   • Control Process
   • Progress Analysis   • Impact Assessment

2. Resource Status   2. Communication
   • Utilization Rates   • Stakeholder Updates
   • Capacity Review   • Progress Reports

3. Risk Management   3. Future Planning
   • Issue Tracking   • Schedule Forecast
   • Mitigation Plans   • Upcoming Changes

4. Compliance Check   4. Best Practices
   • Baseline Alignment   • Lessons Learned
   • Deviation Analysis   • Process Updates

Approval: Prepared by [Name] | Reviewed by [Name] | Approved by [Name]

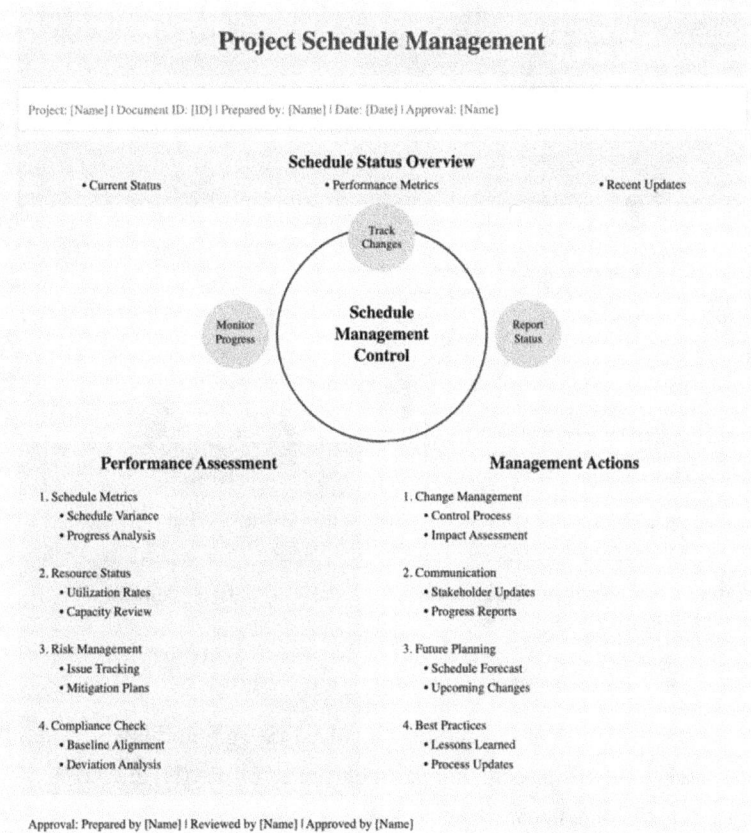

Figure 3.66 Graphical depiction of Project Schedule Management Template

4. *Stakeholder Communications/Decisions Report Template*

   The Stakeholder Communications/Decisions Report Template
   provides a structured approach to stakeholder communication and
   decision-making, ensuring effective management of project stakeholders. Key control measures include regular project status updates, documentation of decisions made, assessment of their impact
   on stakeholders, and evaluation of communication effectiveness.
   The framework also outlines activities for stakeholder communication, feedback collection, and lessons-learned documentation.
   Additionally, it defines the decision-making process, roles, and

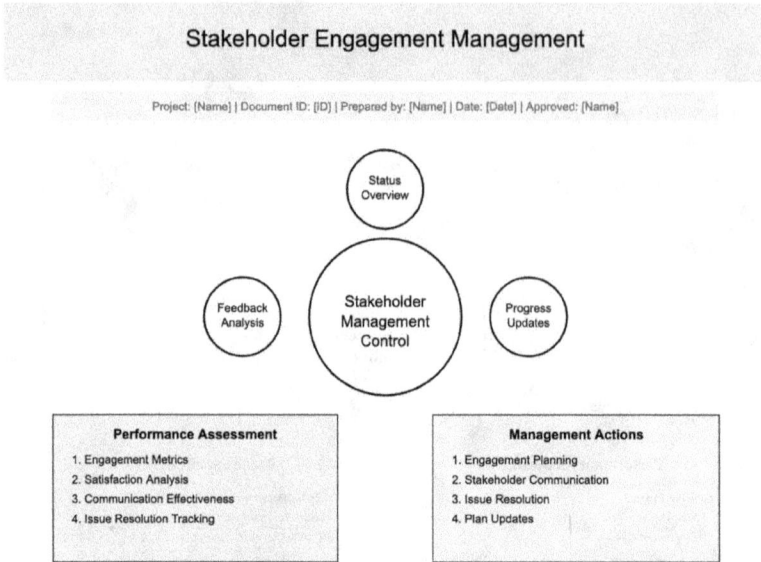

Figure 3.67 Graphical depiction of Stakeholder Engagement Management Template

responsibilities of stakeholders involved. See graphical depiction of Stakeholder Engagement Management Template (Figure 3.67).

5. *Risk and Safety Issue Response Monitoring and Control Report Template*
The Risk and Safety Issue Response Monitoring and Control Report provides a structured approach to managing risks and safety issues in the control phase of a project. Its primary objective is to ensure timely and effective responses to identified risks and safety issues, thereby minimizing their impact on the project. Key control measures include reviewing and evaluating response plans, monitoring response actions, tracking risk and safety issue status, and activating contingency plans as needed. See graphical depiction of Risk and Safety Issue Template (Figure 3.68).

To achieve this, the report outlines several essential activities:

Response Plan Review: Evaluating the effectiveness of response actions taken during the execute phase.
Response Monitoring Metrics: Defining metrics and indicators to measure response effectiveness.

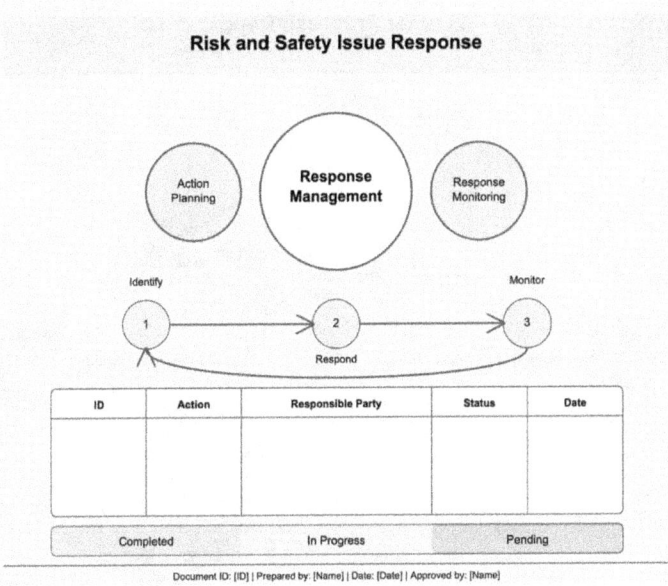

Risk and Safety Issue Response

ID	Action	Responsible Party	Status	Date

Completed	In Progress	Pending

Document ID: [ID] | Prepared by: [Name] | Date: [Date] | Approved by: [Name]

Figure 3.68 Graphical depiction of Risk and Safety Issue Template

Response Monitoring Process: Describing the process and outlining roles and responsibilities.

Risk and Safety Issue Tracking: Monitoring risk likelihood, impact, and severity.

Contingency Activation: Establishing procedures for activating contingency plans.

6. *Budget Variance and Adjustments/Control Report Template*
The Budget Variance and Adjustments/Change-Control process ensures effective financial management in aviation project management. Key control measures include establishing a budget baseline, analyzing variances between planned and actual spending, identifying significant deviations, and documenting change requests with estimated cost impacts. The process proposes budget adjustments based on approved changes, updates the budget baseline, and obtains approval from the project manager. See graphical depiction of Budget Progress Report Template (Figure 3.69).

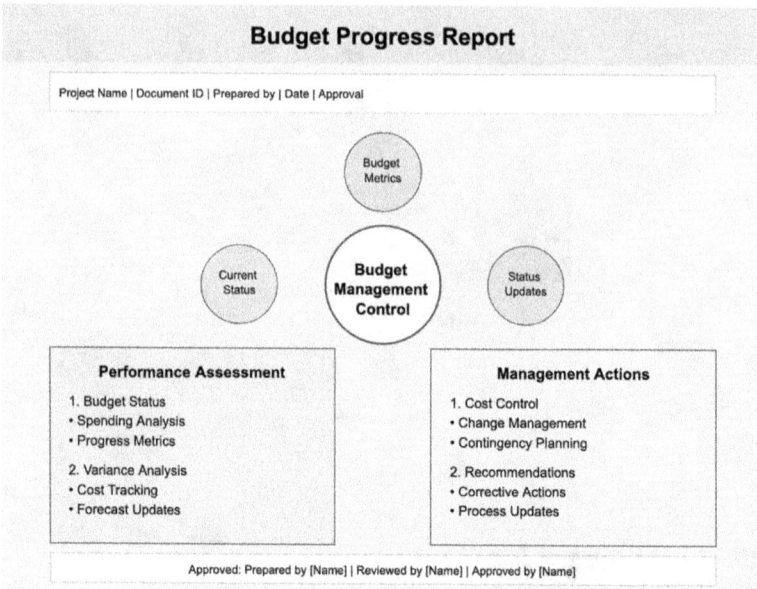

Budget Progress Report

Project Name | Document ID | Prepared by | Date | Approval

Budget Metrics

Current Status

Budget Management Control

Status Updates

Performance Assessment

1. Budget Status
• Spending Analysis
• Progress Metrics

2. Variance Analysis
• Cost Tracking
• Forecast Updates

Management Actions

1. Cost Control
• Change Management
• Contingency Planning

2. Recommendations
• Corrective Actions
• Process Updates

Approved: Prepared by [Name] | Reviewed by [Name] | Approved by [Name]

Figure 3.69 Graphical depiction of Budget Progress Report Template

7. *Team Feedback and Adjustments Template*

The Feedback and Adjustments document provides a structured framework for proactive feedback collection, issue identification, and adjustment implementation to ensure project success. Key control measures include:

A. Feedback collection from team members and stakeholders
B. Feedback analysis and categorization
C. Identification and prioritization of issues
D. Development of adjustment plans with actions, responsibilities, and timelines
E. Communication and implementation of adjustments
F. Evaluation of adjustment effectiveness
G. Continuous improvement through ongoing communication and collaboration.

By implementing these control measures, project managers can address emerging issues, improve project performance, and ensure

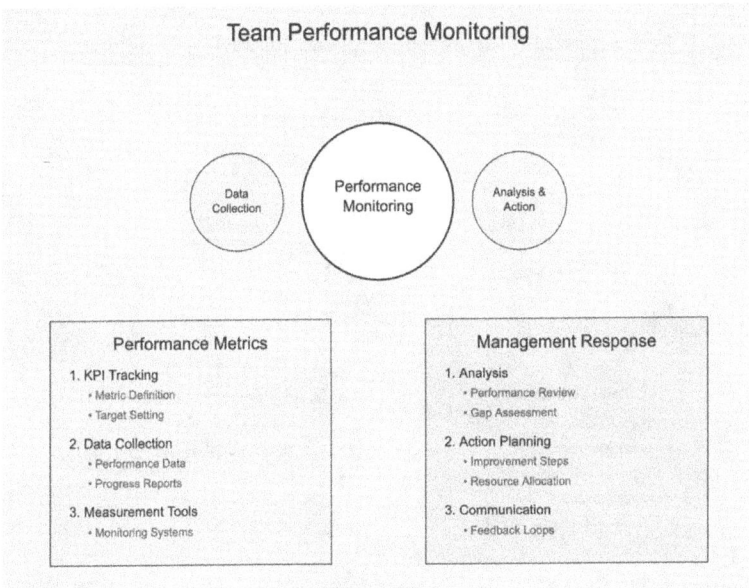

Figure 3.70 *Graphical depiction of Team Performance Monitoring Template*

alignment with project objectives. Effective feedback collection and adjustment enable proactive problem-solving, minimize risks, and foster a culture of continuous improvement. See graphical depiction of Team Performance Monitoring Template (Figure 3.70).

8. *Innovation and Research Adjustments Deliverables Checklist*
The Innovation and Research Adjustments Deliverables Checklist ensures effective management in aviation project management through various control measures. These measures include Review of Research and Innovation Objectives, evaluating alignment with project goals and identifying discrepancies. Other key controls are Assessment of Progress against Plan, Feedback Analysis, and Risk Assessment and Mitigation, which help identify areas for adjustment and minimize risks. Additionally, the checklist outlines Resource Reallocation, Technology Adoption and Integration, and Adjustment of Timeline and Milestones to optimize project performance. Effective communication and stakeholder engagement are also crucial, along with Documentation and Reporting Updates

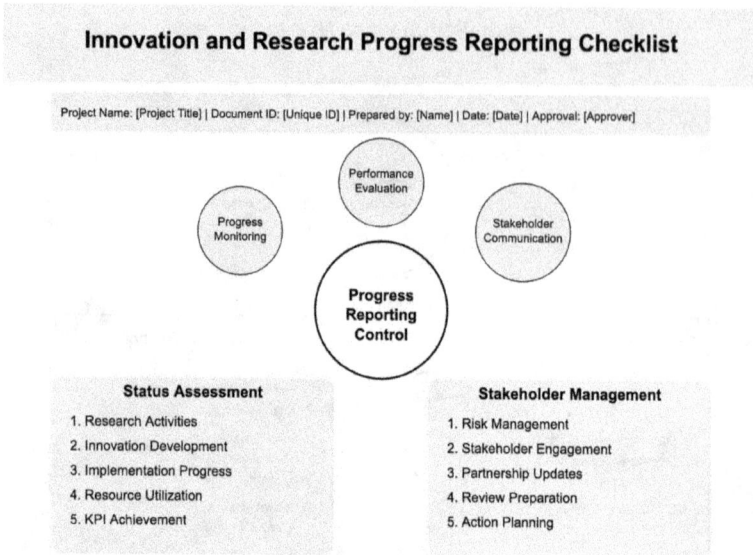

Figure 3.71 *Graphical depiction of Innovation and Research Progress Reporting Checklist*

and Continuous Improvement Initiatives. Finally, a Review and Approval Process ensures adjustments are approved and implemented according to project management protocols. See graphical depiction of Innovation and Research Progress Reporting Checklist (Figure 3.71).

9. *Adjust and Optimize Supply Chain and PROCUREMENT Deliverables Checklist*

The Procurement and Supply Chain Management Deliverables Checklist outlines key control measures to ensure effective management in aviation project management. These measures include Supplier Performance Review, evaluating performance against established key performance indicators (KPIs) and benchmarks, and Contract Compliance Assessment, reviewing contracts to ensure compliance with terms and conditions. Other crucial controls are Cost Analysis and Optimization, Supply Chain Risk Management, and Inventory Management and Optimization, which help identify areas for improvement and mitigate risks. Additionally, the checklist emphasizes Supplier Relationship Management, Continuous

Procurement Deliverables Framework

Procurement
Strategy

Vendor
Management

Procurement
Management
Process

Procurement
Performance

Procurement
Operations

Operational Process

1. Order Processing
2. Receipt Inspection
3. Payment Processing
4. Change Management
5. Risk Mitigation
6. Compliance Checks

Control & Monitoring

1. Quality Control
2. Performance Tracking
3. Supplier Relations
4. Documentation Review
5. Contract Management
6. Process Improvement

Document ID: [Project-ID] | Prepared by: [Name] | Date: [Date]

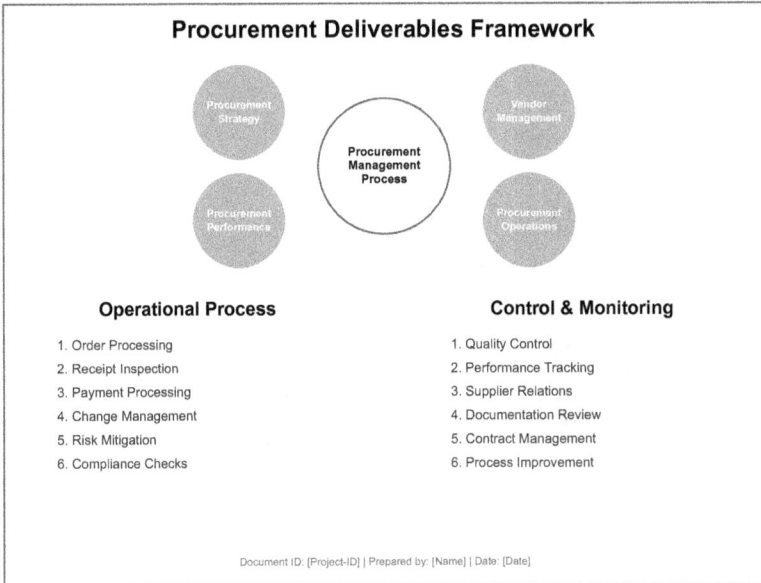

Figure 3.72 Graphical depiction of Procurement Deliverables Checklist

Improvement Initiatives, and Performance Metrics Review to foster positive relationships, streamline processes, and enhance efficiency. Furthermore, it highlights the importance of Technology Adoption and Innovation, Documentation and Reporting, and Stakeholder Communication to ensure transparency, collaboration, and alignment with project objectives. See graphical depiction of Procurement Deliverables Checklist (Figure 3.72).

10. Safety *and Compliance Response and Adjustment Deliverable Checklist* The Safety and Compliance Response and Adjustment Deliverables Checklist outlines key control measures for effective engineering management, focusing on Performance Monitoring to identify areas for improvement, and Root Cause Analysis to determine underlying factors contributing to engineering issues. Continuous Improvement Initiatives are also crucial, involving corrective actions and preventive measures to enhance engineering effectiveness. Additionally, the document highlights the importance of Resource Optimization, Risk Management Updates, Supplier and Vendor

Figure 3.73 Graphical depiction of Safety and Compliance Reports Checklist

Management, Quality Assurance and Control, Feedback Mechanisms, Regulatory Compliance Review, Documentation and Reporting, Training and Development, and Lessons Learned and Best Practices. By implementing these control measures, engineering teams can optimize performance, minimize risks, ensure compliance, and drive continuous improvement. See graphical depiction of Safety and Compliance Reports Checklist (Figure 3.73).

11. *Technical and engineering management: Adjust and Optimize Deliverables Checklist*

The Adjust and Optimize Deliverables Checklist outlines key control measures for effective engineering management, focusing on Performance Monitoring to identify areas for improvement, and Root Cause Analysis to determine underlying factors contributing to engineering issues. Continuous Improvement Initiatives are also crucial, involving corrective actions and preventive measures to enhance engineering effectiveness. Additionally, the document highlights the importance of Resource Optimization, Risk Management

Technology Implementation Management

Planning
Phase

Technology
Implementation
Control

Execution
Phase

Planning Activities	Execution Activities
1. Technology Requirements	1. Training and Support
2. Selection Criteria	2. Testing Procedures
3. Solution Recommendations	3. Communication Plan
4. Implementation Timeline	4. Documentation
5. Resource Allocation	5. Quality Assurance
6. Risk Assessment	6. Review and Approval

Approval: [Project Manager] → [Technical Lead] → [Senior Management]

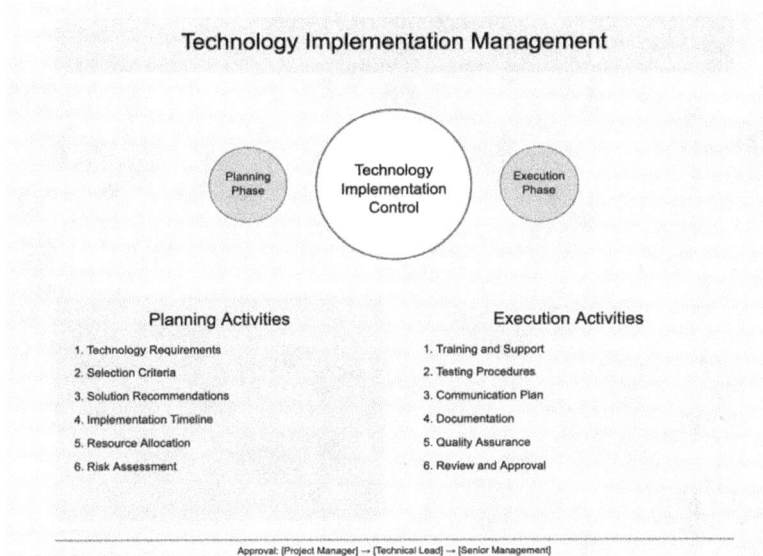

Figure 3.74 Graphical depiction of Technology Implementation Checklist

Updates, Supplier and Vendor Management, Quality Assurance and Control, Feedback Mechanisms, Regulatory Compliance Review, Documentation and Reporting, Training and Development, and Lessons Learned and Best Practices. By implementing these control measures, engineering teams can optimize performance, minimize risks, and ensure compliance. See graphical depiction of Technology Implementation Checklist (Figure 3.74).

12. *Change-Control Deliverables Checklist*

The Change-Control Deliverables Checklist helps ensure effective management of changes in aviation quality assurance during the control phase. Key control measures include Change Request Identification, Documentation, Impact Assessment, Review and Approval, Prioritization, Implementation Planning, Communication, Tracking, and Monitoring. Additionally, the process involves Change-Control Board Meetings, Change Closure and Documentation, and Continuous Improvement Initiatives to ensure that changes are systematically assessed, approved, implemented, and reviewed. These control measures enable the identification and

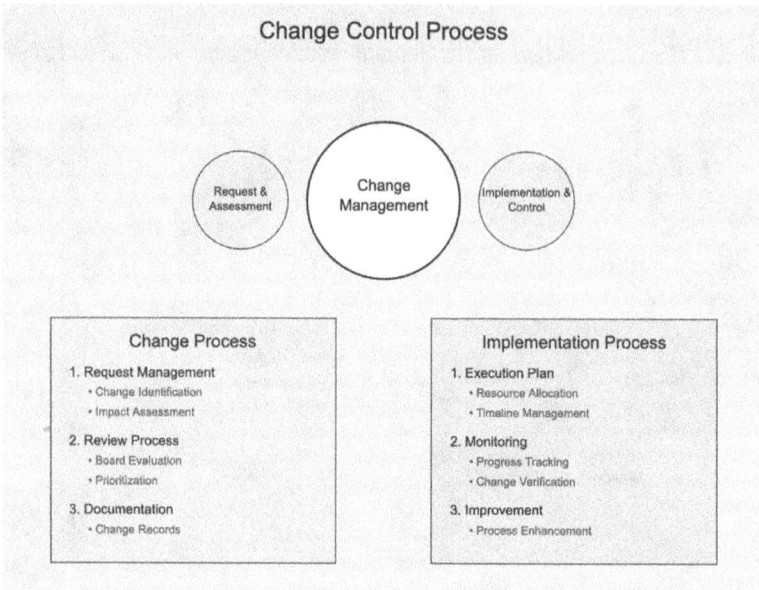

Figure 3.75 *Graphical depiction of Change-Control Process Checklist*

mitigation of potential risks, ensure compliance with project objectives, and facilitate knowledge-sharing and lessons learned. By implementing these controls, project managers can maintain project integrity, minimize disruptions, and ensure successful outcomes, while continually improving change management practices to enhance project efficiency and effectiveness. See graphical depiction of Change-Control Process Checklist (Figure 3.75).

13. *Compliance Monitoring and Adjustment Deliverables Checklist*
    The Compliance Monitoring and Adjustment Deliverables Checklist outlines a comprehensive framework for ensuring regulatory compliance in aviation project management. Key control measures include Regulatory Compliance Review, which involves regularly reviewing regulatory requirements and identifying changes or updates that may impact project activities.

    Other crucial measures include:

    Compliance Monitoring Process: implementing a structured process to track compliance metrics and performance

Data Collection and Analysis: collecting and analyzing data to
  identify trends, patterns, and areas for improvement
Nonconformance Identification: identifying and documenting
  instances of noncompliance
Root Cause Analysis: determining underlying reasons for
  noncompliance
Corrective and Preventive Actions (CAPA): developing and
  implementing plans to address nonconformances
Compliance Documentation Updates: updating documentation to
  reflect changes in regulatory requirements
Compliance Reporting: preparing reports on monitoring activities and
  corrective actions
Stakeholder Communication: communicating compliance issues and
  findings to relevant stakeholders
Regulatory Engagement: engaging with regulatory authorities
  for guidance and clarification *Continuous Improvement Initiatives*:
  implementing initiatives to enhance compliance processes
Compliance Culture Promotion: promoting a culture of compliance
  within the project team and organization.

These control measures enable project managers to identify
and mitigate potential risks, ensure compliance with regulatory
requirements, and maintain project integrity. See graphical depiction of Compliance Monitoring and Adjustment Checklist
(Figure 3.76).

14. *Environmental and Sustainability Performance and Adjustment
Checklist*
The Environmental and Sustainability Performance and Adjustment Checklist outlines a comprehensive framework for ensuring
environmental sustainability in aviation project management,
focusing on control measures to mitigate environmental impacts.
Key control measures include Performance Review, which involves
reviewing environmental KPIs, assessing sustainability initiatives,
and evaluating energy efficiency improvements. See graphical depiction of Environmental Performance and Adjustment Checklist
(Figure 3.77).

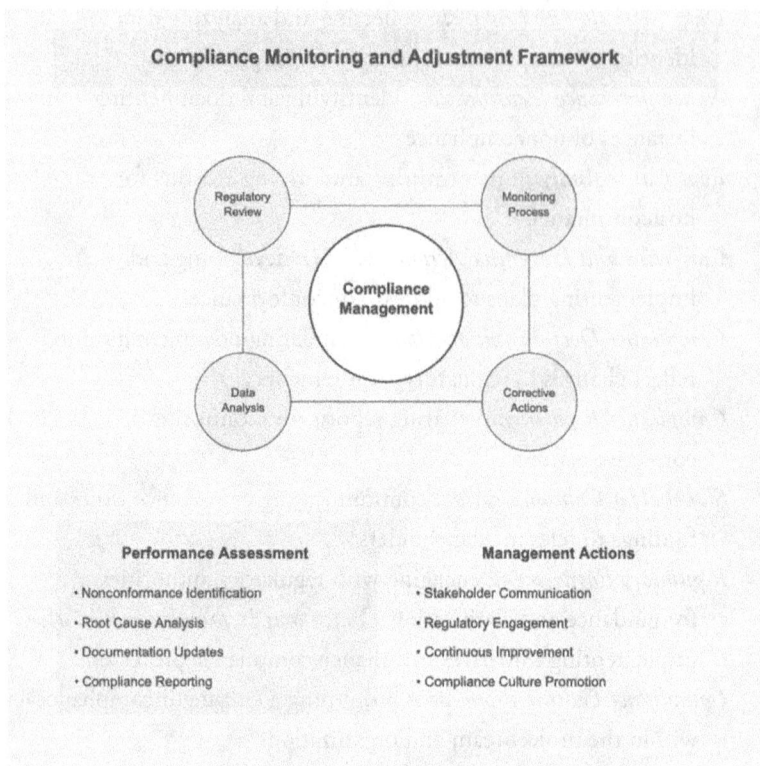

Compliance Monitoring and Adjustment Framework

Regulatory Review

Monitoring Process

Compliance Management

Data Analysis

Corrective Actions

Performance Assessment

· Nonconformance Identification
· Root Cause Analysis
· Documentation Updates
· Compliance Reporting

Management Actions

· Stakeholder Communication
· Regulatory Engagement
· Continuous Improvement
· Compliance Culture Promotion

Figure 3.76 Graphical depiction of Compliance Monitoring and Adjustment Checklist

Other crucial measures include:

Regulatory Compliance: verifying compliance with environmental regulations, reviewing new or updated regulations, and assessing compliance documentation

Stakeholder Feedback: collecting and reviewing environmental feedback from the community and stakeholders

Risk Management: identifying new environmental risks, reviewing risk mitigation measures, and updating the environmental risk register

Adjustments and Corrective Actions: identifying areas for improvement, developing corrective action plans, and adjusting environmental strategies

Environmental Performance and Adjustment Framework

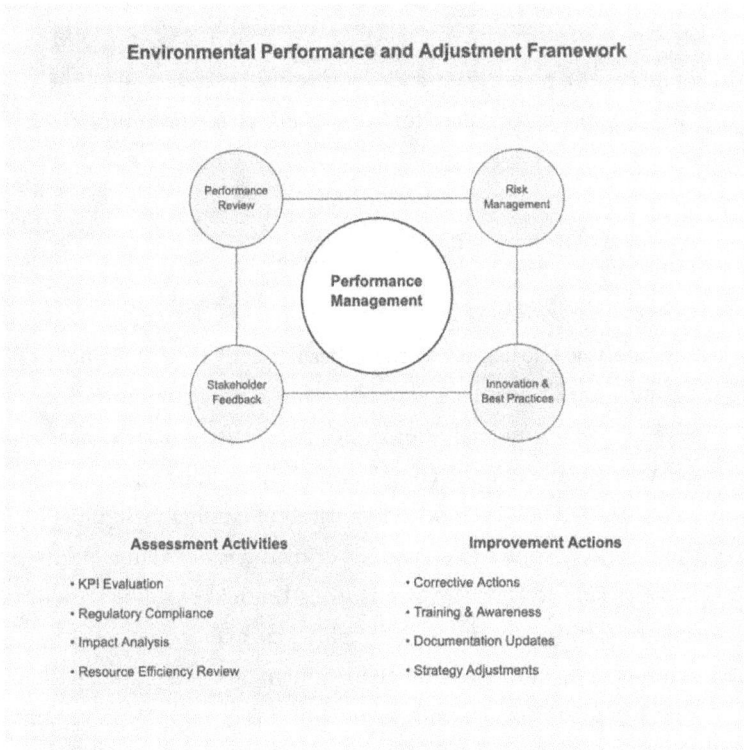

Assessment Activities	Improvement Actions
• KPI Evaluation	• Corrective Actions
• Regulatory Compliance	• Training & Awareness
• Impact Analysis	• Documentation Updates
• Resource Efficiency Review	• Strategy Adjustments

Figure 3.77 Graphical depiction of Environmental Performance and Adjustment Checklist

Innovation and Best Practices: exploring new environmental technologies, benchmarking industry best practices, and recommending innovative solutions

Training and Awareness: reviewing environmental training programs, identifying new training needs, and planning awareness campaigns

Documentation and Reporting: updating environmental management documentation, preparing performance reports, and documenting adjustments and outcomes

Review and Approval: reviewing adjustments, approving proposed changes, and communicating updates to stakeholders

By implementing these control measures, aviation projects can ensure effective environmental management, minimize risks, and promote sustainability.

Control Phase Summary

The templates for plan-driven and iterative lifecycles as well as the primary and supporting practices for the execute phase are summarized in Figure 3.78.

The Close Phase

1. *Lifecycle Closure Report Template*

   The Lifecycle Closure Report outlines key activities for formally closing a project, ensuring that objectives are met, and lessons learned are documented. Project closure activities include Final Status Assessment, verifying completion of deliverables and achievement of project objectives, and Transition Planning, describing handover procedures to operations or maintenance teams. Additional closure activities involve Lessons-Learned Documentation, capturing critical lessons regarding lifecycle management, risk management, and stakeholder engagement, and Recommendations for Future Projects, providing actionable insights for improvement. The report also includes Stakeholder Feedback Summary, Risk Management Overview, and Compliance and Regulatory Adherence Review. Furthermore, the report necessitates Approval and Archiving, involving preparation, review, and approval by designated personnel, and storing project artifacts and documents for future reference. By executing these closure activities, project managers can ensure a systematic and comprehensive project closure, facilitating knowledge-sharing, continuous improvement, and effective transition of project deliverables. See graphical depiction of Lifecycle Closure Report Template (Figure 3.79).

2. *Requirements Management Final Report Template*

   The Requirements Management Final Report Template provides a template for aviation project management, outlining key activities and deliverables for effective requirements management from project inception to closure. See graphical depiction of Requirements Management Final Report Template (Figure 3.80).

Practices	Control
Practice Guide for Lifecycle Management in Aviation Project Management	Lifecycle Control Report Template
AVPMPG-LM-1.000	AVPMP-LM-1.5
Practice Guide for Lifecycle Management in Aviation Project Management	
AVPMPG-LM-1.000	
Practice Guide for Requirements Management in Aviation Project Management	Requirements Measurement and Verification Report Template
AVPMPG-RM-1.000	AVPMP-RM-1.5
Practice Guide for Schedule Management in Aviation Project Management	Schedule Variance and Adjustments/Change Control Report Template
AVPMPC-SM-1.000	AVPMP-SM-1.5
Practice Guide for Stakeholder and Customer Relations Management in Aviation Project Management	Stakeholder Communication/Decisions Report Template
AVPMPG-ST-1.000	AVPMP-ST-1.5
Practice Guide for Risk and Safety Management in Aviation Project Management	Risk and Safety Issue Response Monitoring and Control Report Template
AVPMP3-RS-1.000	AVPMP-RS-1.5
Practice Guide for Financial Management in Aviation Project Management	Budget Variance and Adjustments/Change Control
AVPMPG-FM-1.000	AVPMP-FM-1.5
Practice Guide for Human Resource and Team Management in Aviation Project Management	Team Feedback and Adjustments Template
AVPMPG-HR-1.000	AVPMP-HR-1.5
Practice Guide for Innovation and Research Management in Aviation Project Management	Innovation and Research Adjustments Deliverables Checklist
AVPMPGS-IR-1.000	AVPMS-IR-1.5
Practice Guide for Supply Chain and Procurement Management in Aviation Project Management	Adjust and Optimize Supply Chain and Procurement Deliverable Checklist
AVPM-PGS-SC-1.000	AVPMS-SC-1.5
Practice Guide for Aviation Safety Management in Aviation Project Management	Safety and Compliance Response and Adjustment Deliverable Checklist
AVPMPGS-AS-1.000	AVPMS-AS-1.5
Practice Guide for Technology and Engineering Management in Aviation Project Management	Technical and Engineering Management: Adjust and Optimize Deliverable Checklist
AVPMPGS-TE-1.000	AVPMS-TE-1.5
Practice Guide for Aviation Quality Management in Aviation Project Management	Change Control Deliverable Checklist
AVPMPGS-AQ-1.000	AVPMS-AQ-1.5
Practice Guide for Aviation Regulation Compliance and Certification Management in Aviation Project Management	Compliance Monitoring and Adjustment Deliverable Checklist
AVEMPGS-AR-1.000	AVPMS-AR-1.5
Practice Guide for Environmental and Sustainability Management in Aviation Project Management	Environmental and Sustainability Performance and Adjustment Checklist
AV²MPGS-ES-1.000	AVPMS-ES-1.5

Practices	Iterative Control
Practice Guide for Lifecycle Management in Aviation Project Management	Iteration Plan Adjustment Deliverable Template
	AVPMIT-LM-1.5
Practice Guide for Lifecycle Management in Aviation Project Management	
Practice Guide for Requirements Management in Aviation Project Management	Backlog Adjustment Template
	AVPMIT-RM-1.5
Practice Guide for Requirements Management in Aviation Project Management	Verification Deliverable Template
	AVPMIT-RM-1.5.2

Figure 3.78 Summarizes control phase primary and supporting practices templates for both plan-driven and iterative lifecycles. (Please note that the source text labels this as "execute phase" summary, but based on its placement within the "Control Phase Summary" section, it logically pertains to the control phase)

Lifecycle Closure Report Template

Project: [Name] | Manager: [Name] | Duration: [Start-End] | Report Date: [Date]

Executive Summary
• Project Overview   • Lifecycle Overview   • Key Achievements

Key
Results

Phase
Goals

**Phase
Performance
Review**

Lessons
Learned

Phase Analysis   **Insights and Recommendations**

1. Phase Performance   1. Stakeholder Review
   • Objectives Met   • Engagement Analysis
   • Deliverables Status   • Feedback Summary

2. Risk Overview   2. Key Learnings
   • Mitigation Effectiveness   • Success Factors
   • Unresolved Issues   • Improvement Areas

3. Compliance Status   3. Future Recommendations
   • Regulatory Adherence   • Process Improvements
   • Audit Outcomes   • Best Practices

4. Project Closure   4. Documentation
   • Final Deliverables   • Project Artifacts
   • Transition Plan   • Archive Details

Approval: Prepared by [Name] | Reviewed by [Name] | Approved by [Name]

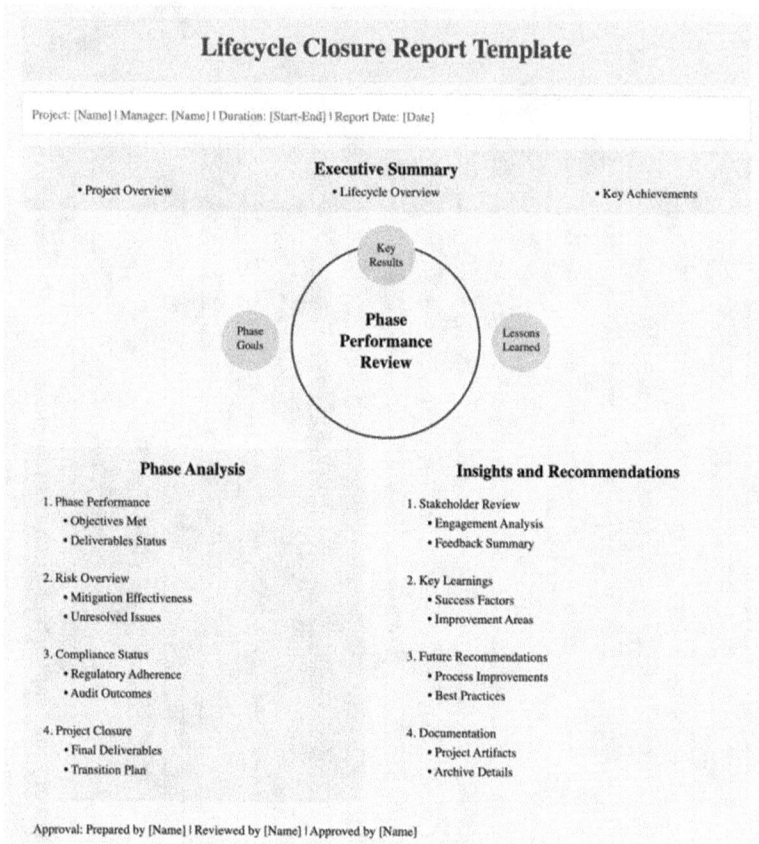

Figure 3.79 Graphical depiction of Lifecycle Closure Report Template

Project closure activities are comprehensive, involving several crucial steps:

Final Requirements Fulfillment Analysis: evaluating the degree to which project deliverables met defined requirements, including successes and challenges

Stakeholder Feedback and Satisfaction Analysis: summarizing stakeholder feedback and assessing satisfaction levels to identify areas for improvement

Lessons-Learned Documentation: capturing key lessons related to requirements management, effective practices, and recommendations for future projects

Requirements Management Final Report

Project: [Name] | Document ID: [ID] | Prepared by: [Name] | Date: [Date] | Approval: [Name]

Executive Summary

• Project Overview   • Key Findings   • Final Outcomes

Resolved
Issues

Met
Goals

**Requirements
Fulfillment
Status**

Lessons
Learned

Requirements Analysis

1. Fulfillment Summary
   • Achievement Status
   • Success Factors

2. Deviation Analysis
   • Identified Issues
   • Resolution Actions

3. Traceability Review
   • Requirements Matrix
   • Change History

4. Documentation
   • Final Records
   • Support Data

Project Outcomes

1. Stakeholder Feedback
   • Satisfaction Levels
   • Key Comments

2. Success Assessment
   • Achievement Analysis
   • Impact Review

3. Lessons Learned
   • Best Practices
   • Improvement Areas

4. Future Guidance
   • Recommendations
   • Process Updates

Approval: Prepared by [Name] | Reviewed by [Name] | Approved by [Name]

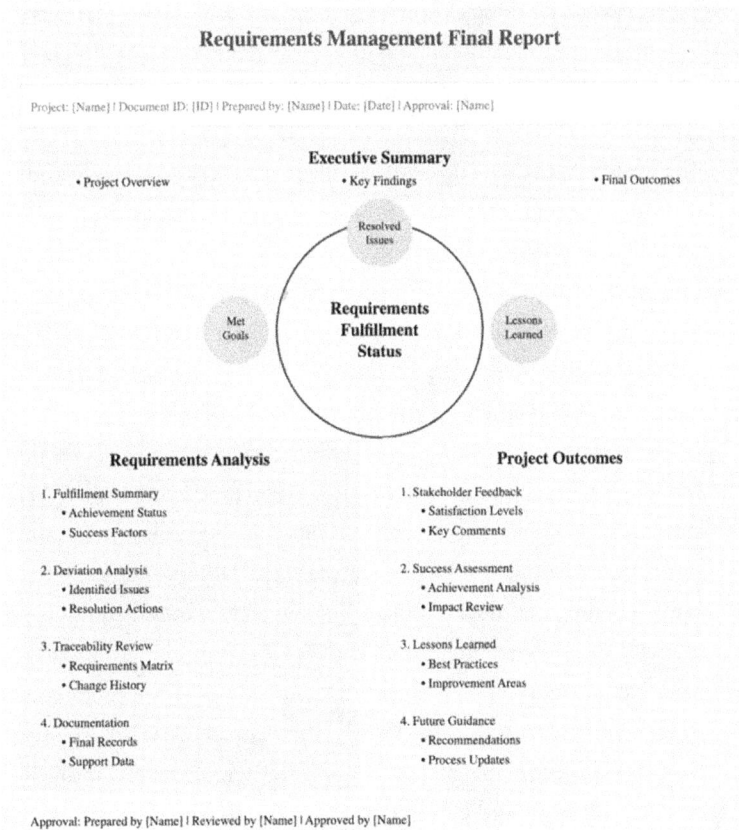

Figure 3.80 Graphical depiction of Requirements Management Final Report Template

Deviations and Resolutions: documenting any deviations from original requirements, impact analyses, and resolution actions taken

Approval and Archiving: obtaining formal approval from the project manager or relevant authority and storing project artifacts and documents for future reference

Requirements Traceability: maintaining a Requirements Traceability Matrix (RTM) to track requirement fulfillment throughout the project lifecycle

Final Project Report: compiling a comprehensive report detailing project outcomes, lessons learned, and recommendations for future improvements

By executing these closure activities, aviation project managers can ensure thorough documentation, knowledge-sharing, and continuous improvement for future projects.

3. *Schedule Closeout and Deliverables Acceptance Template*
The Project Schedule Closeout Template ensures a systematic and comprehensive closure of the project schedule, focusing on deliverables acceptance and documentation. Key closure activities include Schedule Review, verifying task and milestone completion, and Deliverables Acceptance, obtaining stakeholder signoff on completed deliverables. Additional activities involve Schedule Closeout Documentation, compiling relevant documents, and Lessons Learned, reflecting on schedule management successes and challenges. The template also requires a Schedule Closeout Report, summarizing schedule performance, and a Deliverables Acceptance Form, formalizing stakeholder acceptance. Furthermore, it necessitates Schedule Handover, transferring ownership to stakeholders or archives, Acknowledgment of Schedule Closeout, obtaining stakeholder confirmation, and Closure Documentation, compiling final reports and correspondence. Finally, the template requires Approval from the project manager, ensuring formal acknowledgment of the schedule closeout and deliverables acceptance, thereby ensuring a structured project closure process. See graphical depiction of Schedule Closeout and Delivery Acceptance Template (Figure 3.81).

4. *Stakeholder Feedback Report Template*
The Stakeholder Feedback Report Template facilitates comprehensive project closure by gathering and analyzing stakeholder feedback. Key closure activities include Stakeholder Feedback Collection, using surveys, interviews, or focus groups, and Stakeholder Feedback Analysis, identifying common themes and areas of concern or satisfaction. The report also involves Stakeholder Satisfaction Assessment, measuring satisfaction levels, and Lessons Learned, reflecting on successful stakeholder engagement practices. Additionally, the template requires Recommendations for improving stakeholder engagement, Next Steps for addressing feedback, and Approval from the project manager. The report enables project teams to assess stakeholder satisfaction, identify areas for improvement, and incorporate lessons learned into future projects, ensuring

Schedule Closeout and Deliverable Acceptance

Project: [Name] | Document ID: [ID] | Prepared by: [Name] | Date: [Date] | Approved: [Name]

Closeout Process Overview

Final Review

Documentation Handover

Schedule Closeout

Deliverable Acceptance

Review and Documentation

1. **Schedule Review**
   - Task Completion Status
   - Milestone Verification

2. **Documentation Package**
   - Change Control Logs
   - Variance Reports

3. **Lessons Learned**
   - Success Analysis
   - Improvement Areas

Acceptance and Closure

1. **Deliverable Acceptance**
   - Stakeholder Sign-off
   - Acceptance Forms

2. **Schedule Handover**
   - Transfer Documentation
   - Archive Guidelines

3. **Closure Steps**
   - Final Reports
   - Follow-up Actions

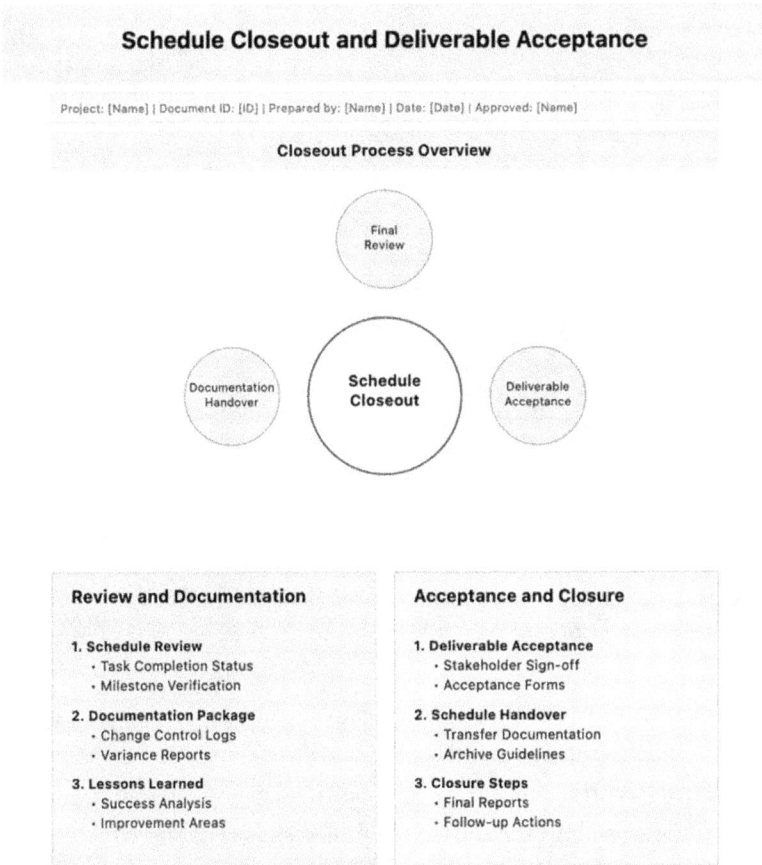

Figure 3.81 Graphical depiction of Schedule Closeout and Delivery Acceptance Template

continuous improvement and effective project closure. See graphical depiction of Stakeholder Feedback Management Template (Figure 3.82).

5. *Risk and Safety Management Final Report Template*

The Risk and Safety Management Final Report Template ensures comprehensive project closure by documenting risk and safety management activities, lessons learned, and recommendations for future improvement. Key closure activities include Risk Register and Safety Issue Log Review, evaluating the effectiveness of risk response actions; Lessons-Learned Documentation, reflecting on successes and challenges; and Recommendations Development, providing actionable steps for improving risk and safety

Stakeholder Feedback Management

Project: [Name] | Document ID: [ID] | Prepared by: [Name] | Date: [Date] | Approved: [Name]

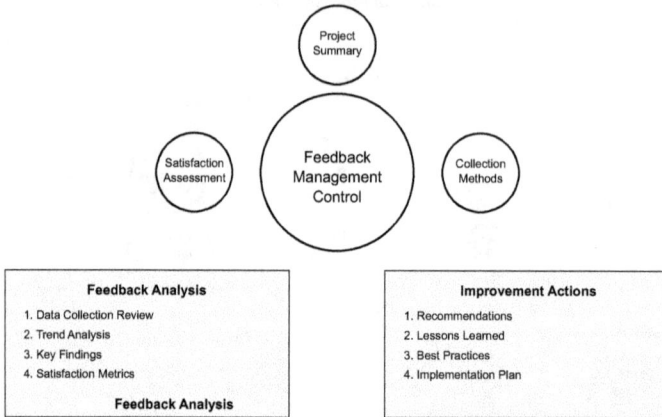

Project Summary

Satisfaction Assessment

Feedback Management Control

Collection Methods

Feedback Analysis
1. Data Collection Review
2. Trend Analysis
3. Key Findings
4. Satisfaction Metrics

Feedback Analysis

Improvement Actions
1. Recommendations
2. Lessons Learned
3. Best Practices
4. Implementation Plan

Figure 3.82 Graphical depiction of Stakeholder Feedback Management Template

management. Additionally, the template requires Response Effectiveness Evaluation, assessing the outcomes of response measures; Final Report Compilation, summarizing key insights and conclusions; and Approval from the project manager. This structured framework enables project teams to capture key insights, document best practices, and inform future risk and safety management efforts, ultimately enhancing project success and continuity. See graphical depiction of Risk and Safety Management Final Report Template (Figure 3.83).

6. *Final Financial Report Template*

The Final Financial Report Template ensures comprehensive project closure by documenting financial performance, expenditures, and outcomes. Key closure activities include Budget Overview, comparing actual spending against the planned budget; Budget Variance Analysis, identifying significant deviations and their causes; and Financial Lessons Learned, reflecting on successes and challenges. Additionally, the template requires Cost Performance Index (CPI) and Schedule Performance Index (SPI) Calculation, assessing cost and schedule performance; Financial Recommendations, providing

Risk and Safety Management Final Report

Risk & Safety Management Overview

Key Activities

1. Risk Identification
2. Safety Assessments
3. Mitigation Strategies
4. Response Implementation
5. Monitoring & Control
6. Documentation

Recommendations

1. Process Improvements
2. Best Practices
3. Training Needs
4. Tool Enhancements
5. Communication Strategy
6. Future Considerations

Document ID: [Project-ID] | Prepared by: [Name] | Date: [Date]

Figure 3.83 Graphical depiction of Risk and Safety Management Final Report Template

strategies for improving financial management; and Final Report Approval, obtaining project manager signoff. This structured framework enables project teams to evaluate financial performance, document best practices, and inform future financial management efforts, ultimately ensuring transparency, accountability, and project success. See graphical depiction of Final Financial Report Template (Figure 3.84).

7. *Final Human Resource and Team Management Report Template*
The Final Human Resource and Team Management Report Template ensures comprehensive project closure by documenting team management activities, lessons learned, and recommendations for future improvement. Key closure activities include Team Performance Evaluation, assessing strengths and weaknesses; Conflict Resolution Review, analyzing conflict management strategies; Lessons-Learned Documentation, reflecting on successes and challenges; and Recommendations Development, providing actionable steps for enhancing recruitment, training, and team dynamics. Additionally, the template requires Final Report Compilation, summarizing key findings and conclusions, and Approval from the project

Final Financial Report

Project Name | Document ID | Prepared by | Date | Approval

Performance Metrics

Budget Overview

Final Financial Analysis

Lessons Learned

Financial Performance

1. Expenditure Analysis
• Cost Categories
• Variance Review

2. Performance Indices
• CPI Analysis
• SPI Analysis

Future Recommendations

1. Process Improvements
• Best Practices
• Success Factors

2. Strategic Planning
• Cost Optimization
• Risk Mitigation

Approved: Prepared by [Name] | Reviewed by [Name] | Approved by [Name]

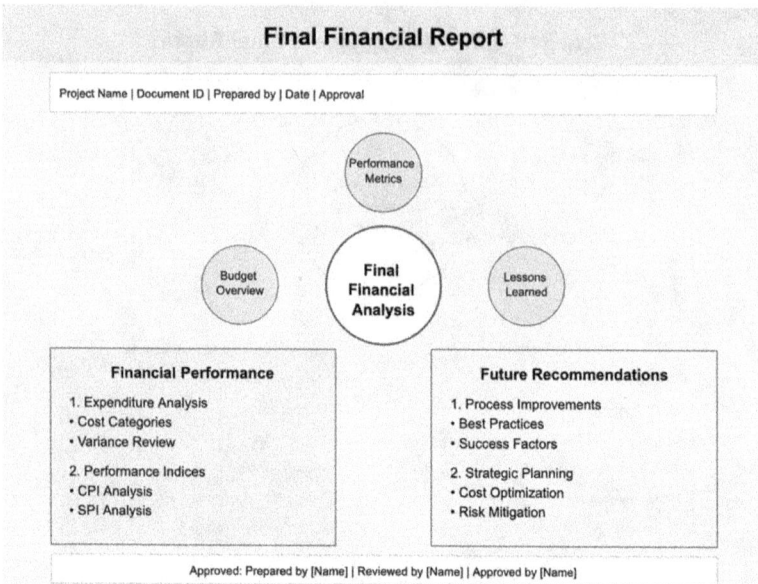

Figure 3.84 Graphical depiction of Final Financial Report Template

manager. This structured framework enables project teams to evaluate team performance, capture best practices, and inform future human resource and team management efforts, ultimately enhancing project outcomes and team effectiveness. See graphical depiction of final HR and Team Management Report Template (Figure 3.85).

8. *Roadmap Updates/Future Opportunities Deliverables Checklist*

The Roadmap Updates/Future Opportunities Deliverables Checklist outlines the essential activities for closing a project, focusing on research and innovation initiatives. To effectively wrap up the project, consider the following key steps:

Review and Evaluation: Assess completed research and innovation activities, evaluating outcomes against original objectives and goals.

Lessons Learned: Document key takeaways, successes, challenges, and best practices to inform future innovation efforts.

Future Opportunities: Identify new research and innovation avenues based on project insights and emerging trends.

Roadmap Updates: Revise timelines, milestones, and objectives to reflect completed activities and new opportunities.

Final HR and Team Management Report

Team Performance

Project Outcomes

Lessons Learned

Project Review

1. Team Management
- Composition & Structure
- Recruitment Process

2. Development
- Training Activities
- Skill Enhancement

3. Team Dynamics
- Collaboration Assessment

Future Recommendations

1. Best Practices
- Success Factors
- Process Improvements

2. Strategy Updates
- Resource Planning
- Team Development

3. Future Focus
- Growth Opportunities

Figure 3.85 Graphical depiction of final HR and Team Management Report Template

Stakeholder Communication: Inform stakeholders about roadmap updates and potential collaboration areas.

Strategic Alignment: Ensure the updated roadmap aligns with organizational priorities and supports long-term vision.

Resource Planning: Allocate necessary resources for future initiatives.

Documentation and Closure: Complete administrative tasks, document updates, and obtain final signoff from project sponsors.

By following these steps, the project team may systematically complete necessary activities during the project's close phase, thereby capturing valuable insights and lessons learned to facilitate continuous improvement and strategic planning for future initiatives. See graphical depiction of Roadmap Updates and Future Opportunities Checklist (Figure 3.86).

9. *Supplier Report Card Deliverables Checklist*

The project closure activities involve a comprehensive evaluation of supplier performance, ensuring accountability and identifying areas for improvement. This 12-step process includes evaluating supplier performance based on predefined KPIs, collecting and analyzing

Roadmap Updates & Future Opportunities Checklist

Completed Activities

Innovation Roadmap

Future Opportunities

Current Assessment

1. Research Review
- Completed Activities
- Outcomes Evaluation

2. Remaining Items
- Incomplete Milestones
- Forward Planning

3. Lessons Learned
- Successes & Challenges

Future Planning

1. New Opportunities
- Emerging Trends
- Technology Insights

2. Strategic Alignment
- Organizational Goals
- Resource Planning

3. Communication
- Stakeholder Updates

Figure 3.86 Graphical depiction of roadmap updates and future opportunities Checklist

data, and assigning scores or ratings. A performance review meeting is held with stakeholders and suppliers to discuss findings, strengths, and weaknesses. Constructive feedback and improvement plans are developed, and contractual obligations are assessed. The process also involves documenting and reporting findings, soliciting supplier feedback, and verifying final deliverables before contract closure and final payments. Lessons learned and best practices are captured, and results are communicated to stakeholders. Finally, all documentation is archived and stored, and procurement contracts are closed out according to organizational policies and regulatory requirements, ensuring a thorough and structured project closure. See graphical depiction of Supplier Report Card Framework Checklist (Figure 3.87).

10. *Aviation Safety and Compliance Final Report Deliverables Checklist* Project closure activities are crucial to ensure a project's success and provide valuable lessons for future projects. For aviation projects, the closure activities involve a comprehensive evaluation of safety and compliance management throughout the project lifecycle. This includes Safety Performance Summary, analyzing incident rates, near misses, and safety initiatives implemented (Figure 3.88).

Supplier Report Card Deliverable Checklist

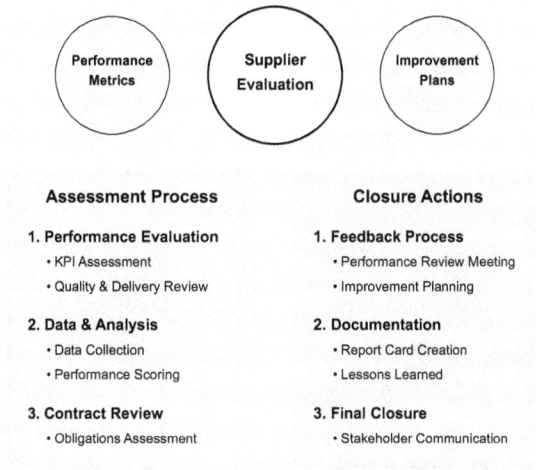

Performance Metrics

Supplier Evaluation

Improvement Plans

Assessment Process

1. Performance Evaluation
- KPI Assessment
- Quality & Delivery Review

2. Data & Analysis
- Data Collection
- Performance Scoring

3. Contract Review
- Obligations Assessment

Closure Actions

1. Feedback Process
- Performance Review Meeting
- Improvement Planning

2. Documentation
- Report Card Creation
- Lessons Learned

3. Final Closure
- Stakeholder Communication

Figure 3.87 Graphical depiction of Supplier Report Card Framework Checklist.

Aviation Safety and Compliance Final Report

Performance Review

Safety Management

Risk Assessment

Safety Analysis

1. Performance Summary
- Incident Rates & Metrics
- Compliance Status

2. Incident Analysis
- Root Cause Evaluation
- Corrective Actions

3. Risk Management
- Control Effectiveness

Program Assessment

1. Training Evaluation
- Competency Assessment
- Emergency Response

2. Documentation Review
- Compliance Verification
- Regulatory Confirmation

3. Future Recommendations
- Lessons Learned

Figure 3.88 Graphical depiction of aviation safety and compliance final report Checklist

11. *Technical and Engineering Management: Roadmap Updates and Future Opportunities*

The project closure checklist focuses on capturing lessons learned, evaluating emerging trends, and informing future opportunities in aviation project management. Key activities include reviewing project progress, updating the technology roadmap, and identifying new technologies and methodologies. The checklist also involves capturing lessons learned, recommending future projects, and considering resource allocation, risk assessment, and regulatory compliance. Stakeholder engagement and communication are crucial, with documentation of updates and rationales for reference and accountability. Additionally, the checklist promotes continuous improvement initiatives and establishes monitoring and review mechanisms to track progress against the updated roadmap. By following this checklist, project teams can ensure a comprehensive evaluation of project outcomes, identify areas for improvement, and provide valuable insights for strategic planning and decision-making in future aviation projects. See graphical depiction of Roadmap Updates Management Checklist (Figure 3.89).

Technical & Engineering Management Roadmap

Project Review — Technology Roadmap — Future Innovations

Current Evaluation

1. Progress Review
• Technical Activities
• Achievements Assessment

2. Lessons Captured
• Success Factors
• Improvement Areas

3. Industry Analysis
• Emerging Trends

Future Planning

1. Project Recommendations
• Innovation Opportunities
• Priority Assessment

2. Implementation Planning
• Resource Allocation
• Risk Mitigation

3. Stakeholder Engagement
• Communication Strategy

Figure 3.89 Graphical depiction of Roadmap Updates Management Checklist

12. *Quality Management Final Report Deliverables Checklist*

The project closure activities for aviation quality management involve compiling a comprehensive final report that captures the project's objectives, scope, achievements, and quality performance. The report outlines the quality assurance approach, quality control activities, and performance evaluation, highlighting successes, challenges, and lessons learned. It also assesses supplier and vendor performance, confirms regulatory compliance, and captures customer feedback and satisfaction levels. Additionally, the report provides recommendations for improving quality assurance practices in future projects and identifies areas for further research and innovation. The report concludes by reinforcing the importance of quality assurance in achieving project success and meeting stakeholder expectations and includes supporting documents, acknowledgments, and references. This structured approach ensures knowledge transfer and continuous improvement in aviation quality management practices. See graphical depiction of Quality Management Final Report Checklist (Figure 3.90).

Quality Management Final Report Checklist

Process Review

Quality Assurance

Improvement Initiatives

Quality Assessment

1. Quality Control
   • Inspection Results
   • Testing Outcomes

2. Performance Evaluation
   • Metrics Assessment
   • Supplier Performance

3. Compliance Review
   • Regulatory Standards

Future Improvements

1. Lessons Learned
   • Success Factors
   • Improvement Areas

2. Recommendations
   • Process Enhancements
   • Future Initiatives

3. Customer Satisfaction
   • Feedback Analysis

Figure 3.90 Graphical depiction of Quality Management Final Report Checklist

13. *Compliance Report Deliverables Checklist*

The project closure checklist ensures that all compliance activities are formally completed and documented. This involves a final review of regulatory requirements, verification of documentation and certifications, and preparation of compliance reports. The process also includes closing out compliance-related tasks, documenting lessons learned, and conducting a project review meeting with stakeholders. Regulatory closure documentation is prepared, and compliance records are archived securely. Formal signoff is obtained from stakeholders, regulatory authorities, and management, confirming successful completion of compliance activities. Finally, project closure documentation is completed, and compliance responsibilities are handed over to designated parties, ensuring a smooth transition and ongoing compliance management. See graphical depiction of Compliance Final Report Checklist (Figure 3.91).

14. *Environmental and Sustainability Final Report Checklist*

The project closure checklist for environmental and sustainability management involves compiling a comprehensive final report that

Completion & Report Deliverable Checklist

Documentation Review — Regulatory Compliance — Certification Process

Compliance Verification

1. Final Review
   • Regulatory Requirements
   • Corrective Actions

2. Documentation Check
   • Records Verification
   • Certification Validation

3. Reporting
   • Compliance Summary

Closure Activities

1. Lessons Learned
   • Process Improvement
   • Best Practices

2. Closure Documentation
   • Formal Sign-off
   • Records Archiving

3. Handover Process
   • Documentation Transfer

Figure 3.91 Graphical depiction of Compliance Final Report Checklist

Environmental & Sustainability Final Report

Impact
Assessment

Environmental
Management

Sustainability
Initiatives

Performance Review

1. Environmental Impact
- Impact Assessment
- Compliance Status

2. Performance Metrics
- KPI Evaluation
- Resource Consumption

3. Stakeholder Engagement
- Community Feedback

Future Planning

1. Lessons Learned
- Best Practices
- Challenges & Solutions

2. Innovative Approaches
- New Technologies
- Sustainable Solutions

3. Recommendations
- Continuous Improvement

Figure 3.92 Graphical depiction of Environmental and Sustainability Final Report Checklist

summarizes the project's environmental objectives, achievements, and outcomes. The report covers key aspects including environmental impact assessments, sustainability initiatives, compliance with regulations, performance metrics, stakeholder engagement, and lessons learned. It also highlights best practices, innovative solutions, and challenges overcome, providing recommendations for future improvements. The report is supported by appendixes and verified through approval and signoff from the environmental management team and project leadership. This structured approach ensures a thorough documentation of environmental and sustainability efforts, facilitating knowledge transfer and continuous improvement for future aviation projects. See graphical depiction of Environmental and Sustainability Final Report Checklist (Figure 3.92).

Close Phase Summary

The templates for plan-driven and iterative lifecycles as well as the primary and supporting practices for the execute phase are summarized in Figure 3.93.

Practices	Execute	Control
Practice Guide for Lifecycle Management in Aviation Project Management	Lifecycle Execution Report Template	Lifecycle Control Report Template
AVPMPG-LM-1.000	AVPMP-LM-1.4	AVPMP-LM-1.5
Practice Guide for Lifecycle Management in Aviation Project Management		
AVPMPG-LM-1.000		
Practice Guide for Requirements Management in Aviation Project Management	Requirements Validation Report Template	Requirements Measurement and Verification Report Template
AVPMPG-RM-1.000	AVPMP-RM-1.4	AVPMP-RM-1.5
Practice Guide for Schedule Management in Aviation Project Management	Project Schedule Management Template	Schedule Variance and Adjustments/Change Control Report Template
AVPMPG-SM-1.000	AVPMP-SM-1.4	AVPMP-SM-1.5
Practice Guide for Stakeholder and Customer Relations Management in Aviation Project Management	Stakeholder Engagement Report Template	Stakeholder Communication/Decisions Report Template
AVPMPG-ST-1.000	AVPMP-ST-1.4	AVPMP-ST-1.5
Practice Guide for Risk and Safety Management in Aviation Project Management	Risk and Safety Issue Response Report Template	Risk and Safety Issue Response Monitoring and Control Report Template
AVPMPG-RS-1.000	AVPMP-RS-1.4	AVPMP-RS-1.5
Practice Guide for Financial Management in Aviation Project Management	Budget Progress Report Template	Budget Variance and Adjustments/Change Control
AVPMPG-FM-1.000	AVPMP-FM-1.4	AVPMP-FM-1.5
Practice Guide for Human Resource and Team Management in Aviation Project Management	Team Performance Monitoring Template	Team Feedback and Adjustments Template
AVPMPG-HR-1.000	AVPMP-HR-1.4	AVPMP-HR-1.5
Practice Guide for Innovation and Research Management in Aviation Project Management	Innovation and Research Progress Reporting Checklist	Innovation and Research Adjustments Deliverables Checklist
AVPMPG-IR-1.000	AVPMS-IR-1.4	AVPMS-IR-1.5
Practice Guide for Supply Chain and Procurement Management in Aviation Project Management	Procurement Deliverable Checklist	Adjust and Optimize Supply Chain and Procurement Deliverable Checklist
AVPMPG-SC-1.000	AVPMS-SC-1.4	AVPMS-SC-1.5
Practice Guide for Aviation Safety Management in Aviation Project Management	Safety and Compliance Reports Deliverable Checklist	Safety and Compliance Response and Adjustment Deliverable Checklist
AVPMPG-AS-1.000	AVPMS-AS-1.4	AVPMS-AS-1.5
Practice Guide for Technology and Engineering Management in Aviation Project Management	Technology Implementation Plan Deliverables Checklist	Technical and Engineering Management: Adjust and Optimize Deliverable Checklist
AVPMPG-TE-1.000	AVPMS-TE-1.4	AVPMS-TE-1.5
Practice Guide for Aviation Quality Management in Aviation Project Management	Quality Control Reports Deliverable Checklist	Change Control Deliverable Checklist
AVPMPG-AQ-1.000	AVPMS-AQ-1.4	AVPMS-AQ-1.5
Practice Guide for Aviation Regulation Compliance and Certification Management in Aviation Project Management	Compliance Management Deliverable Checklist	Compliance Monitoring and Adjustment Deliverable Checklist
AVPMPG-AR-1.000	AVPMS-AR-1.4	AVPMS-AR-1.5
Practice Guide for Environmental and Sustainability Management in Aviation Project Management	Environmental/Sustainability Reports Checklist	Environmental and Sustainability Performance and Adjustment Checklist
AVPMPG-ES-1.000	AVPMS-ES-1.4	AVPMS-ES-1.5
Practices	**Iterative Execute**	**Iterative Control**
Practice Guide for Lifecycle Management in Aviation Project Management	Daily Standup Meeting Template	Iteration Plan Adjustment Deliverable Template
	AVPMIT-LM-1.4	AVPMIT-LM-1.5
Practice Guide for Lifecycle Management in Aviation Project Management	Sprint Plan Deliverable Template	
	AVPMIT-LM-1.4.2	
Practice Guide for Requirements Management in Aviation Project Management	Validation Deliverable Template	Backlog Adjustment Template
	AVPMIT-RM-1.4	AVPMIT-RM-1.5
Practice Guide for Requirements Management in Aviation Project Management	Verification Deliverable Template	
	AVPMIT-RM-1.5.2	

Figure 3.93 *Summarizes close phase primary and supporting practices templates for both plan-driven and iterative lifecycles. (Please note that the source text labels this as "execute phase" summary, but based on its placement within the "Close Phase Summary" section, it logically pertains to the close phase).*

CHAPTER 4

Aviation Plan–Driven Project Case: AirCare

The project for a plan-driven case example begins with a Request for Proposal (RFP) for an engine overhaul project from Cargo Lift Aviation. Often a project team will engage in some limited pre-project and start phase activity in anticipation of winning the RFP. This is the case with the AirCare project team while waiting for the final award of the RFP. The RFP for the project is provided below.

Request for Proposal (RFP)
Company: Cargo Lift Aviation
Project: Aircraft Engine Overhaul and Conversion Services
Date: August 27, 2024

1. **Introduction**
   Cargo Lift Aviation, a regional air cargo carrier operating a fleet of six Short 330 aircraft, is seeking proposals from qualified vendors to provide engine overhaul and conversion services. The objective of this project is to enhance the reliability, fuel efficiency, and environmental sustainability of our fleet. We are open to rebuilding existing engines and exploring potential conversions to different fuel types or engine models.

2. **Project Scope**
   This project encompasses the following key components:
   2.1. The selected vendor will conduct a thorough inspection and evaluation of our existing engines to determine the feasibility and benefits of overhaul versus conversion. Based on this assessment, the vendor will recommend suitable engine models or fuel types for conversion, considering performance, cost, and environmental impact.

2.2. The project will involve either the complete overhaul of existing engines, including disassembly, inspection, repair or replacement of components, reassembly, and testing, or the conversion of existing engines to a different fuel type or engine model, including all necessary modifications, installations, and testing.

2.3. The vendor must ensure strict adherence to all relevant engine maintenance manuals, service bulletins, and airworthiness directives. This includes obtaining all required inspections, certifications, and approvals from regulatory authorities, ensuring proper engine performance, and ensuring compliance with emissions standards.

2.4. The vendor will implement rigorous quality control processes to prevent improper assembly, component failures, and engine malfunctions, providing comprehensive documentation and traceability of all work performed.

3. **Requirements**

To be considered, vendors must meet the following requirements:

2.1. Demonstrate extensive experience in aircraft engine overhaul and/or conversion projects, particularly for the models in our fleet.

3.2. Possess access to specialized tooling, equipment, and facilities required for engine overhaul/conversion.

3.3. Display in-depth understanding of aviation regulations and certification processes related to engine maintenance and modifications.

3.4. Maintain a strong safety culture with a proven track record of minimizing risks and prioritizing quality.

3.5. Provide clear project plans with well-defined timelines, milestones, and communication protocols.

3.6. Offer transparent and detailed cost breakdown, including labor, parts, materials, and any potential contingencies.

4. **Proposal Submission**

Proposals should include the following information:

4.1. A company overview, highlighting experience in engine overhaul/conversion, technical capabilities, and certifications.

4.2. A detailed explanation of the proposed approach to engine assessment, overhaul/conversion, and compliance with regulations.

4.3. A comprehensive project timeline with key milestones and estimated completion dates.

4.4. A clear and itemized cost breakdown of all services and deliverables.

4.5. Contact information for at least three references from previous engine overhaul/conversion projects.

4.6. An outline of procedures for ensuring safety, quality control, and risk mitigation.

5. **Evaluation Criteria**

Proposals will be evaluated based on the following criteria:

5.1. Technical expertise and experience in performing high-quality engine overhaul/conversions.

5.2. Proven ability to navigate and adhere to complex aviation regulations.

5.3. Commitment to maintaining the highest safety standards.

5.4. Clear and organized project plan with effective communication.

5.5. Value proposition and transparent pricing.

6. **Submission Deadline**

Proposals must be submitted by NLT 30 days from RFP release to DK89@CLA.com.

7. **Contact Information**

For inquiries, please contact:

Dan Kooper

MRO Administrator DK89@CLA.com

Pre-Project Activities

The initial project activities involve setting basic direction and ground rules prior to the start of the project. The place to begin such preparation is with the primary practices and pre-project activities as shown in Figure 4.1:

Practices
Practice Guide for Lifecycle Management in Aviation Project Management
AVPMPG-LM-1.000
Practice Guide for Lifecycle Management in Aviation Project Management
AVPMPG-LM-1.000
Practice Guide for Requirements Management in Aviation Project Management
AVPMPG-RM-1.000
Practice Guide for Schedule Management in Aviation Project Management
AVPMPG-SM-1.000
Practice Guide for Stakeholder and Customer Relations Management in Aviation Project Management
AVPMPG-ST-1.000
Practice Guide for Risk and Safety Management in Aviation Project Management
AVPMPG-RS-1.000
Practice Guide for Financial Management in Aviation Project Management
AVPMPG-FM-1.000
Practice Guide for Human Resource and Team Management in Aviation Project Management
AVPMPG-HR-1.000

Figure 4.1 Primary practices and pre-project activities for aviation project management

Lifecycle Selection

AirCare has already determined that the lifecycle selection that best fits the project is the plan-driven lifecycle. Given that iterative projects are often software intensive and lend themselves to presenting features for evaluation at the end of each of the iterations, the project team has decided early on that the iterative lifecycle is not the best fit for this project.

Requirements Sources

While preparing for the announcement of the winning bid, AirCare has already been engaged in identifying the sources of project requirements. This was carried out by closely studying the RFP and conducting additional research. Some high-level sources are identified as follows.

Operational Needs: Cargo Lift's desire to enhance their fleet's reliability, fuel efficiency, and environmental sustainability drives the core requirements.

Technical Considerations: The need for thorough engine assessments, feasible conversion options, and compliance with maintenance manuals and airworthiness directives shapes the technical requirements.

Regulatory Compliance: Adherence to aviation regulations, certification processes, and emissions standards forms a crucial set of requirements.

Safety Assurance: Prioritizing safety through rigorous quality control, preventing malfunctions, and ensuring comprehensive documentation adds another layer of requirements.

Vendor Capabilities: The RFP outlines requirements for vendors to demonstrate expertise, technical capabilities, regulatory knowledge, a strong safety commitment, and effective project management.

Schedule Management

Prior to AirCare submitting the bid for the RFP, the project team carried out a very high-level "Rough Order of Magnitude" (ROM) schedule to obtain a feel for the overall scale of the project. The findings in the resulting report are as follows.

Phase	Estimated Duration	Key Activities
Project Initiation and Planning	24 weeks	* Finalize project scope and objectives. * Select a vendor and establish a contract. * Develop a detailed project plan and schedule. * Secure necessary resources and funding.
Engine Assessment and Recommendation	46 weeks	* Thorough inspection and evaluation of existing engines. * Determine feasibility and benefits of overhaul versus conversion. * Recommend suitable engine models or fuel types for conversion.
Engineering and Procurement	812 weeks	* Detailed engineering design for overhaul or conversion. * Procure necessary parts, components, and materials. * Prepare tooling and facilities for engine work.
Engine Overhaul/ Conversion	1,216 weeks	* Disassembly, inspection, and repair/ replacement of components. * Complete overhaul of existing engines OR * Conversion of engines to a different fuel type or model. * Engine testing and validation.
Regulatory Compliance and Certification	48 weeks	* Obtain necessary certifications and approvals from regulatory authorities. * Ensure compliance with all relevant regulations and airworthiness directives.
Installation and Testing	46 weeks	* Install overhauled/converted engines on aircraft. * Conduct ground and flight tests to verify performance.
Project Closure	24 weeks	* Final documentation and reporting. * Project closeout and handover to Cargo Lift.

Total Estimated Duration: 3,660 weeks

Important Notes

1. **ROM Estimate:** This is a rough estimate based on the high-level information in the RFP. The actual duration of each phase may vary significantly depending on factors such as the chosen vendor, engine conditions, complexity of conversions, and regulatory processes.
2. **Dependencies:** There are likely dependencies between phases. For example, the "Engine Overhaul/Conversion" phase cannot start until "Engineering and Procurement" is complete.
3. **Flexibility:** This schedule is intended to provide a general timeline and should be refined as the project progresses and more detailed information becomes available.
4. **Contingency:** It's always advisable to include a contingency buffer in the schedule to accommodate potential delays or unforeseen issues.

Stakeholder Landscape

The AirCare project team has conducted an initial analysis of the stakeholder landscape for the aircraft engine overhaul and conversion project. This report identifies key internal and external stakeholders, their interests, and levels of influence.

Internal Stakeholder Categories

Cargo Lift Aviation has several internal stakeholders who play critical roles in the project's success.

Cargo Lift Management, comprising key decision-makers responsible for project approval, budget allocation, and overall project success.

The flight operations team, consisting of personnel directly impacted by the project, such as pilots, maintenance crews, and flight operations managers.

The Technical Team, composed of Cargo Lift's internal technical experts who will assess vendor proposals, evaluate technical feasibility, and oversee project implementation.

The Procurement/Contracts department, responsible for managing the RFP process, vendor selection, contract negotiation, and ensuring compliance with procurement policies.

External Stakeholder Categories

Several external stakeholders will also impact the project's outcome. Vendors specializing in aircraft engine overhaul and conversion services.

Regulatory Authorities, specifically aviation regulatory bodies such as the Federal Aviation Administration (FAA) in the United States.

Engine Manufacturers, who may be consulted for technical specifications, recommendations, or specialized support.

Parts Suppliers, providing the necessary parts and components for engine overhaul or conversion.

Stakeholder Engagement

Understanding the interests and influence of each stakeholder group is essential to the project's success. By recognizing and engaging with these stakeholders, AirCare can ensure a collaborative and successful project outcome that meets the needs of all parties involved.

Risk and Safety

In pre-project activities, the risk and safety practice involves assessing the risk appetite as well as a historical look-back at previous similar projects.

This report provides historical data for AirCare, a company bidding on the RFP for Cargo Lift Aviation's engine overhaul and conversion project. The data cover historical performance, risk-level assessment, and risk appetite.

Historical Performance

AirCare has a proven track record of successfully completing similar engine overhaul/conversion projects. Over the past 5 years, we have completed five such projects, with an average project completion time of 42 weeks, ranging from 38 to 48 weeks. Our average cost overrun has been

5 percent, with a range of 2 to 10 percent. Notably, our customer satisfaction rating has consistently averaged 4.5 out of 5 across these projects.

In addition, AirCare possesses specialized technical expertise that aligns well with the requirements of the RFP. Our team has extensive experience working with Short 330 engines and similar turboprop engines. Furthermore, we have successfully completed three engine conversions to alternative fuel types within the past 3 years. AirCare also maintains a strong track record of meeting aviation safety regulations and certification requirements.

Risk-Level Assessment

AirCare has conducted a thorough risk assessment associated with this project, identifying potential technical, regulatory, and project management risks. From a technical standpoint, we recognize a moderate risk related to engine condition, as unforeseen damage or wear may require additional repairs. Conversion complexity also poses a moderate to high risk, depending on the chosen conversion option, due to potential technical challenges and integration issues. Additionally, parts availability presents a low to moderate risk due to potential delays in procuring specific components.

On the regulatory front, certification delays pose a moderate risk due to potential delays in obtaining necessary approvals from regulatory authorities. However, compliance changes are considered a low risk, as aviation regulations are generally stable, although minor changes could still impact the project.

From a project management perspective, AirCare has assessed resource availability as a low risk, given our sufficient skilled personnel and resources. Schedule slippage poses a moderate risk due to potential delays from technical challenges or external factors. Cost overruns are also considered a low to moderate risk, potentially resulting from unforeseen repairs, parts availability, or project extensions.

Risk Appetite

AirCare has a moderate risk appetite, willingness to take on projects with reasonable risk levels, provided the potential rewards outweigh the risks. Specifically, we are willing to accept minor schedule delays of up to 10 percent, if necessary to ensure quality and safety. We also tolerate cost overruns within a 5 percent range. Our technical expertise gives us confidence in overcoming moderate technical challenges, and we are committed to strict adherence to regulatory requirements, investing necessary time and resources for compliance.

Risk and Safety Report Summary

The risk and safety pre-project report provides a comprehensive overview of AirCare's capabilities and risk profile for the aircraft engine overhaul and conversion project. Our relevant experience and moderate risk appetite make us a potentially suitable vendor for Cargo Lift Aviation. However, we recognize the importance of carefully assessing specific project risks and developing effective mitigation strategies to ensure successful project delivery.

High-Level ROM Budget Estimate

The AirCare management team developed a high-level ROM budget estimate to facilitate bidding on the RFP as part of the pre-project work. The ROM estimate is provided in the following report.

Assumptions:

- Engine overhaul/conversion costs will vary depending on the complexity of the project.
- Regulatory compliance and certification costs will be influenced by the specific requirements of the project.

High-Level Estimated Costs by Phase:

1. Project Initiation and Planning (24 weeks)
   - Vendor selection and contract establishment: $50,000 to $100,000
   - Project planning and resource allocation: $20,000 to $40,000
     Total: $70,000 to $140,000
2. Engine Assessment and Recommendation (46 weeks)
   - Engine inspection and evaluation: $100,000 to $200,000

- Feasibility study and recommendation report: $30,000 to $60,000

  Total: $130,000 to $260,000

3. Engineering and Procurement (812 weeks)
   - Detailed engineering design: $200,000 to $400,000
   - Parts and materials procurement: $500,000 to $1,000,000
   - Tooling and facility preparation: $100,000 to $200,000

     Total: $800,000 to $1,600,000

4. Engine Overhaul/Conversion (1,216 weeks)
   - Labor costs for overhaul/conversion: $500,000 to $1,000,000
   - Parts and materials costs for overhaul/conversion: $1,000,000 to $2,000,000
   - Testing and validation: $100,000 to $200,000 Total: $1,600,000 to $3,200,000

5. Regulatory Compliance and Certification (48 weeks)
   - Regulatory consulting and support: $50,000 to $100,000
   - Certification and approval costs: $20,000 to $40,000 Total: $70,000 to $140,000

6. Installation and Testing (46 weeks)
   - Labor costs for installation: $100,000 to $200,000
   - Testing and validation: $20,000 to $40,000

     Total: $120,000 to $240,000

7. Project Closure (24 weeks)
   - Documentation and reporting: $10,000 to $20,000
   - Project closeout and handover: $5,000 to $10,000

     Total: $15,000 to $30,000

Total ROM Estimated Budget: $3,515,000 to $6,410,000

Contingency Buffer: 10 to 20 percent of total estimated budget ($351,500 to $1,282,000) Important Notes from the AirCare pre-project ROM estimate:

- This ROM budget estimate is based on rough assumptions and should be refined as the project progresses.
- Actual costs may vary significantly depending on factors such as vendor selection, engine conditions, and regulatory requirements.

- A contingency buffer is included to accommodate potential cost overruns or unforeseen expenses.

Talent Needs Assessment Report

The AirCare project team has evaluated the RFP in pre-project activity to obtain a high-level needs assessment to understand the resource needs. The Cargo Lift Aviation RFP requires a skilled vendor to provide aircraft engine overhaul and conversion services for its fleet of six Short 330 aircraft. The project aims to enhance reliability, fuel efficiency, and environmental sustainability.

Key Talent Requirements

To successfully execute this project, the vendor will need to possess the following key talents:

1. Aircraft Engine Experts: Experienced professionals with in-depth knowledge of Short 330 engine models, overhaul, and conversion processes.
2. Aviation Regulations Specialists: Experts familiar with aviation regulations, certification processes, and airworthiness directives.
3. Quality Control Specialists: Professionals skilled in implementing rigorous quality control processes to prevent improper assembly, component failures, and engine malfunctions.
4. Project Managers: Experienced project managers with expertise in planning, scheduling, and communication.
5. Technical Writers: Professionals skilled in creating comprehensive documentation and traceability records.
6. Safety Specialists: Experts committed to maintaining the highest safety standards and minimizing risks.

Estimated Talent Requirements by Phase

1. Project Initiation and Planning (24 weeks)
   ○ 1 Project Manager
   ○ 1 Aircraft Engine Expert
   ○ 1 Aviation Regulations Specialist
2. Engine Assessment and Recommendation (46 weeks)
   ○ 2 Aircraft Engine Experts
   ○ 1 Aviation Regulations Specialist
   ○ 1 Technical Writer
3. Engineering and Procurement (812 weeks)
   ○ 3 Aircraft Engine Experts
   ○ 2 Engineers (mechanical, electrical)
   ○ 1 Procurement Specialist
4. Engine Overhaul/Conversion (1,216 weeks)
   ○ 68 Aircraft Engine Technicians
   ○ 2 Quality Control Specialists
   ○ 1 Safety Specialist
5. Regulatory Compliance and Certification (48 weeks)
   ○ 1 Aviation Regulations Specialist
   ○ 1 Quality Control Specialist
6. Installation and Testing (46 weeks)
   ○ 4 Aircraft Engine Technicians
   ○ 1 Safety Specialist
7. Project Closure (24 weeks)
   ○ 1 Project Manager
   ○ 1 Technical Writer

Total Estimated Talent Requirements: 2,535 fulltime equivalents (FTEs) for the duration of the project.

Skills Matrix

Skill	Required Level	Estimated FTEs
Aircraft Engine Expertise	Advanced	810
Aviation Regulations	Advanced	23
Quality Control	Intermediate	34
Project Management	Intermediate	23
Technical Writing	Intermediate	12
Safety Management	Advanced	23
Engineering (mechanical, electrical)	Intermediate	23
Procurement	Intermediate	12

Supporting Practices in the Pre-Project Environment

The primary practices in aviation projects form the traditional essence of the project as they lead directly to plans and decision-making associated with the lifecycle and its governance, the scope, schedule, budget, risk, safety, and resources. Because of the centrality of these practices in the project, the decisions, deliverables, artifacts, templates, and other project work products, these practice deliverables were created by the AirCare project team directly. The supporting practices are equally important but tend to be developed in concert with the extended functional organization—hence, the rationale behind checklists for confirming and collecting information by way of engagement and interaction with the larger AirCare team (Figure 4.2).

Innovation and Research Technology Needs Checklist

The AirCare project team followed the general process outlined below to engage with the extended organization in order to complete the Innovation and Research Technology Needs Checklist (process flow depicted in Figure 4.3).

The meeting with the extended organization focused on identifying potential innovations and research needs to ensure a competitive proposal. Discussions centered around leveraging predictive maintenance data and advanced diagnostics to optimize engine assessment (2.1),

Practices
Practice Guide for Innovation and Research Management in Aviation Project Management
AVPMPGS-IR-1.000
Practice Guide for Supply Chain and Procurement Management in Aviation Project Management
AVPMPGS-SC-1.000
Practice Guide for Aviation Safety Management in Aviation Project Management
AVPMPGS-AS-1.000
Practice Guide for Technology and Engineering Management in Aviation Project Management
AVPMPGS-TE-1.000
Practice Guide for Aviation Quality Management in Aviation Project Management
AVPMPGS-AQ-1.000
Practice Guide for Aviation Regulation Compliance and Certification Management in Aviation Project Management
AVPMPGS-AR-1.000
Practice Guide for Environmental and Sustainability Management in Aviation Project Management
AVPMPGS-ES-1.000

Figure 4.2 Supporting practices in the pre-project environment for aviation project management

Innovation and Research Management

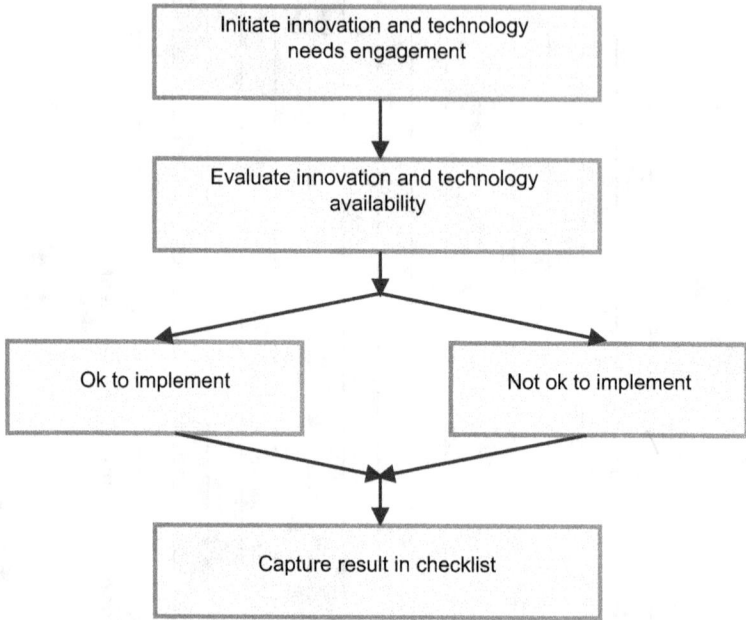

Figure 4.3 Process flow for Innovation and Research Management and completing the Technology Needs Checklist

exploring cutting-edge coating technologies to improve fuel efficiency and reduce emissions in the overhaul/conversion process (2.2), and investigating the feasibility of incorporating sustainable aviation fuels (SAF) as a conversion option to align with Cargo Lift's environmental goals (2.1). The team also emphasized the importance of thorough research on the latest regulatory requirements and certification processes to ensure compliance (2.3).

These insights informed the completion of the innovation and research needs technology checklist, guiding the proposal development and positioning AirCare as a forward-thinking and technologically advanced solution provider.

Supply Chain and Procurement Management

The AirCare project team followed up with a meeting with the organization's supply chain team using the general decision-making and information collection (process flow depicted in Figure 4.4).

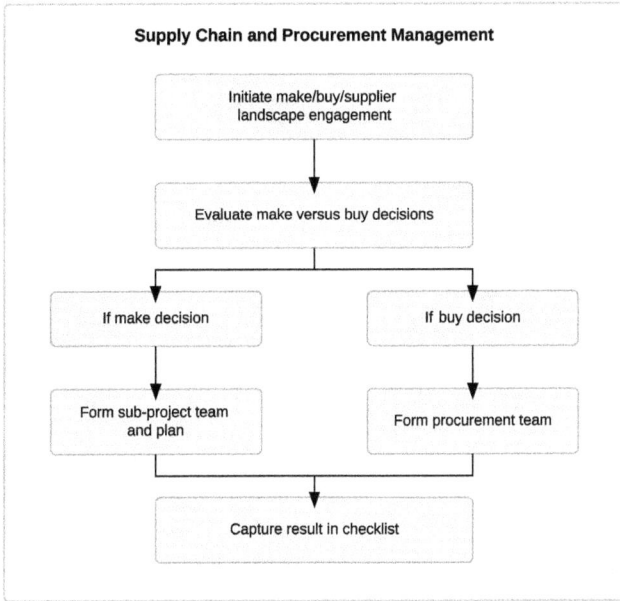

Supply Chain and Procurement Management

Initiate make/buy/supplier landscape engagement

Evaluate make versus buy decisions

If make decision

If buy decision

Form sub-project team and plan

Form procurement team

Capture result in checklist

Figure 4.4 Process flow for Supply Chain and Procurement Management

The AirCare team pre-project meeting was convened to specifically address supply chain and procurement aspects of the Cargo Lift Aviation engine overhaul and conversion project RFP. Discussions revolved around the supplier landscape for required parts and components, with a focus on identifying reliable vendors for both new and refurbished parts to ensure quality and cost-effectiveness (3.2, 3.6). The team analyzed potential "make-or-buy" decisions, considering the feasibility and cost–benefit analyses' findings on overhauling certain components in-house versus outsourcing to specialized repair shops. This analysis focused on factors like in-house expertise, capacity, turnaround time, and cost comparisons to optimize the supply chain strategy and ensure timely project delivery (3.5, 4.2). The meeting's insights will be used to populate the supply chain and procurement management checklist, guiding the selection of suppliers, negotiation of contracts, and efficient management of materials throughout the project lifecycle.

Aviation Safety Management

The AirCare team also conducted a pre-project meeting dedicated to aviation safety management aspects of the Cargo Lift Aviation engine overhaul and conversion project (process flow depicted in Figure 4.5).

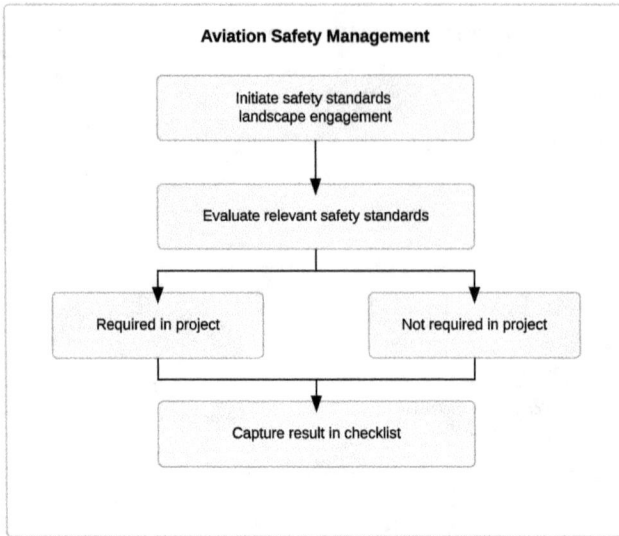

Figure 4.5 Process flow for Aviation Safety Management

The AirCare team conducted a pre-project meeting dedicated to aviation safety management aspects of the Cargo Lift Aviation engine overhaul and conversion project. Discussions centered on risk assessment and mitigation strategies for potential hazards throughout the project lifecycle (3.4, 4.6). Specific areas of focus included ensuring the competency and certification of personnel involved in engine work; establishing rigorous quality control procedures for disassembly, inspection, and reassembly processes; and implementing robust testing protocols to verify engine performance and safety after overhaul or conversion (2.3, 2.4). The team also explored strategies for proactive hazard identification and risk management, emphasizing the importance of clear communication and documentation to maintain a strong safety culture throughout the project. This information will be incorporated into the Aviation Safety Management Checklist, guiding the development of safety protocols and ensuring compliance with all relevant aviation safety regulations.

Technology and Engineering Management

Following the aviation safety management meeting, the AirCare team held a pre-project meeting to delve into the technology and engineering

Technology and Engineering Management

Initiate technology and engineering
needs engagement

Evaluate technology and
engineering requirements

Ok to implement in project

Not ok to implement in project

Capture result in checklist

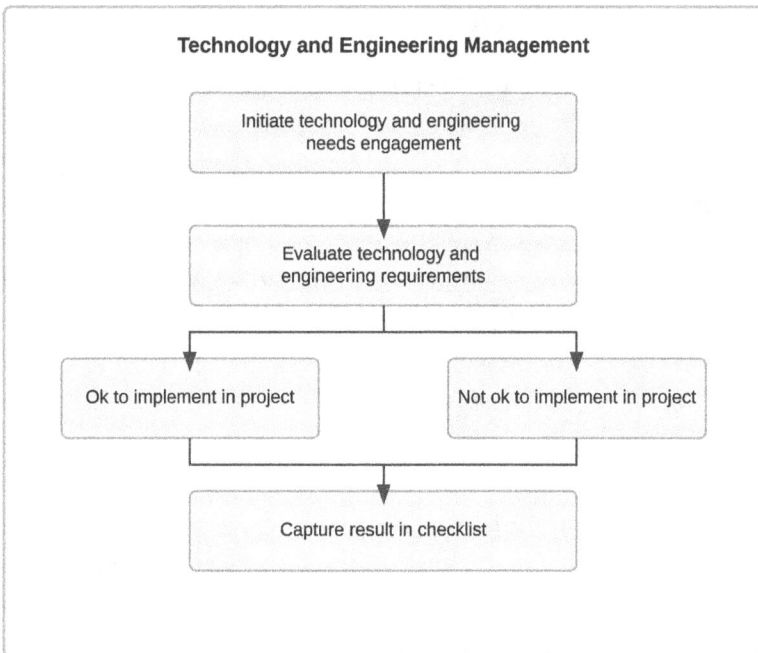

Figure 4.6 Process flow for Technology and Engineering Management

management aspects of the Cargo Lift Aviation engine overhaul and conversion project (process flow depicted in Figure 4.6).

Discussions focused on evaluating the suitability of existing tooling and equipment for the proposed engine work and identifying any necessary upgrades or investments to ensure efficiency and precision (3.2). The team also explored potential applications of advanced technologies, such as 3D scanning and modeling for precise component inspection and analysis, and the use of simulation software to optimize engine performance after conversion (4.2). Furthermore, the team discussed knowledge management strategies to capture and leverage engineering expertise throughout the project, ensuring effective documentation and transfer of technical information (2.3). These insights will be used to inform the Technology and Engineering Management Checklist, guiding the selection of tools, adoption of innovative techniques, and effective management of engineering resources throughout the project lifecycle.

Aviation Quality Management

The next AirCare extended team meeting was convened to specifically address aviation quality management aspects crucial to the Cargo Lift Aviation engine overhaul and conversion project (process flow depicted in Figure 4.7).

The project focused on establishing a robust QMS that complies with industry standards and regulatory requirements (3.3, 5.2). This included defining quality control procedures for each stage of the project, from initial engine assessment and disassembly to component repair/replacement, reassembly, and final testing (2.2, 2.4). The team emphasized the importance of meticulous documentation and traceability throughout the process to ensure accountability and compliance. Additionally, the team explored strategies for continuous improvement within the QMS, including regular audits, data analysis, and feedback mechanisms to identify and address any potential quality issues proactively. This information will be used to develop a comprehensive quality management plan, ensuring that the project meets the highest standards of safety, reliability, and airworthiness.

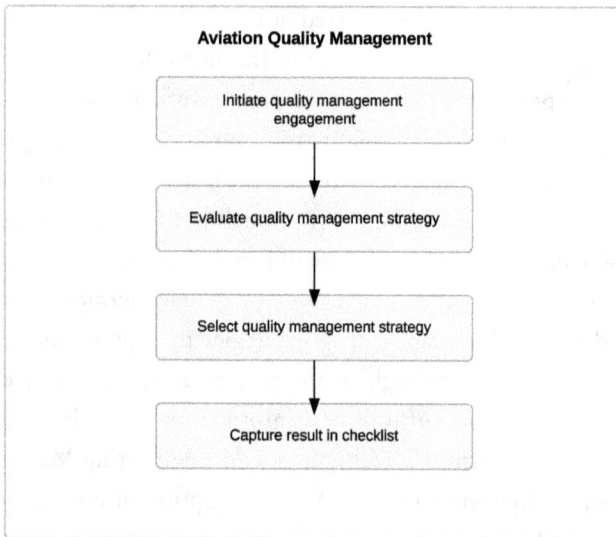

Figure 4.7 Process flow for Aviation Quality Management

Aviation Regulation, Compliance, and Certification

The AirCare team held a pre-project meeting with the regulatory and certification team. The meeting was dedicated to navigating the complex landscape of aviation regulations, compliance, and certification for the Cargo Lift Aviation engine overhaul and conversion project (process flow depicted in Figure 4.8).

While engaging with the regulatory team, the central focus was on ensuring adherence to all applicable airworthiness directives, maintenance manuals, and service bulletins relevant to the Short 330 aircraft and its engine types (2.3). The team meticulously reviewed the regulatory requirements for engine modifications, including those related to potential conversions to different fuel types or engine models, to ensure full compliance with certification processes and emissions standards (2.2, 2.3). Furthermore, they emphasized the importance of meticulous recordkeeping and documentation to demonstrate compliance throughout the project lifecycle and during interactions with regulatory authorities (2.4). This information will be compiled into a Comprehensive Compliance Checklist, guiding the team to navigate the regulatory landscape effectively and ensure the project meets all necessary aviation safety and compliance standards.

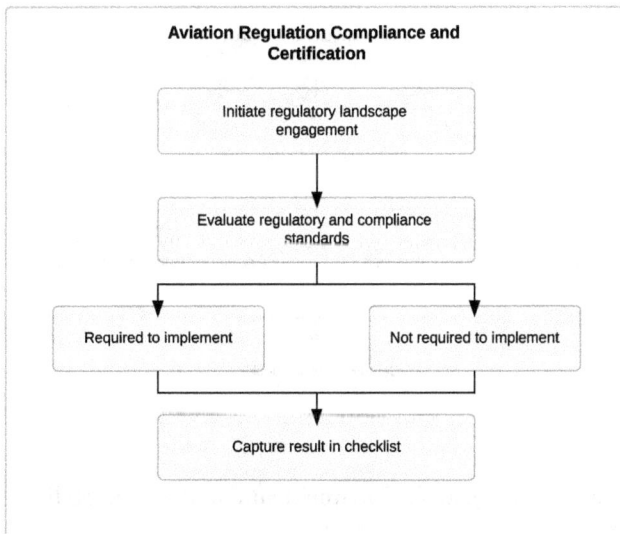

Figure 4.8 Process flow for Aviation Regulation, Compliance, and Certification Management

Environmental and Sustainability Management

The AirCare team then held a pre-project meeting specifically to address environmental and sustainability considerations within the Cargo Lift Aviation engine overhaul and conversion project (process flow depicted in Figure 4.9).

The meeting revolved around minimizing the environmental impact of the project activities, with a focus on responsible waste management and disposal procedures for hazardous materials (e.g., oils, solvents) used during engine maintenance (4.6). The team explored opportunities to incorporate ecofriendly practices, such as utilizing biodegradable cleaning agents and optimizing energy consumption in their facilities. Furthermore, they investigated the feasibility of recommending and implementing sustainable aviation fuels (SAF) as part of the engine conversion options, aligning with Cargo Lift's stated objectives (2.1). This information will be used to develop an environmental and sustainability plan, guiding the team to minimize the project's ecological footprint and contribute to a more sustainable aviation industry.

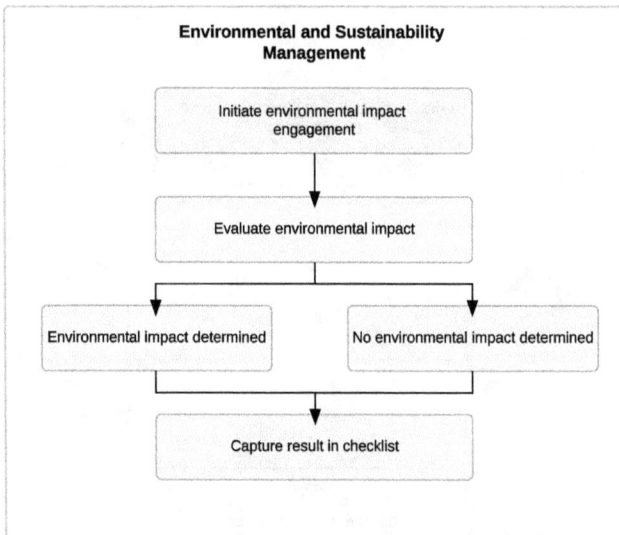

Figure 4.9 Process flow for Environmental and Sustainability Management

Start Phase Activities

With pre-project work complete, the AirCare team proceeded to formally move into the start phase. As was the case with pre-project work, the team focused on not only completing the important work of the start phase as documented in AVPM practices but also recording the work in templates and checklists depending on whether the practices were primary or supporting (Figure 4.10).

Lifecycle Management

The lifecycle practice in the start phase was straightforward for the Air-Care team. Given that the decision was made in the pre-project phase to employ a plan-driven lifecycle, the main deliverable was to formally kick off the lifecycle and document it in the Lifecycle Management Initiation Template.

Requirement Collection and Statement of Work

Requirements and the statement of work are critical to capture at the start of a project. The AirCare project team held several working meetings to flesh out requirements as well as the statement of work as follows:

Requirements

Cargo Lift Aviation requires engine overhaul and conversion services for their fleet of six Short 330 aircraft. The selected vendor must:

1. Conduct a thorough assessment of existing engines to determine the feasibility of overhaul versus conversion to alternative fuel types or engine models (2.1).
2. Perform either a complete overhaul of existing engines or convert them to a different fuel type or model, adhering to all relevant maintenance manuals and airworthiness directives (2.2, 2.3).
3. Implement rigorous quality control processes to ensure safety and prevent engine malfunctions, providing comprehensive documentation of all work performed (2.4).

	Start
Lifecycle Management Initiation Template	
AVPMP-LM-1.2	
Requirements Collection and Statement of Work Template	
AVPMP-RM-1.2	
Project Schedule Management Plan Template	
AVPMP-SM-1.2	
Stakeholder Identification Matrix Template	
AVPMP-ST-1.2	
Risk and Safety Issues Identification Report Template	
AVPMP-RS-1.2	
Top Down Refined Budget Estimate Template	
AVPMP-FM-1.2	
Talent Analysis/Source Template	
AVPMP-HR-1.2	

Figure 4.10 Primary practice deliverables for the Start Phase of the AirCare plan-driven project

4. Demonstrate extensive experience in aircraft engine overhaul/conversion, possess the necessary tooling and facilities, and display in-depth knowledge of aviation regulations and certification processes (3.1, 3.2, and 3.3).

5. Maintain a strong safety culture and provide clear project plans with transparent cost breakdowns (3.4, 3.5, and 3.6).

Statement of Work (SOW)

The selected vendor will provide comprehensive engine overhaul and conversion services for Cargo Lift Aviation's fleet of six Short 330 aircraft. This includes:

1. **Engine Assessment:** Thorough inspection and evaluation of existing engines to determine the feasibility and benefits of overhaul versus conversion, recommending suitable engine models or fuel types for conversion (2.1).

2. **Overhaul/Conversion:** Complete overhaul of existing engines OR conversion to a different fuel type or model, including all necessary modifications, installations, and testing (2.2).

3. **Regulatory Compliance:** Ensuring strict adherence to all relevant engine maintenance manuals, service bulletins, airworthiness directives, and obtaining necessary certifications and approvals (2.3).

4. **Quality Assurance:** Implementing rigorous quality control processes to prevent improper assembly, component failures, and engine malfunctions, providing comprehensive documentation and traceability (2.4).

The vendor will deliver a fully functional and compliant aircraft fleet with enhanced reliability, fuel efficiency, and environmental sustainability.

Upon completion of these deliverables, the AirCare project team documented them in the Requirements Collection and Statement of Work Template.

Project Schedule Management

Prior to carrying out work in the project schedule, the AirCare project team reviewed the initial ROM schedule and discussed how to approach the management of the overall project schedule. The project team documented the result in the Project Schedule Management Plan Template deliverables.

Stakeholder Identification

Drawing upon the stakeholder landscape, the AirCare team evaluated and identified all of the relevant stakeholders of the Cargo Lift organization and used the findings of their evaluation to populate a stakeholder table and complete the Stakeholder Matrix Template deliverables.

Stakeholder Group	Name	Title	Description	Interests	Level of Influence
Cargo Lift Management	Emily Chen	CEO	Oversees overall project success	Maximize ROI, efficiency, and minimize downtime	High
	David Lee	CFO	Manages project budget and finances	Cost-effectiveness and financial sustainability	High
	Rachel Patel	Board Member	Ensures strategic alignment	Long-term growth and competitiveness	High
Flight Operations	Captain James Johnson	Flight Operations Manager	Ensures safe and reliable flight operations	Safety, reliability, and performance	Medium
	Michael Rodriguez	Maintenance Manager	Oversees maintenance crew	Efficient maintenance and minimal downtime	Medium
	Captain Sarah Taylor	Pilot Representative	Represents pilot concerns	Safety, performance and comfort	Medium
Technical Team	Dr. John Kim	Chief Technical Officer	Evaluates technical feasibility	Technical soundness and innovation	Medium
	Mark Davis	Engineering Manager	Oversees project implementation	Technical success and timeline adherence	Medium
Procurement/ Contracts	Karen Brown	Procurement Manager	Manages RFP process and vendor selection	Compliance with procurement policies	Low to Medium
	Tom Harris	Contract Negotiator	Ensures favorable contract terms	Cost-effectiveness and risk mitigation	Low to Medium

Stakeholder Group	Name	Title	Description	Interests	Level of Influence
Vendors	Brian Smith	CEO, EngineTech, Inc.	Secures contract and delivers project	Secure contract and reputation enhancement	Medium
Regulatory Authorities	Dr. Lisa Nguyen	FAA Representative	Ensures compliance with safety regulations	Safety and regulatory adherence	High
Engine Manufacturers	Robert Johnson	Technical Support Manager, Engine Co.	Provides technical specifications and recommendations	Technical support and expertise	Low to Medium
Parts Suppliers	David Kim	Sales Manager, Parts-R-Us	Delivers quality parts and components	Timely delivery and quality products	Low

Risk and Safety

The AirCare project team revisited the risk and safety report developed in the pre-project phase and proceeded to capture specific risk and safety issues in detail. The team assessed the category and severity of each risk and safety concern and, along with response measures, documented the result in the Risk and Safety Issues Identification Practice Template for the start phase (Figure 4.11).

Top-Down Refined Budget Estimate

The AirCare project team referred to the ROM budget estimate completed in the pre-project phase and developed a more detailed top-down estimate of the budget as follows:

Estimated Costs by Phase:

1. Project Initiation and Planning (24 weeks)
   a. Vendor selection and contract establishment: $60,000 to $120,000
   b. Project planning and resource allocation: $25,000 to $50,000
   c. Project management and coordination: $15,000 to $30,000
   d. Total: $100,000 to $200,000
2. Engine Assessment and Recommendation (46 weeks)
   a. Engine inspection and evaluation: $120,000 to $240,000

Risk Assessment

ID	Risk/Safety Issue	Description	Category	Risk Level	Safety Severity
1	Engine Damage	Unforeseen engine damage or failure	Technical	Moderate	Medium
2	Conversion Complexity	Conversion complexity and integration issues	Technical	Moderate-High	Medium
3	Parts Availability	Parts availability and procurement delays	Supply Chain	Low-Moderate	Low
4	Certification Delays	Certification delays or regulatory issues	Regulatory	Moderate	Low
5	Regulation Changes	Regulation changes or updates	Regulatory	Low	Low
6	Schedule Slippage	Schedule slippage due to technical challenges	Project Management	Moderate	Medium
7	Cost Overruns	Cost overruns due to unforeseen repairs or extensions	Project Management	Moderate	Low
8	Quality Control	Quality control issues or defects	Technical	Moderate	Medium
9	Safety Risks	Safety risks during engine overhaul/conversion	Safety	High	High
10	Fire Hazards	Fire hazards during engine overhaul/conversion	Safety	High	High
11	Electrical Shock	Electrical shock risks during engine overhaul/conversion	Safety	Medium	Medium
12	Fall Hazards	Fall hazards during engine overhaul/conversion	Safety	Medium	Medium

Figure 4.11 Risk Assessment table detailing identified risk and safety issues for the start phase

b. Feasibility study and recommendation report: $40,000 to $80,000

c. Technical writing and documentation: $10,000 to $20,000

d. Total: $170,000 to $340,000

3. Engineering and Procurement (812 weeks)

a. Detailed engineering design: $240,000 to $480,000

b. Parts and materials procurement: $600,000 to $1,200,000

c. Tooling and facility preparation: $120,000 to $240,000

d. Supply chain management: $20,000 to $40,000

e. Total: $980,000 to $2,000,000

4. Engine Overhaul/Conversion (1,216 weeks)

a. Labor costs for overhaul/conversion: $600,000 to $1,200,000

b. Parts and materials costs for overhaul/conversion: $1,200,000 to $2,400,000

c. Testing and validation: $120,000 to $240,000

d. Quality control and assurance: $20,000 to $40,000

e. Total: $1,940,000 to $3,880,000

5. Regulatory Compliance and Certification (48 weeks)

a. Regulatory consulting and support: $60,000 to $120,000

b. Certification and approval costs: $25,000 to $50,000

c. Compliance documentation: $10,000 to $20,000

d. Total: $95,000 to $190,000

6. Installation and Testing (46 weeks)

a. Labor costs for installation: $120,000 to $240,000

b. Testing and validation: $25,000 to $50,000

c. Quality control and assurance: $10,000 to $20,000

d. Total: $155,000 to $310,000

7. Project Closure (24 weeks)

a. Documentation and reporting: $15,000 to $30,000

b. Project closeout and handover: $10,000 to $20,000

c. Lessons learned and knowledge management: $5,000 to $10,000

d. Total: $30,000 to $60,000

Total Estimated Budget: $4,070,000 to $8,230,000

Contingency Buffer: 10 to 20 percent of total estimated budget ($407,000 to $1,646,000)

AirCare observed that the more detailed top-down budget increased by approximately 20 percent. This is within the range of typical error range of ROM estimates.

Talent Landscape/Source

The AirCare project team used the talent needs assessment developed in the pre-project phase and employed it to evaluate possible sources of talent within the overall talent landscape.

The talent landscape for aircraft engine overhaul and conversion services is highly specialized and competitive. Key talent requirements include:

- Aircraft Engine Experts
- Aviation Regulations Specialists
- Quality Control Specialists
- Project Managers
- Technical Writers
- Safety Specialists

Talent Availability:

- Aircraft Engine Experts: Limited availability due to specialized knowledge requirements (Short 330 engine models).
- Aviation Regulations Specialists: Moderate availability, with most experts working for regulatory bodies or large aviation companies.
- Quality Control Specialists: Moderate availability, with opportunities to train and develop internal talent.
- Project Managers: High availability, with many experienced professionals in the industry.
- Technical Writers: Moderate availability, with opportunities to outsource documentation services.
- Safety Specialists: Limited availability due to high demand and strict regulatory requirements.

Talent Sources:

1. Industry Partnerships: Collaborate with aviation industry partners, such as engine manufacturers, maintenance providers, and regulatory bodies.
2. Professional Associations: Utilize professional associations, such as the Aircraft Engineers Association, Aviation Regulations Association, and International Air Transport Association.
3. Job Boards: Post job openings on specialized job boards, such as Aviation JobNet, Aerospace Crossing, and Engineered Jobs.
4. Social Media: Leverage social media platforms, such as LinkedIn, Twitter, and Facebook, to reach potential candidates.
5. Employee Referrals: Encourage employee referrals and offer incentives for successful hires.
6. Training and Development: Invest in training and development programs to up-skill existing employees and address talent gaps.
7. Contractors and Consultants: Consider hiring contractors or consultants for specific phases or tasks.

Upon capturing the talent source and landscape information, the AirCare team documented their findings in the Talent Landscape/Source Template associated with the start phase of the human resource and team management practice.

Start Phase Supporting Practice Deliverables

As was the case in the pre-project phase, in the start phase, the AirCare project team engages with the extended organization to capture and document important information required for the project. The overall series of engagement activities is captured in the Table of Practices for the Start Phase (Figure 4.12).

Innovation and Research Commercialization Plan Deliverables and Checklist

The AirCare team has reviewed innovation and research observations as recorded in the pre-project work. The team has determined that the

Start				
J&R Commercialization Plan Deliverable Checklist				
AVPMS-IR-1.2				
Approved Suppliers Deliverable Checklist				
AVPMS-SC-1.2				
Safety and Compliance Framework Deliverable Checklist				
AVPMS-AS-1.2				
Commercialization Plan Deliverable Checklist				
AVPMS-CT-1.2				
Quality Systems and Assurance Deliverable Checklist				
AVPMS-AQ-1.2				
Certification Plan Deliverable Checklist				
AVPMS-AR-1.2				
Environmental and Sustainability Policy Checklist				
AVPMS-ES-1.2				

Figure 4.12 Supporting practice deliverables for the Start Phase of the AirCare plan-driven project

Cargo Lift Aviation project is expected to yield innovative technologies and research with significant commercialization potential. The project's focus on aircraft engine overhaul and conversion services has led to advancements in areas such as sustainable aviation fuel integration, digital twin technology, artificial intelligence (AI)–powered predictive maintenance, and additive manufacturing. To capitalize on these innovations, AirCare aims to develop new revenue streams, enhance its competitive advantage, and expand its market share in the aviation industry.

A comprehensive commercialization plan has been developed, involving licensing and partnerships, productization, consulting and training, and joint ventures. Target markets include the aviation industry, defense and government agencies, and emerging markets such as electric vertical takeoff and landing and urban air mobility. Initial investment is estimated at $5 million, with projected revenue growth of $20 million, $50 million, and $100 million in years 2, 3, and 5, respectively. A dedicated commercialization team will be established to execute the plan, with KPIs tracking revenue growth, market share expansion, customer acquisition, and innovation pipeline development.

The team has documented the plan and, while engaging with the extended organization, has completed the associated start phase checklist.

Approved Suppliers Deliverables and Checklist

The AirCare team met once again with the logistics and supply chain group with the organization and, in doing so, developed a list of approved suppliers for each of the major categories of project deliverables. The listing is as follows:

Engine Components:

1. General Electric Aviation (GEA): Engine overhaul kits, components, and spare parts
2. Pratt & Whitney (P&W): Engine components, spare parts, and repair services
3. Honeywell Aerospace: Engine control systems, avionics, and electrical components
4. Safran Aircraft Engines: Engine components, spare parts, and repair services

Avionics and Electronics:

1. Rockwell Collins: Avionics systems, communication equipment, and navigation systems
2. Garmin International: Avionics systems, GPS navigation, and communication equipment
3. Honeywell Aerospace: Avionics systems, flight control systems, and electrical components

Airframe and Structural Components:

1. Boeing Distribution Services: Airframe components, spare parts, and repair services
2. Airbus Defense and Space: Airframe components, spare parts, and repair services
3. Lockheed Martin Aeronautics: Airframe components, spare parts, and repair services`

Safety and Survival Equipment:

1. Cobham, plc.: Safety equipment, survival gear, and emergency oxygen systems
2. UTC Aerospace Systems: Safety equipment, survival gear, and emergency oxygen systems
3. Zodiac Aerospace: Safety equipment, survival gear, and emergency oxygen systems

Maintenance, Repair, and Overhaul (MRO) Services:

1. ST Aerospace: MRO services for airframe, engine, and component repair
2. HAECO Group: MRO services for airframe, engine, and component repair
3. AAR Corp.: MRO services for airframe, engine, and component repair

Logistics and Supply Chain Services:

1. DB Schenker: Logistics and supply chain management services

2. Kuehne + Nagel: Logistics and supply chain management services
3. DHL Supply Chain: Logistics and supply chain management services

Approval Criteria:
- Quality management systems (ISO 9001, AS9100)
- Industry certifications (FAA, EASA, CAAC)
- Supply chain reliability and stability
- Compliance with regulatory requirements
- Performance history and customer satisfaction

The project team then proceeded to document the results in the approved supplier's deliverables checklist.

Technology and Engineering Commercialization Plan Deliverables and Checklist

The AirCare project team met with the engineering group and identified technologies with significant commercialization potential, including advanced engine overhaul and conversion techniques, sustainable aviation fuel integration, digital twin technology, artificial intelligence (AI)–powered predictive maintenance, and additive manufacturing. To capitalize on these innovations, for its commercialization plan, AirCare aims to license and productize these technologies, targeting the $80 billion aviation MRO market and $10 billion SAF market. Through strategic partnerships with industry leaders, joint ventures, and targeted marketing efforts, AirCare seeks $50 million in revenue growth within the first 3 years, with a high potential ROI. Key focus areas include developing modular, scalable solutions for engine overhaul and conversion, integrating digital twin technology with AI-powered predictive maintenance, and establishing a SAF supply chain. By commercializing these technologies, AirCare is expected to establish itself as a leader in aviation innovation, drive revenue growth, and enhance its competitive advantage.

After summarizing the plan, the project documented the details in the Commercialization Plan Deliverables checklist.

Quality Systems and Assurance Plan Deliverables and Checklist

During the Start phase of the AirCare project, the team has determined that the quality systems and assurance deliverables will focus on establishing a robust quality management framework. Key deliverables include the development of a Project Quality Plan (PQP) outlining quality objectives, policies, and procedures; establishment of a Quality Management System (QMS) aligned with ISO 9001 and AS9100 standards; definition of quality metrics and key performance indicators (KPIs); identification and mitigation of potential risks and nonconformities; and development of a Supply Chain Quality Assurance Plan (SCQAP) to ensure supplier compliance. Additionally, the project team will conduct a Quality Risk Assessment (QRA) to identify potential areas of noncompliance and develop corrective actions.

Deliverables will also include quality documentation, such as quality procedures, work instructions, and inspection checklists, to ensure consistency and repeatability throughout the project lifecycle. These quality systems and assurance deliverables will provide a solid foundation, and the AirCare team will proceed to complete the relevant practice template checklist.

Certification Plan Deliverables and Checklist

The AirCare project team has developed a comprehensive Regulatory Certification Plan (RCP) to ensure compliance with relevant aviation regulations and standards. The plan outlines the necessary steps to obtain certification from regulatory bodies, including the Federal Aviation Administration (FAA) and European Aviation Safety Agency (EASA). Key elements of the RCP include identification of applicable regulations (e.g., FAR 33, FAR 43, and EASA Part 21); development of a certification matrix; establishment of a Design Assurance Level (DAL) and Safety Integrity Level (SIL); creation of a testing and validation plan; and definition of documentation requirements (e.g., Type Certification Data Sheet, Instructions for Continued Airworthiness). The team has also identified necessary certifications, such as Supplemental Type Certificate (STC) and Production Certificate (PC), and established a timeline for submission of certification applications. Additionally, the RCP includes a plan for ongoing compliance and post-certification activities, ensuring the modified aircraft meet regulatory requirements throughout its lifecycle. The AirCare team then documented the effort in the Certification Plan Deliverables Checklist.

Environmental and Sustainability Policy Deliverables and Checklist

The AirCare project team has developed in conjunction with the extended organization a comprehensive Environmental and Sustainability Policy (ESP) to minimize the project's ecological footprint and promote environmentally responsible practices. The policy aligns with international standards (ISO 14001) and industry best practices, emphasizing reduction of greenhouse gas emissions, conservation of natural resources, and mitigation of waste. Key objectives include achieving a 20 percent reduction in carbon emissions through sustainable aviation fuel integration, minimizing hazardous waste generation through responsible supply chain management, and implementing a recycling program for aircraft materials. The ESP also outlines guidelines for energy efficiency, water conservation, and biodiversity protection.

Additionally, the team has established a Sustainability Steering Committee to monitor progress, identify areas for improvement, and ensure compliance with regulatory requirements. The policy serves as a framework for integrating environmental considerations into all aspects of the project and is documented in the Environmental and Sustainability Policy Checklist.

Plan Phase

The foundation of the project built by the AirCare project in the preproject and start phases now culminates in complete plans for each of the practices that are to be employed as the basis for all work in the execute phase of the project (Figure 4.13).

Lifecycle Management Plan

The AirCare project team met with the client and the extended organization while at the same time reviewing the lifecycle management practice documents from the pre-project and start phases. The team created the resulting outline of the plan and proceeded to flesh out the details and document the result in the Lifecycle Management Plan Template.

Initial Lifecycle Management Plan Outline

1. Introduction

   The AirCare Project Lifecycle Management Plan outlines the structured approach to managing the project from concept to closure. This plan ensures that the project meets its objectives, delivers value to stakeholders, and minimizes risks.

2. Lifecycle Management Objectives
   a. Ensure compliance with regulatory requirements (FAR 33, FAR 43, and EASA Part 21)
   b. Achieve 20 percent reduction in carbon emissions
   c. Improve aircraft reliability and availability
   d. Enhance customer satisfaction
   e. Minimize lifecycle costs

3. Lifecycle Phases

   Pre-Project Phase (Conceptualization)

   Define project scope and objectives

   Conduct feasibility studies

   Develop business case

   Start Phase (Initiation)

   Establish project team

   Define project schedule and budget

   Develop project charter

   Plan Phase (Planning)

   Develop detailed project plan

   Define requirements and specifications

   Establish quality and risk management plans

   Execute Phase (Implementation)

   Procure materials and services

Plan
Lifecycle Management Plan Template
AVPMP-LM-1.3
Scope Development Based on Requirements Document Template
AVPMP-RM-1.3
Project Schedule Development Template
AVPMP-SM-1.3
Stakeholder Assessment Report Template
AVPMP-ST-1.3
Risk Register and Safety Issue Log Template
AVPMP-RS-1.3
Project Budget Baseline/Time-Phased Deliverable Template
AVPMP-FM-1.3
Team Development Plan Template
AVPMP-HR-1.3

Figure 4.13 Primary practice deliverables for the Plan Phase of the AirCare plan-driven project

       Conduct engineering and design activities

       Implement configuration management

Control Phase (Monitoring and Control)

       Track project progress and performance

       Identify and mitigate risks

       Conduct quality assurance activities

Close Phase (Closure)

       Formalize project completion

       Document lessons learned

       Evaluate project success

4. Phase Gate Reviews

   Pre-Project to Start: Project charter approval

   Start to Plan: Project plan approval

   Plan to Execute: Design and specification approval

   Execute to Control: Configuration management implementation

   Control to Close: Project completion and handover

5. Governance and Organization

   Project Manager: (Names to be added in practice template)

   Project Team: (List team members to be added in practice template)

   Stakeholders: (List stakeholders to be added in practice template)

   Governance Board: (List board members to be added in practice template)

6. Monitoring and Control

   Performance metrics: (Include metrics to be added in practice template)

   Progress monitoring: (Include schedule to be added in practice template)

   Issue management: (Include process to be added in practice template)

7. Review and Revision

   Review frequency: Quarterly

   Revision process: (Include process to be added in practice template)

Scope and Baseline

The AirCare project team carefully examined all of the requirements of the RFP, including all of the requirements generated from practices, and employed them to develop the complete project scope. The resulting WBS is depicted in Figure 4.14:

Schedule Plan and Baseline

Once the project scope was fully elaborated in the form of a WBS, the project team then proceeded to identify activities required to produce the project deliverables. This was followed by duration estimates as well as identification of predecessors. The result of the work was the following schedule baseline (Figures 4.15–4.20).

WBSID	Deliverable	WBS ID	Deliverable
1	Project Management Plan	5	Modified Airframe and Structure
1.1	Project Charter	5.1	Airframe Components
1.2	Project Schedule	5.2	Structural Components
1.3	Risk Management Plan	5.3	Fasteners and Hardware
1.4	Quality Management Plan	6	Safety and Survival Equipment
2	Modified Aircraft	6.1	Safety Equipment
2.1	Aircraft Design	6.2	Survival Equipment
2.1.1	Aircraft Design Requirements	6.3	Emergency Oxygen Systems
2.1.2	Aircraft Design Specifications	7	Testing and Validation Report
2.1.3	Aircraft Design Review Report	7.1	Testing and Validation Plan
2.2	Structural Analysis Report	7.2	Functional Test Results
2.3	Systems Integration Plan	7.3	Performance Test Results
3	Overhauled and Converted Engine	8	Deployment and Training Materials
3.1	Engine Selection Report	8.1	Deployment Plan
3.2	Engine Overhaul Procedures	8.2	Training Materials
3.3	Engine Conversion Procedures	8.3	Training Completion Records
4	Upgraded Avionics and Electronics	9	Operations and Maintenance Manual
4.1	Avionics System	9.1	Operations Plan
4.1.1	Avionics System Requirements	9.2	Maintenance Plan
4.1.2	Avionics System Design	9.3	Logistics Support Plan
4.1.3	Avionics System Test Report	10	Disposal and Recycling Plan
4.2	Electronics System	10.1	Disposal Plan
4.3	Communication System	10.2	Recycling Plan
		10.3	Environmental Impact Assessment

Figure 4.14 Work Breakdown Structure (WBS) for the Modified Aircraft project

WBS ID	Deliverable	Activity	Duration	Start Date	End Date	Milestone	Predecessors
1	Project Management Plan						
1.1	Project Charter	1.1 Project Charter	2 days	20241014	20241015	Project Charter Complete	
		1.1.a Define project objectives and scope	1 day	20241014	20241015		
		1.1.b Draft charter document	2 days	20241016	20241016		1.1.a
		1.1.c Review and approve charter	2 days	20241017	20241018		1.1.b
1.2	Project Schedule	1.2.a Develop WBS	3 days	20241018	20241020	WBS Complete	1.1
		1.2.b Define activities	5 days	20241021	20241025	Activity Definition Complete	1.2.a
		1.2.c Estimate durations	3 days	20241026	20241028	Duration Estimation Complete	1.2.b
		1.2.d Sequence activities and determine dependencies	2 days	20241029	20241030	Activity Sequencing Complete	1.2.c
		1.2.e Create schedule (Gantt chart)	2 days	20241031	20241101	Project Schedule Complete	1.2.d
1.3	Risk Management Plan	1.3.a Identify potential risks	3 days	20241102	20241104	Risk Identification Complete	1.2
		1.3.b Analyze risk probability and impact	2 days	20241105	20241106	Risk Analysis Complete	1.3.a
		1.3.c Develop risk response strategies	3 days	20241107	20241109	Risk Response Strategies Complete	1.3.b
		1.3.d Document risk management plan	2 days	20241110	20241111	Risk Management Plan Complete	1.3.c
1.4	Quality Management Plan	1.4.a Define quality standards and metrics	3 days	20241112	20241114	Quality Standards Defined	1.2
		1.4.b Establish quality control procedures	2 days	20241115	20241116	Quality Control Procedures Established	1.4.a
		1.4.c Develop quality assurance plan	3 days	20241117	20241119	Quality Assurance Plan Developed	1.4.b
		1.4.d Document quality management plan	2 days	20241120	20241121	Quality Management Plan Complete	1.4.c
2	Modified Aircraft						
2.1	Aircraft Design	2.1 Aircraft Design		20241122			1.2
2.1.1	Aircraft Design Requirements	2.1.1 Aircraft Design Requirements		20241122			2
		2.1.1.a Gather stakeholder requirements	5 days	20241122	20241126	Stakeholder Requirements Gathered	2.1
		2.1.1.b Analyze existing aircraft data	3 days	20241127	20241129	Existing Aircraft Data Analyzed	2.1.1.a
		2.1.1.c Define performance and safety requirements	5 days	20241130	20241204	Performance and Safety Requirements Defined	2.1.1.b
		2.1.1.d Document requirements	2 days	20241205	20241206	Aircraft Design Requirements Documented	2.1.1.c
2.1.2	Aircraft Design Specifications	2.1.2.a Develop initial design concepts	10 days	20241207	20241216	Initial Design Concepts Developed	2.1.1
		2.1.2.b Create detailed design specifications	15 days	20241217	20241231	Aircraft Design Specifications Complete	2.1.2.a
2.1.3	Aircraft Design Review Report	2.1.3.a Conduct design review	5 days	20250101	20250105	Design Review Conducted	2.1.2
		2.1.3.b Document review findings and recommendations	3 days	20250106	20250108	Aircraft Design Review Report Complete	2.1.3.a
2.2	Structural Analysis Report	2.2.a Analyze structural loads and stresses	10 days	20241207	20241216	Structural Analysis Completed	2.1.2
		2.2.b Perform finite element analysis (FEA)	10 days	20241217	20241226	FEA Completed	2.2.a
		2.2.c Document analysis results	5 days	20241227	20241231		2.2.b

Figure 4.15 Initial portion of the project schedule baseline for the AirCare project

WBS ID	Deliverable	Activity	Duration	Start Date	End Date	Milestone	Predecessors
3	Overhauled and Converted Engine						2,3
3.1	Engine Selection Report	3.1 Engine Selection Report		20250109			3
		3.1.a Define engine selection criteria	3 days	20250109	20250111	Engine Selection Criteria Defined	
		3.1.b Research and evaluate engine options	5 days	20250112	20250116	Engine Options Evaluated	3.1.a
		3.1.c Select engine and document rationale	2 days	20250117	20250118	Engine Selected	3.1.b
3.2	Engine Overhaul Procedures	3.2.a Develop engine disassembly procedures	5 days	20250119	20250123	Disassembly Procedures Developed	3.1
		3.2.b Define inspection and repair procedures	5 days	20250124	20250128	Inspection and Repair Procedures Defined	3.2.a
		3.2.c Develop engine reassembly procedures	5 days	20250129	20250202	Reassembly Procedures Developed	3.2.b
		3.2.d Document overhaul procedures	3 days	20250203	20250205	Engine Overhaul Procedures Documented	3.2.c
3.3	Engine Conversion Procedures	3.3.a Define conversion requirements	3 days	20250206	20250208	Conversion Requirements Defined	3.1
		3.3.b Develop conversion procedures	10 days	20250209	20250218	Conversion Procedures Developed	3.3.a
		3.3.c Document conversion procedures	3 days	20250219	20250221	Engine Conversion Procedures Documented	3.3.b
4	Upgraded Avionics and Electronics			20250222			3
4.1	Avionics System	4.1 Avionics System		20250222			4
4.1.1	Avionics System Requirements	4.1.1 Avionics System Requirements		20250222			4.1
		4.1.1.a Gather avionics system requirements	5 days	20250222	20250226	Avionics System Requirements Gathered	
		4.1.1.b Define functionality and performance	5 days	20250227	20250303	Functionality and Performance Defined	4.1.1.a
		4.1.1.c Document requirements	2 days	20250304	20250305	Avionics System Requirements Documented	4.1.1.b
4.1.2	Avionics System Design	4.1.2.a Develop avionics system architecture	10 days	20250306	20250315	Avionics System Architecture Developed	4.1.1
		4.1.2.b Design avionics system components	15 days	20250316	20250330	Avionics System Components Designed	4.1.2.a
		4.1.2.c Create avionics system schematics	5 days	20250331	20250404	Avionics System Design Complete	4.1.2.b
4.1.3	Avionics System Test Report	4.1.3.a Develop test plan	3 days	20250405	20250407	Test Plan Developed	4.1.2
		4.1.3.b Conduct avionics system testing	10 days	20250408	20250417	Avionics System Testing Completed	4.1.3.a
		4.1.3.c Document test results	3 days	20250418	20250420	Avionics System Test Report Complete	4.1.3.b
4.2	Electronics System	4.2.a Define electronics system requirements	3 days	20250421	20250423	Electronics System Requirements Defined	4.1
		4.2.b Design electronics system	10 days	20250424	20250503	Electronics System Designed	4.2.a
		4.2.c Integrate electronics with avionics	5 days	20250504	20250508	Electronics System Integrated	4.2.b, 4.1.3
4.3	Communication System	4.3.a Define communication system requirements	3 days	20250509	20250511	Communication System Requirements Defined	4.1
		4.3.b Design communication system	10 days	20250512	20250521	Communication System Designed	4.3.a
		4.3.c Integrate communication system	5 days	20250522	20250526	Communication System Integrated	4.3.b, 4.2

Figure 4.16 Continued portion of the project schedule baseline for the AirCare project

WBS ID	Deliverable	Activity	Duration	Start Date	End Date	Milestone	Predecessors
5	Modified Airframe and Structure	5.1 Airframe Components		20250527			2,3
5.1	Airframe Components	5.1.a Procure airframe components	10 days	20250527	20250605	Airframe Components Procured	5
		5.1.b Inspect and verify components	3 days	20250606	20250608	Components Inspected	5.1.a
		5.1.c Modify airframe components (if needed)	7 days	20250609	20250615	Airframe Components Ready	5.1.b
5.2	Structural Components	5.2.a Procure structural components	10 days	20250616	20250625	Structural Components Procured	5
		5.2.b Inspect and verify components	3 days	20250626	20250628	Components Inspected	5.2.a
		5.2.c Modify structural components (if needed)	7 days	20250629	20250705	Structural Components Ready	5.2.b
5.3	Fasteners and Hardware	5.3.a Procure fasteners and hardware	5 days	20250706	20250710	Fasteners and Hardware Procured	5
		5.3.b Inspect and verify components	2 days	20250711	20250712	Components Inspected	5.3.a
		5.3.c Prepare components for assembly	3 days	20250713	20250715	Fasteners and Hardware Ready	5.3.b
6	Safety and Survival Equipment	6.1 Safety Equipment		20250716			5
6.1	Safety Equipment	6.1.a Procure safety equipment	7 days	20250716	20250722	Safety Equipment Procured	6
		6.1.b Inspect and verify equipment	2 days	20250723	20250724	Equipment Inspected	6.1.a
		6.1.c Install and test safety equipment	5 days	20250725	20250729	Safety Equipment Installed	6.1.b
6.2	Survival Equipment	6.2.a Procure survival equipment	7 days	20250730	20250805	Survival Equipment Procured	6
		6.2.b Inspect and verify equipment	2 days	20250806	20250807	Equipment Inspected	6.2.a
		6.2.c Install and test survival equipment	5 days	20250808	20250812	Survival Equipment Installed	6.2.b
6.3	Emergency Oxygen Systems	6.3.a Procure emergency oxygen systems	5 days	20250813	20250817	Emergency Oxygen Systems Procured	6
		6.3.b Inspect and verify systems	2 days	20250818	20250819	Systems Inspected	6.3.a
		6.3.c Install and test oxygen systems	5 days	20250820	20250824	Emergency Oxygen Systems Installed	6.3.b

Figure 4.17 *Continued portion of the project schedule baseline for the AirCare project*

WBS ID	Deliverable	Activity	Duration	Start Date	End Date	Milestone	Predecessors
7	Testing and Validation Report	7.1 Testing and Validation Plan		20250825			6 0, 4.0
7.1	Testing and Validation Plan	7.1.a Define testing objectives and scope	3 days	20250825	20250827	Testing Objectives and Scope Defined	7
		7.1.b Develop test procedures and cases	7 days	20250828	20250903	Test Procedures and Cases Developed	7.1.a
		7.1.c Establish acceptance criteria	3 days	20250904	20250906	Testing and Validation Plan Complete	7.1.b
7.2	Functional Test Results	7.2.a Conduct functional testing	10 days	20250907	20250916	Functional Testing Conducted	7.1
		7.2.b Analyze and document results	3 days	20250917	20250919	Functional Test Results Documented	7.2.a
7.3	Performance Test Results	7.3.a Conduct performance testing	10 days	20250920	20250929	Performance Testing Conducted	7.1
		7.3.b Analyze and document results	3 days	20250930	20251002	Performance Test Results Documented	7.3.a
8	Deployment and Training Materials	8.1 Deployment Plan		20251003			7
8.1	Deployment Plan	8.1.a Define deployment strategy	3 days	20251003	20251005	Deployment Strategy Defined	8
		8.1.b Develop deployment schedule	5days	202			8.1
8.2	Training Materials	8.2.a Identify training needs	3 days	20251011	20251013	Training Needs Identified	8.1
		8.2.b Develop training curriculum	10 days	20251014	20251023	Training Curriculum Developed	8.2.a
		8.2.c Create training materials (manuals, presentations, etc.)	7 days	20251024	20251030	Training Materials Created	8.2.b
8.3	Training Completion Records	8.3.a Conduct training sessions	5days	20251031	20251104	Training Sessions Conducted	8.2
		8.3.b Evaluate training effectiveness	3 days	20251105	20251107	Training Effectiveness Evaluated	8.3.a
		8.3.c Document training completion	2 days	20251108	20251109	Training Completion Records Documented	8.3.b

Figure 4.18 Continued portion of the project schedule baseline for the AirCare project

WBS ID	Deliverable	Activity	Duration	Start Date	End Date	Milestone	Predecessors
9	Operations and Maintenance Manual	9.1 Operations Plan		20251110			8
9.1	Operations Plan	9.1.a Define operational procedures	5 days	20251110	20251114	Operational Procedures Defined	9
		9.1.b Develop operating checklists	5 days	20251115	20251119	Operating Checklists Developed	9.1.a
		9.1.c Document operations plan	3 days	20251120	20251122	Operations Plan Documented	9.1.b
9.2	Maintenance Plan	9.2.a Define maintenance procedures	5 days	20251123	20251127	Maintenance Procedures Defined	9
		9.2.b Develop maintenance schedules	5 days	20251128	20251202	Maintenance Schedules Developed	9.2.a
		9.2.c Document maintenance plan	3 days	20251203	20251205	Maintenance Plan Documented	9.2.b
9.3	Logistics Support Plan	9.3.a Define logistics requirements	3 days	20251206	20251208	Logistics Requirements Defined	9
		9.3.b Establish supply chain processes	5days	20251209	20251213	Supply Chain Processes Established	9.3.a
		9.3.c Document logistics support plan	3 days	20251214	20251216	Logistics Support Plan Documented	9.3.b
10	Disposal and Recycling Plan	10.1 Disposal Plan		20251217			9
10.1	Disposal Plan	10.1.a Define aircraft disposal procedures	5days	20251217	20251221	Aircraft Disposal Procedures Defined	10
		10.1.b Identify disposal sites and partners	5days	20251222	20251226	Disposal Sites and Partners Identified	10.1.a
		10.1.c Document disposal plan	3 days	20251227	20251229	Disposal Plan Documented	10.1.b
10.2	Recycling Plan	10.2.a Identify recyclable materials	3 days	20251230	20260101	Recyclable Materials Identified	10
		10.2.b Develop recycling procedures	5 days	20260102	20260106	Recycling Procedures Developed	10.2.a
		10.2.c Document recycling plan	3 days	20260107	20260109	Recycling Plan Documented	10.2.b
10.3	Environmental Impact Assessment	10.3.a Assess environmental impacts	7 days	20260110	20260116	Environmental Impacts Assessed	10
		10.3.b Develop mitigation strategies	5 days	20260117	20260121	Mitigation Strategies Developed	10.3.a
		10.3.c Document environmental impact assessment	3 days	20260122	20260124	Environmental Impact Assessment Documented	10.3.b

Figure 4.19 Continued portion of the project schedule baseline for the AirCare project

WBS ID	Deliverable	Cost Category	Item/Activity	Budgeted Cost
1	Project Management Plan	Labor	Project Manager (100 hours @ $100/hr)	$10,000.00
		Labor	Project Coordinator (50 hours @ $50/hr)	$4,125.00
		Software	Project Management Software License	$825.00
2	Modified Aircraft	Material	Aircraft Acquisition	$375,000.00
2.1	Aircraft Design	Labor	Design Engineer (200 hours @ $80/hr)	$26,400.00
		Software	CAD Software License	$1,650.00
3	Overhauled and Converted Engine	Material	Engine Overhaul Parts	$33,000.00
		Labor	Engine Technician (150 hours @ $60/hr)	$14,850.00
4	Upgraded Avionics and Electronics	Material	Avionics Systems	$247,500.00
		Labor	Avionics Technician (200 hours @ $75/hr)	$24,750.00
		Material	Electronics Systems	$49,500.00
		Labor	Electronics Engineer (100 hours @ $80/hr)	$13,200.00
		Material	Communication Systems	$41,250.00
		Labor	Communication System Engineer (80 hours @ $70/hr)	$9,240.00
5	Modified Airframe and Structure	Material	Airframe Components	$132,000.00
		Labor	Airframe Mechanic (250 hours @ $65/hr)	$16,987.50
		Material	Structural Components	$99,000.00
		Labor	Structural Engineer (75 hours @ $90/hr)	$7,425.00
		Material	Fasteners and Hardware	$16,500.00
6	Safety and Survival Equipment	Material	Safety Equipment	$24,750.00
		Labor	Safety Equipment Technician (40 hours @ $50/hr)	$3,300.00
		Material	Survival Equipment	$19,800.00
		Material	Emergency Oxygen Systems	$13,200.00
7	Testing and Validation Report	Labor	Test Pilot (50 hours @ $150/hr)	$12,375.00
		Equipment Rental	Testing Equipment and Facilities	$16,500.00
		Labor	Test Engineer (100 hours @ $70/hr)	$11,550.00
8	Deployment and Training Materials	Labor	Deployment Manager (60 hours @ $60/hr)	$5,940.00
		Travel	Travel to Deployment Site	$3,300.00
		Labor	Training Instructor (80 hours @ $80/hr)	$10,560.00
		Material	Training Materials Development	$1,650.00
9	Operations and Maintenance Manual	Labor	Technical Writer (100 hours @ $60/hr)	$9,900.00
		Printing	Manual Printing and Distribution	$1,650.00
10	Disposal and Recycling Plan	Labor	Environmental Consultant (50 hours @ $100/hr)	$8,250.00
		Disposal Fees	Aircraft Disposal	$8,250.00
		Recycling Fees	Materials Recycling	$3,300.00
				$1,736,377.50
	Contingency		(15% of total costs)	$260,456.63

Figure 4.20 Budgeted Cost table for the project deliverables, supporting the schedule baseline

Stakeholder Plan

The AirCare project team referred to the stakeholder landscape and identification work from the previous phases and proceeded to assess project stakeholders. This resulted in the following stakeholder assessment report and communication plan.

Cargo Lift Project Stakeholder Assessment Report

Document ID: ACSAR001 Revision: 1.0
Date: March 10, 2023
Approved by: [Name], Project Manager

Table of Contents

1. Introduction

The AirCare project stakeholder assessment report identifies and analyzes the stakeholders impacted by the project. This report provides a comprehensive understanding of stakeholder interests, expectations, and influence levels.

2. Stakeholder Identification

The following stakeholders have been identified:

1. AirCare Project Team
2. AirCare Customers
3. Regulatory Agencies (FAA, EASA)
4. Aircraft Manufacturers
5. Engine Suppliers
6. Avionics and Electronics Suppliers
7. Airframe and Structural Component Suppliers
8. Safety and Survival Equipment Suppliers
9. Testing and Validation Service Providers
10. Deployment and Training Service Providers
11. Operations and Maintenance Personnel
12. Environmental Groups
13. Local Communities

3. Stakeholder Analysis

Stakeholder	Interest	Expectation	Influence Level
AirCare Project Team	Successful project delivery	On-time, within budget	High
AirCare Customers	Reliable, efficient aircraft	Safe, cost-effective operations	High
Regulatory Agencies	Compliance with regulations	Adherence to standards	High
Aircraft Manufacturers	Protection of intellectual property	No design or manufacturing flaws	Medium
Engine Suppliers	Quality engine performance	Reliable, efficient engine operation	Medium
Avionics and Electronics Suppliers	Advanced system integration	Seamless system operation	Medium
Airframe and Structural Component Suppliers	Quality component delivery	No defects or delays	Medium
Safety and Survival Equipment Suppliers	Effective safety solutions	Reliable equipment operation	Medium
Testing and Validation Service Providers	Successful testing and validation	Accurate results, no delays	Low
Deployment and Training Service Providers	Effective deployment and training	Smooth transition, minimal downtime	Low
Operations and Maintenance Personnel	Efficient operations and maintenance	Minimal downtime, easy maintenance	Medium
Environmental Groups	Reduced carbon emissions	Ecofriendly operations	Low
Local Communities	Minimal disruption	No noise or pollution issues	Low

4. Stakeholder Classification

Based on the analysis, stakeholders can be classified into three categories:

1. High-Influence Stakeholders: AirCare Project Team, AirCare Customers, and Regulatory Agencies
2. Medium-Influence Stakeholders: Aircraft Manufacturers, Engine Suppliers, Avionics and Electronics Suppliers, Airframe and

Structural Component Suppliers, Safety and Survival Equipment Suppliers, and Operations and Maintenance Personnel
3. Low-Influence Stakeholders: Testing and Validation Service Providers, Deployment and Training Service Providers, Environmental Groups, and Local Communities
5. Stakeholder Engagement Strategy
To effectively engage stakeholders:
1. Establish regular communication channels
2. Conduct stakeholder meetings and workshops
3. Provide project updates and progress reports
4. Encourage feedback and concerns
5. Address stakeholder expectations and interests
6. Stakeholder Communication Plan

Stakeholder	Communication Method	Frequency
AirCare Project Team	Project meetings, e-mail	Weekly
AirCare Customers	Progress reports, phone calls	Biweekly
Regulatory Agencies	Compliance reports, meetings	Quarterly
Aircraft Manufacturers	Technical meetings, e-mail	Monthly
Engine Suppliers	Technical meetings, e-mail	Monthly
Avionics and Electronics Suppliers	Technical meetings, e-mail	Monthly
Airframe and Structural Component Suppliers	Technical meetings, e-mail	Monthly
Safety and Survival Equipment Suppliers	Technical meetings, e-mail	Monthly
Testing and Validation Service Providers	Progress reports, phone calls	Biweekly
Deployment and Training Service Providers	Progress reports, phone calls	Biweekly
Operations and Maintenance Personnel	Training sessions, e-mail	Quarterly
Environmental Groups	Progress reports, meetings	Quarterly
Local Communities	Public meetings, newsletters	Quarterly

7. Stakeholder Monitoring and Review
Regularly review stakeholder engagement and communication:
1. Monitor stakeholder feedback and concerns
2. Assess stakeholder satisfaction
3. Adjust engagement strategy as needed
Revision 1.0

Risk and Safety Plan

The AirCare team considered the initial identification of risk and safety concerns from previous phases and successfully completed the project risk and safety plan as follows.

Cargo Lift Project Risk and Safety Plan

Document ID: ACRSP001
Revision: 1.0
Date: March 10, 2023
Approved by: [Name], Project Manager

Table of Contents

1. Introduction
2. Risk Management Objectives
3. Risk Identification
4. Risk Assessment
5. Risk Mitigation Strategies
6. Safety Management
7. Hazard Identification
8. Hazard Assessment
9. Hazard Control Measures
10. Emergency Response Plan
11. Monitoring and Review

1. Introduction
   The AirCare project risk and safety plan identifies, assesses, and mitigates risks and hazards associated with the project.
2. Risk Management Objectives
   i. Ensure compliance with regulatory requirements (FAR 33, FAR 43, and EASA Part 21)
   ii. Minimize risks to personnel, equipment, and the environment
   iii. Maintain project schedule and budget
   iv. Ensure quality and reliability of modified aircraft

3. Risk Identification

Technical Risks:

   i. Engine failure

   ii. Avionics system malfunction

   iii. Airframe structural integrity issues

   iv. Safety equipment failure

Operational Risks:

   i. Human error

   ii. Weather-related issues

   iii. Air traffic control errors

   iv. Emergency landing procedures

Project Management Risks:

   i. Schedule delays

   ii. Budget overruns

   iii. Stakeholder communication breakdown

   iv. Team member turnover

4. Risk Assessment

Risk	Likelihood	Impact	Risk Level
Engine failure	Medium	High	Medium High
Avionics system malfunction	Low	Medium	Low Medium
Airframe structural integrity issues	High	Critical	High Critical
Safety equipment failure	Medium	High	Medium High
Human error	High	Medium	High Medium
Weather-related issues	Medium	Low	Medium Low
Air traffic control errors	Low	Medium	Low Medium
Emergency landing procedures	Medium	High	Medium High
Schedule delays	Medium	Medium	Medium Medium
Budget overruns	Medium	High	Medium High
Stakeholder communication breakdown	Low	Medium	Low Medium
Team member turnover	Medium	Low	Medium Low

5. Risk Response Strategies

   i. Engine failure: Regular maintenance, backup systems

   ii. Avionics system malfunction: Redundant systems, testing

   iii. Airframe structural integrity issues: Regular inspections, material selection

    iv. Safety equipment failure: Regular maintenance, backup systems

    v. Human error: Training, procedures

    vi. Weather-related issues: Weather monitoring, contingency planning

    vii. Air traffic control errors: Communication protocols

    viii. Emergency landing procedures: Training, drills

6. Safety Management

    i. Safety policy: [Include policy]

    ii. Safety objectives: [Include objectives]

    iii. Safety metrics: [Include metrics]

    iv. Safety monitoring and review

7. Hazard Identification

Physical Hazards:

    i. Falling objects

    ii. Electrical shock

    iii. Fire

    iv. Explosions

Health Hazards:

    i. Chemical exposure

    ii. Noise exposure

    iii. Radiation exposure

    iv. Ergonomic hazards

8. Hazard Assessment

Hazard	Likelihood	Impact	Risk Level
Falling objects	Medium	High	Medium High
Electrical shock	Low	Critical	Low Critical
Fire	Medium	High	Medium High
Explosions	Low	Critical	Low Critical
Chemical exposure	Medium	Medium	Medium Medium
Noise exposure	Medium	Low	Medium Low
Radiation exposure	Low	Critical	Low Critical
Ergonomic hazards	Medium	Low	Medium Low

9. Hazard Control Measures
    i. Falling objects: Safety nets, hard hats
    ii. Electrical shock: Grounding, insulation
    iii. Fire: Fire suppression systems, emergency response plan
    iv. Explosions: Explosion-proof equipment, safe handling procedures
    v. Chemical exposure: Personal protective equipment, ventilation
    vi. Noise exposure: Hearing protection, noise reduction measures
    vii. Radiation exposure: Shielding, personal protective equipment
    viii. Ergonomic hazards: Ergonomic design, training
10. Emergency Response Plan
    i. Emergency response team
    ii. Emergency procedures (fire, explosion, medical)
    iii. Communication protocols
    iv. Training and drills
11. Monitoring and Review
    Regularly review risk and safety plan:
    i. Monitor risk and hazard levels
    ii. Assess effectiveness of mitigation strategies
    iii. Update plan as needed

Budget Plan and Baseline

With the scope, schedule, stakeholder, and risk plans in place, resources are assigned to all activities. The project absorbs costs based on the assignment of resources. This is captured in the project budget as well as the time-phased project budget baseline (Figure 4.21).

Team Development Plan

AirCare is focused on creating a smoothly functioning team for the purpose of carrying out the complete project. The team development efforts are captured in the formal team development plan.

Budget Baseline

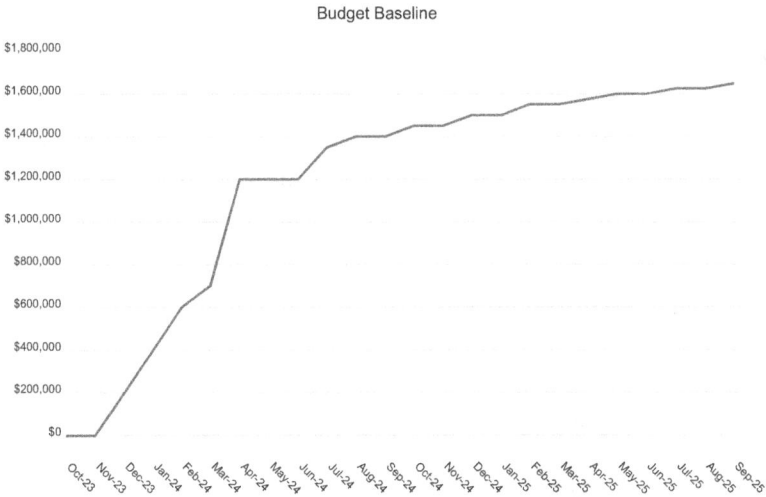

Figure 4.21 Time-phased project budget baseline (S-Curve) for the AirCare project

Team Development Plan

1. Team Formation and Roles:
   a. Identify Required Skills: Review the project schedule and WBS to determine the specific skills and expertise needed (e.g., aircraft design, engine overhaul, avionics, testing, etc.).
   b. Select Team Members: Choose individuals with the right skills, experience, and a collaborative mindset. Consider diversity in backgrounds and perspectives.
   c. Define Roles and Responsibilities: Clearly define each team member's role and responsibilities within the project. Create a responsibility assignment matrix (RAM) to document this.
2. Team Kickoff and Goal Setting:
   a. Project Kickoff Meeting: Hold a kickoff meeting to formally introduce the team, review the project goals, and discuss expectations.
   b. Team Charter: Collaboratively create a team charter that outlines the team's mission, values, communication guidelines, and decision-making processes.
   c. SMART Goals: Set specific, measurable, achievable, relevant, and time-bound (SMART) goals for the team.

3. Skills Development and Training:
   a. Identify Skill Gaps: Assess the team's current skills and identify any gaps that need to be addressed.
   b. Training Plan: Develop a training plan to provide team members with the necessary skills and knowledge. This could include:
      a. Technical training (e.g., avionics systems, engine conversion)
      b. Project management training
      c. Teamwork and communication workshops
   c. Mentoring and Coaching: Pair experienced team members with those who need guidance and support.
4. Communication and Collaboration:
   a. Communication Plan: Establish a clear communication plan that outlines how information will be shared within the team and with stakeholders.
   b. Regular Meetings: Schedule regular team meetings (e.g., weekly) to discuss progress, address challenges, and make decisions.
   c. Collaboration Tools: Utilize collaboration tools like project management software, shared documents, and communication platforms (e.g., Slack, Microsoft Teams) to facilitate communication and information-sharing.
5. Performance Management and Feedback:
   a. Performance Metrics: Define clear performance metrics to track individual and team progress.
   b. Regular Feedback: Provide regular feedback to team members on their performance, both positive and constructive.
   c. Performance Reviews: Conduct formal performance reviews at regular intervals (e.g., quarterly) to assess progress and identify areas for improvement.
6. Teambuilding and Motivation:
   a. Teambuilding Activities: Organize teambuilding activities to foster camaraderie and strengthen relationships.
   b. Recognition and Rewards: Recognize and reward team members for their contributions and achievements.
   c. Celebrate Successes: Celebrate milestones and successes to boost morale and maintain motivation.

7. Conflict Resolution:
   a. Conflict Management Training: Provide training on conflict resolution techniques.
   b. Open Communication: Encourage open and honest communication to address conflicts early on.
   c. Mediation: If needed, provide a neutral third party to help resolve conflicts.
8. Monitoring and Evaluation:
   a. Regularly assess the team's progress in achieving its goals.
   b. Monitor team dynamics and address any issues that arise.
   c. Evaluate the effectiveness of the team development plan and adjust as needed.

Plan Phase Supporting Practices

The primary practices form the core of the project plan. The supporting practices may include additional deliverables, activities, and milestones. It is for this reason that the supporting practices within the plan phase do not involve additional plans but, instead, result in possible additions to the primary practice project plans. For the supporting practices in the plan phase, the action is to review each supporting practice, complete the associated checklist, and updating the project scope schedule and budget process flow depicted in Figure 4.22.

The complete list of checklists (Figure 4.23) for supporting practices in the plan phase is provided below as follows:

The AirCare team, upon review of all supporting practices, made the determination that all supporting practice deliverables were either already incorporated in the project plan or resulted in no further scope, schedule, and budget.

Execute and Control Phases

The execution and control of the AirCare project involves doing the work as outlined in the complete project plan and adjusting as necessary. The execution and control actions for the primary practices are provided in Figure 4.24.

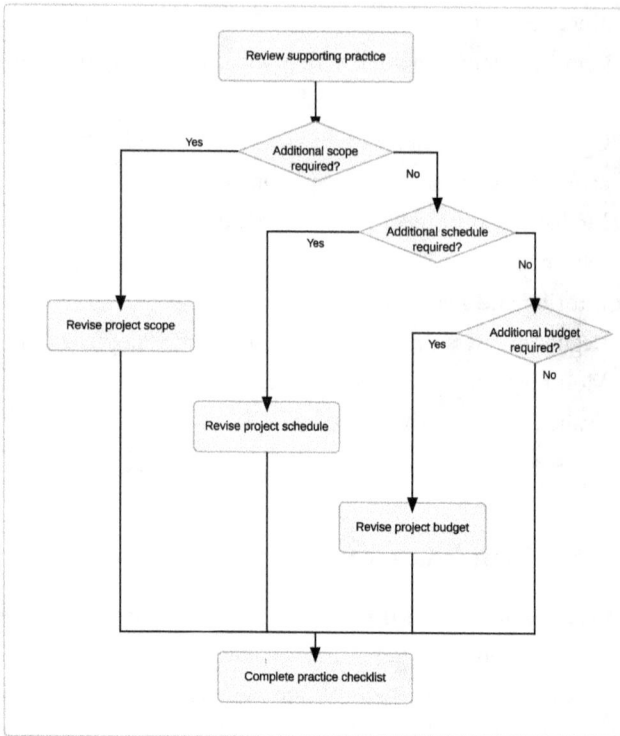

Figure 4.22 Process flow for reviewing supporting practice deliverables and updating project scope, schedule, and budget in the plan phase

Lifecycle Practice in Execution and Control

The lifecycle of the project involves the end-to-end governance of the overall project. During the execution phase, as the lifecycle unfolds, the focus of the AirCare project team is on confirming the progress to plan and adjusting the process flow as depicted in Figure 4.25.

Any updates or necessary adjustments are documented in the Lifecycle Practice Template.

Requirements Practice in Execution and Control

As the AirCare project team is focused on meeting the client requirements and executes and produces deliverables, AirCare evaluates progress, makes revisions as necessary, and performs validation and verification (process flow depicted in Figure 4.26).

Plan
Technology Implementation Plan Deliverables Checklist
AVPMS-IR-1.3
Supplier Selection Deliverable Checklist
AVPMS-SC-1.3
Safety and Compliance Plan Deliverable Checklist
AVPMS-AS-1.3
Engineering Strategy Deliverable Checklist
AVPMS-TE-1.3
Quality Management Plan Deliverable Checklist
AVPMS-AQ-1.3
Compliance Plan Deliverable Checklist
AVPMS-AR-1.3
Environmental and Sustainability Plan Checklist
AVPMS-ES-1.3

Figure 4.23 Supporting practice checklists for the Plan Phase of the AirCare plan-driven project

Execute	Control
Lifecycle Execution Report Template	Lifecycle Control Report Template
AVPMP-LM-1.4	AVPMP-LM-1.5
Requirements Validation Report Template	Requirements Measurement and Verification Report Template
AVPMP-RM-1.4	AVPMP-RM-1.5
Project Schedule Management Template	Schedule Variance and Adjustments/Change Control Report Template
AVPMP-SM-1.4	AVPMP-SM-1.5
Stakeholder Engagement Report Template	Stakeholder Communication/Decisions Report Template
AVPMP-ST-1.4	AVPMP-ST-1.5
Risk and Safety Issue Response Report Template	Risk and Safety Issue Response Monitoring and Control Report Template
AVPMP-RS-1.4	AVPMP-RS-1.5
Budget Progress Report Template	Budget Variance and Adjustments/Change Control
AVPMP-FM-1.4	AVPMP-FM-1.5
Team Performance Monitoring Template	Team Feedback and Adjustments Template
AVPMP-HR-1.4	AVPMP-HR-1.5

Figure 4.24 Primary practice deliverables for the Execute and Control Phases of the AirCare plan-driven project

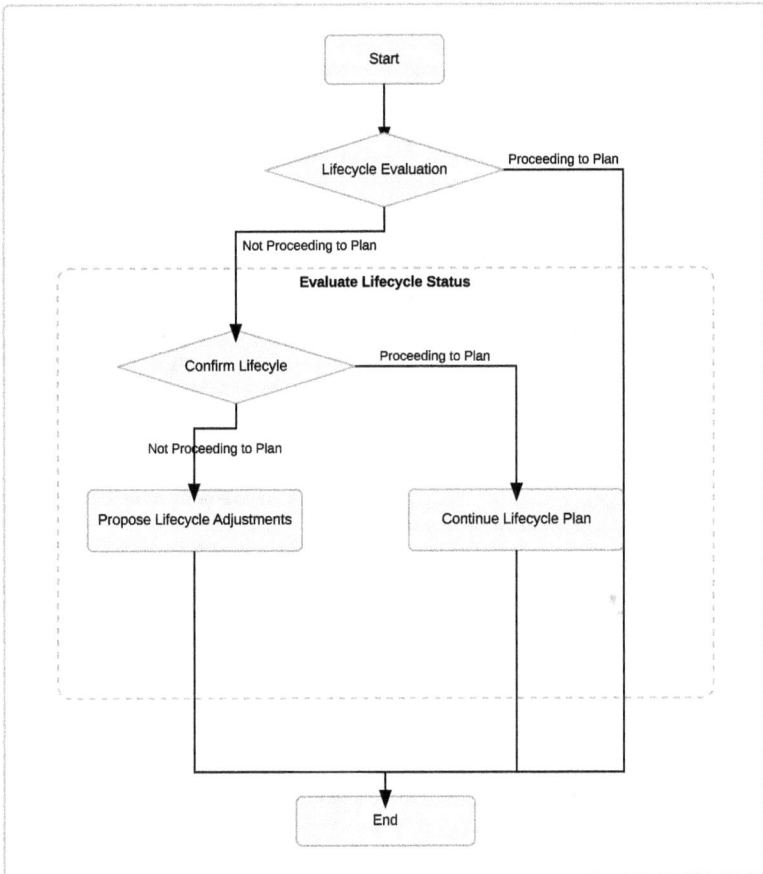

Figure 4.25 Process flow for Lifecycle Practice in Execution and Control

As the project team works through the project requirements evaluation process, the results are documented accordingly in the Requirements
Practice Template.

Schedule Management Practice in Execution and Control

As AirCare works through the execution of the project, the schedule is
monitored to confirm progress to plan. The AirCare team adjusts the
schedule as necessary (process flow depicted in Figure 4.27).

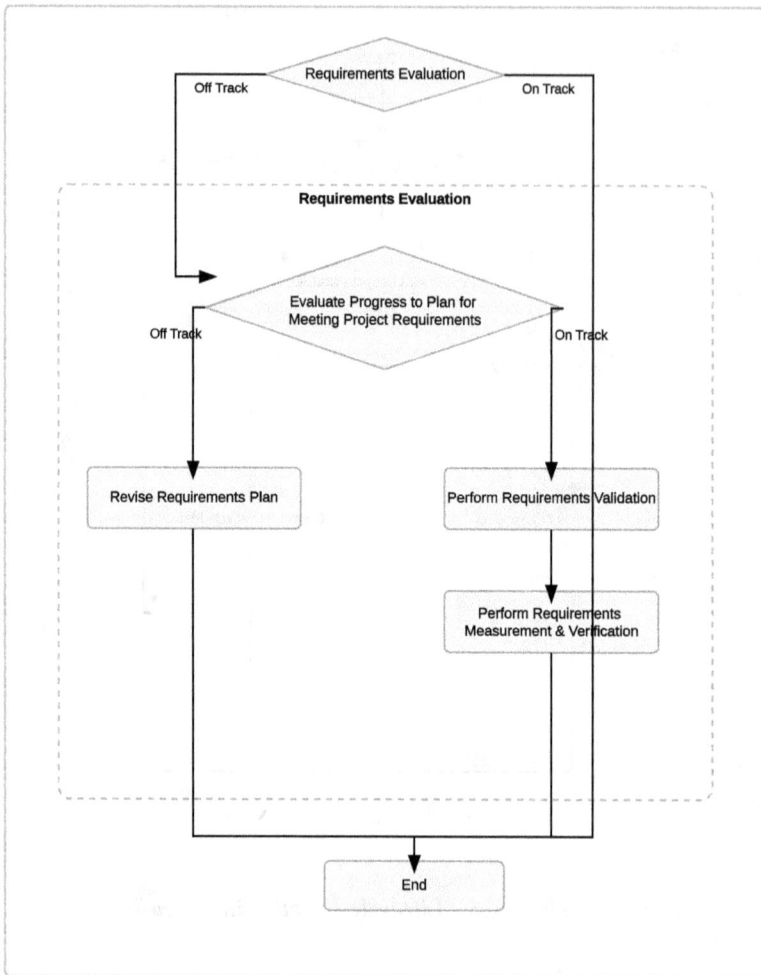

Figure 4.26 Process flow for Requirements Practice in Execution and Control

Stakeholder Management Practice in Execution and Control

The AirCare team, after developing the stakeholder management plan, has been communicating and engaging with stakeholders throughout the execution phase of the project. In the same manner as it did with the other facets of the project, the level and quality of stakeholder engagement are continuously monitored. AirCare observes issues in communication and engagement and makes necessary adjustments (process flow depicted in Figure 4.28).

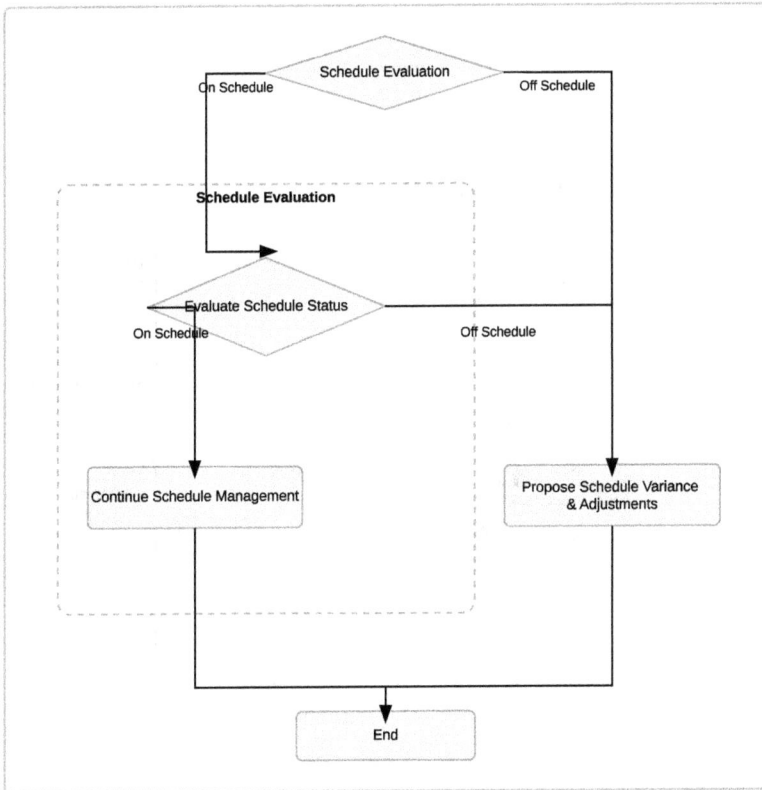

Figure 4.27 Process flow for Schedule Management Practice in Execution and Control

Risk and Safety Management Practice in Execution and Control

The AirCare project team recognizes that project risks identified and assessed in the plan phase are often fluid. New risks arise, while other risks originally identified and assessed may no longer be a concern and are retired from the risk register. Just as importantly, AirCare monitors the effectiveness of the execution of the risk management plan and makes necessary adjustments (process flow depicted in Figure 4.29).

Safety concerns are closely managed in a manner similar to risk management. AirCare therefore monitors safety incidents as well as risks and performs adjustments as necessary employing the following process flow (see Figure 4.30).

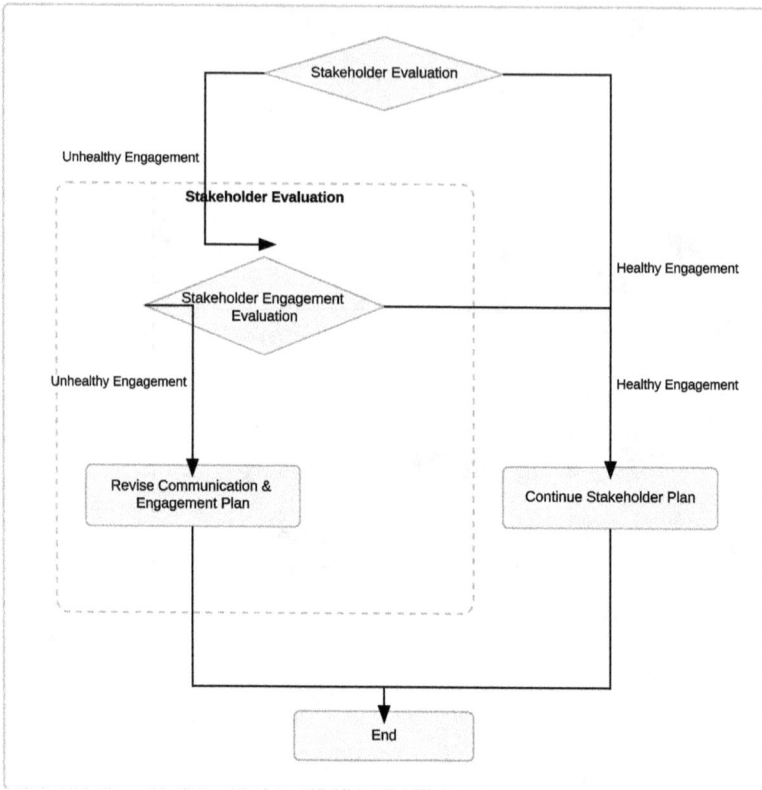

Figure 4.28 Process flow for Stakeholder Management Practice in Execution and Control

Financial Management Practice in Execution and Control

The primary financial focus of the AirCare team in the execution phase is on the project budget. The project budget is complicated by the fact that any changes to scope or schedule as the project unfolds also impact the project budget. AirCare therefore continuously tracks the project budget, identifies variances, and proposes changes using the following process flow depicted in Figure 4.31.

Human Resource and Team Management Practice in Execution and Control

AirCare recognizes the importance of a smoothly functioning and effective project team. To this end, the AirCare team monitors team performance,

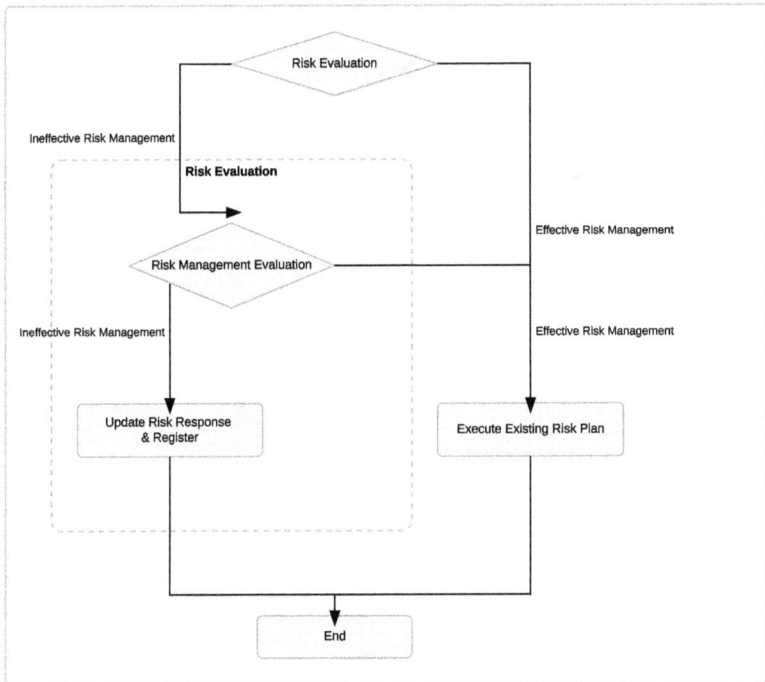

Figure 4.29 *Process flow for Risk Management Practice in Execution and Control*

provides feedback, and adjusts as necessary using the following process flow depicted in Figure 4.32.

For all primary practices, the results of the team management are documented in the relevant practice templates.

Supporting Practices in Execution and Control

The AirCare project team closely monitors and evaluates the supporting practices in project execution to the extent that revisions to scope, schedule, and budget are required. The mechanism for accomplishing this follows the same process as described in the supporting practice activities in the plan phase. Also, while this process is carried out, any updates or revisions are captured in each supporting process checklist. Also, each checklist is updated as necessary. The table of supporting practices and deliverables for the AirCare project are provided in Figure 4.33:

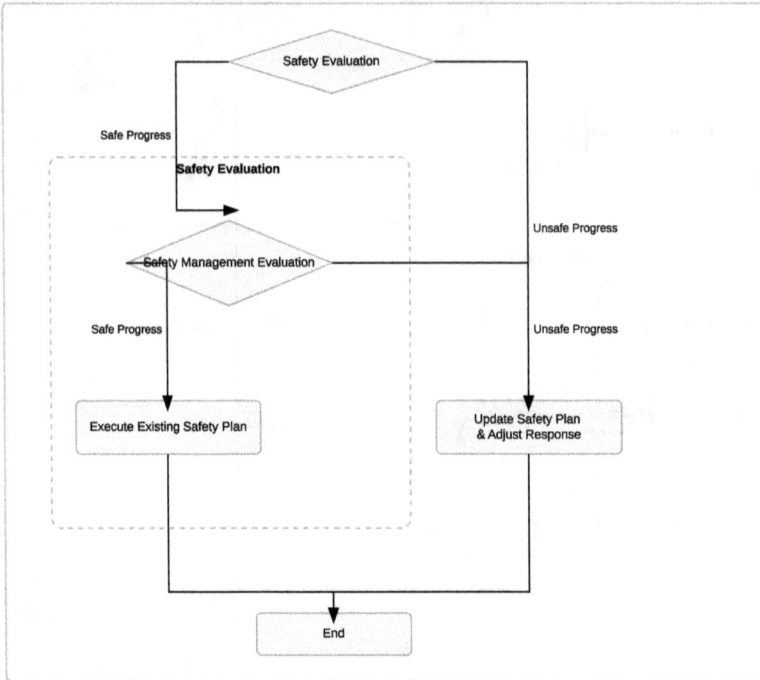

Figure 4.30 Process flow for Safety Management Practice in Execution and Control

Close Phase

The primary activity of the close phase for the AirCare delivery of the Cargo Lift project is the completion of the end of the close phase report. A succinct outline of the AirCare close report for the Cargo Lift project is provided below.

Cargo Lift Project: End of Close Phase Report

1. Introduction

   This report summarizes the successful completion of the AirCare engine overhaul and conversion project for Cargo Lift Aviation. The Close Phase encompassed finalizing deliverables, obtaining stakeholder acceptance, and archiving project records.

2. Complete Lifecycle

   The project successfully met its objectives, delivering overhauled/ converted engines that enhance the Cargo Lift fleet's reliability,

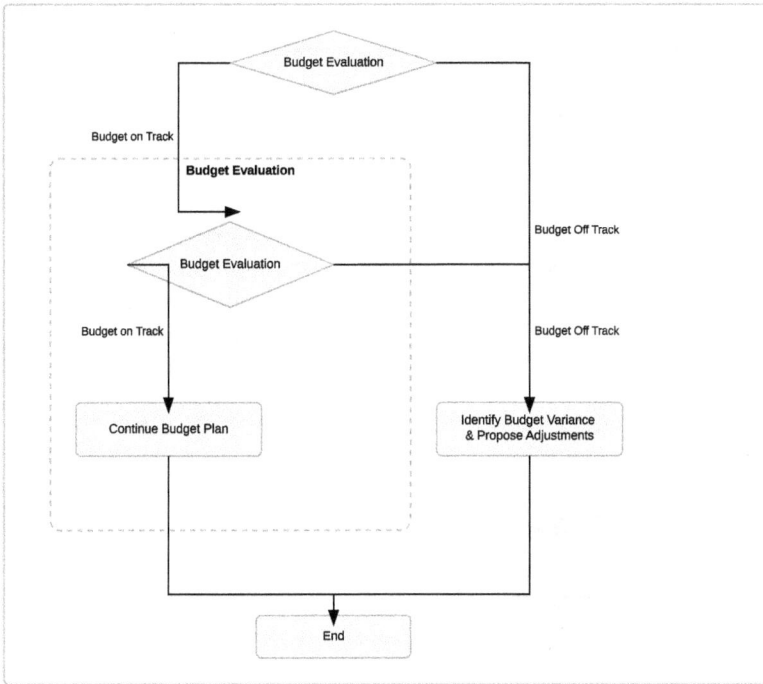

Figure 4.31 Process flow for Financial Management Practice in Execution and Control

fuel efficiency, and environmental sustainability. A lessons-learned session was conducted to capture insights for future projects.

3. Stakeholder Feedback

Final communication with Cargo Lift Aviation confirmed their satisfaction with the project outcomes. Feedback highlighted the improved engine performance and compliance with safety standards.

4. Confirm Requirements

All project requirements outlined in the RFP were met, and the deliverables satisfied Cargo Lift Aviation's needs. The requirements traceability matrix reflects the successful verification and validation of results.

5. R&S Final Report

The final risk and safety assessment confirmed the effectiveness of risk mitigation measures. No major safety concerns remained unresolved. A comprehensive risk and safety report was compiled.

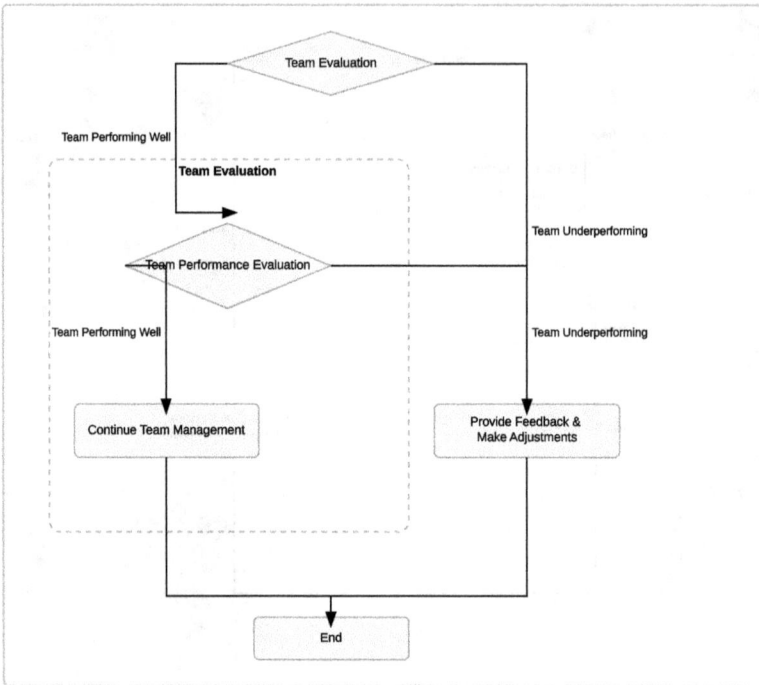

Figure 4.32 Process flow for Human Resource and Team Management Practice in Execution and Control

6. Deliver Schedule

   All tasks were completed within the approved schedule baseline, with minor delays mitigated through proactive actions. The final schedule performance analysis demonstrates overall schedule effectiveness.

7. Final Budget Report

   The final project costs were slightly under the approved budget due to efficient resource management. The cost performance analysis identified specific areas of cost-savings. Financial closure was completed, including final payments and account closure.

8. Final Team Report

   The project team's performance was commendable, with individuals demonstrating strong collaboration and technical expertise. Team members were recognized for their contributions. Knowledge transfer sessions ensured valuable project knowledge was shared.

Practices	Execute	Control
Practice Guide for Innovation and Research Management in Aviation Project Management	Innovation and Research Progress Reporting Checklist (AVPMS-IR-1.4)	Innovation and Research Adjustments Deliverables Checklist (AVPMS-IR-1.5)
Practice Guide for Supply Chain and Procurement Management in Aviation Project Management	Procurement Deliverable Checklist (AVPMS-SC-1.4)	Adjust and Optimize Supply Chain and Procurement Deliverable Checklist (AVPMS-SC-1.5)
Practice Guide for Aviation Safety Management in Aviation Project Management	Safety and Compliance Reports Deliverable Checklist (AVPMS-AS-1.4)	Safety and Compliance Response and Adjustment Deliverable Checklist (AVPMS-AS-1.5)
Practice Guide for Technology and Engineering Management in Aviation Project Management	Technology Implementation Plan Deliverables Checklist (AVPMS-TE-1.4)	Technical and Engineering Management: Adjust and Optimize Deliverable Checklist (AVPMS-TE-1.5)
Practice Guide for Aviation Quality Management in Aviation Project Management	Quality Control Reports Deliverable Checklist (AVPMS-AQ-1.4)	Change-Control Deliverable Checklist (AVPMS-AQ-1.5)
Practice Guide for Aviation Regulation Compliance and Certification Management in Aviation Project Management	Compliance Management Deliverable Checklist (AVPMS-AR-1.4)	Compliance Monitoring and Adjustment Deliverable Checklist (AVPMS-AR-1.5)
Practice Guide for Environmental and Sustainability Management in Aviation Project Management	Environmental/Sustainability Reports Checklist (AVPMS-ES-1.4)	Environmental and Sustainability Performance and Adjustment Checklist (AVPMS-ES-1.5)

Figure 4.33 Supporting practice deliverables for the Execute and Control Phases of the AirCare plan-driven project

9. Roadmap Updates

   The project roadmap was updated to reflect the actual timeline and archived for future reference.

10. Certification and Safety Compliance

    All required certifications were obtained, demonstrating compliance with aviation regulations and safety standards. Comprehensive reports document the project's adherence to these standards.

11. Supplier Report Card

    Supplier performance was evaluated, and feedback was provided. All suppliers met quality and delivery expectations.

12. Quality Report

    The final quality assurance review confirmed that all deliverables met the defined quality standards. The quality performance analysis identified minor areas for potential improvement in future projects.

13. Environment/Sustainability Report

    The project's environmental impact was minimal, with effective waste management and energy-saving measures implemented. The sustainability performance met the established goals, particularly regarding the exploration of sustainable aviation fuels.

14. Conclusions and Recommendations

    The project was successfully completed, exceeding Cargo Lift Aviation's expectations. Key success factors included proactive risk management, strong stakeholder collaboration, and a commitment to quality and safety. Recommendations for future projects emphasize continuous improvement in estimation accuracy and knowledge transfer processes.

CHAPTER 5

Aviation Iterative Project Case

AirCare encountered another opportunity, and this involved an RFP for a software-intensive Flight Management System project. For AirCare, this represents an opportunity to carry the first iterative project. The AirCare management team therefore responded to the following RFP from Blue Yonder and, in anticipation of a winning bid, began carrying out initial pre-project and start phase activities.

Request for Proposal (RFP)
Company: Blue Yonder
Project: Flight Management System (FMS) Software Development & Update
Date: August 27, 2024

1. *Introduction*

   Blue Yonder, a regional airline operating a fleet of seven small jets, is seeking proposals from qualified vendors to develop and/or update the Flight Management System (FMS) software for our aircraft. The goal is to modernize our FMS capabilities, improve operational efficiency, enhance flight safety, and ensure compliance with current and future aviation regulations.

2. *Project Scope*

   This project entails the following:

   A. Assessment of Existing FMS: Thorough evaluation of the current FMS software to identify limitations, areas for improvement, and compatibility with modern avionics systems.

   B. Development/Update of FMS Software:

      a. Design and development of new FMS software OR

      b. Update and enhancement of existing FMS software

    c. Incorporation of the following features:
   - i. Advanced navigation capabilities (e.g., RNAV, RNP)
   - ii. Optimized flight planning and fuel efficiency calculations
   - iii. Enhanced situational awareness and terrain avoidance
   - iv. Integration with modern communication and surveillance systems (e.g., ADSB, CPDLC)
   - v. Compliance with future airspace mandates and regulatory requirements

C. Testing and Certification: Rigorous testing of the developed/updated software to ensure functionality, accuracy, and compliance with all relevant aviation standards.

D. Deployment and Training: Installation of the new/updated software on all seven aircraft and provision of comprehensive training to pilots and maintenance personnel.

3. *Requirements*

A. Proven Experience: Vendors must demonstrate a strong track record in FMS software development or updates for commercial aircraft, preferably with experience on similar jet models.

B. Technical Expertise: In-depth knowledge of FMS architecture, avionics systems, aviation regulations, and software development best practices.

C. Regulatory Compliance: Ensure the developed/updated software meets all FAA and other relevant regulatory requirements and standards.

D. Safety Focus: Prioritize safety throughout the development and testing process, with robust quality assurance measures in place.

E. Project Management: Clear project plan with well-defined milestones, deliverables, and timelines.

F. Cost-effectiveness: Competitive pricing and transparent cost breakdown.

4. *Proposal Submission*

Proposals should include:

A. Company Overview: Details about your company, including experience in FMS development, relevant certifications, and technical capabilities.

    B. Technical Approach: Detailed description of your proposed solution, development methodology, testing procedures, and compliance strategy.

    C. Project Timeline: A comprehensive project timeline with key milestones and estimated completion date.

    D. Cost Breakdown: A clear and itemized cost breakdown of all project phases and deliverables.

    E. References: Contact information for at least three references from previous FMS development or update projects.

5. *Evaluation Criteria*

    Proposals will be evaluated based on the following:

    A. Technical Capability: Ability to meet project requirements and deliver a high-quality FMS solution.

    B. Experience and Expertise: Demonstrated track record in FMS development and relevant industry knowledge.

    C. Regulatory Compliance: Commitment to adhering to all applicable aviation regulations and standards.

    D. Safety Focus: Prioritization of safety throughout the project lifecycle.

    E. Project Management: Clear and realistic project plan with effective management processes.

    F. Cost-Competitiveness: Competitive pricing and value proposition.

6. *Submission Deadline*

    Proposals must be submitted by [submission deadline] to [contact e-mail address].

7. *Contact Information*

    For any questions or clarifications, please contact:

Clark Westerfeld
Procurement Officer
CW001@BY.com

We look forward to receiving your proposals and partnering with a qualified vendor to enhance our FMS capabilities.
Blue Yonder

The Plan Phase

The AirCare project team referred to the iterative practices and acknowledged once again that the practices that differ substantially from plan-driven projects involve the project lifecycle as well as the management of requirements. Given that the team early on recognized the importance of the use of the iterative lifecycle, such a lifecycle was assumed, and the team proceeded to vet requirements and incorporate the results into the product backlog as follows:

Product Backlog for Flight Management System (FMS) Software Development and Update

Iteration 1: Assessment and Planning

A. User Story 1: As a project manager, I want to conduct a thorough assessment of the existing FMS software to identify its limitations, areas for improvement, and compatibility with modern avionics systems.

B. User Story 2: As a software architect, I want to define the scope and requirements for the new/updated FMS software, including features like advanced navigation, optimized flight planning, and enhanced situational awareness.

Iteration 2: FMS Software Development Core Features

A. User Story 3: As a developer, I want to develop the core features of the FMS software, including advanced navigation capabilities (RNAV, RNP) and optimized flight planning and fuel efficiency calculations.

B. User Story 4: As a tester, I want to create and execute unit tests for the developed core features to ensure their functionality and accuracy.

Iteration 3: FMS Software Development Additional Features

A. User Story 5: As a developer, I want to develop additional features of the FMS software, such as enhanced situational awareness, terrain avoidance, and integration with modern communication and surveillance systems (ADSB, CPDLC).

B. User Story 6: As a tester, I want to create and execute integration tests to verify the interaction between the new/updated FMS software and other avionics systems.

Iteration 4: Testing and Certification

A. User Story 7: As a tester, I want to conduct comprehensive testing of the developed/updated FMS software to ensure its functionality, accuracy, and compliance with all relevant aviation standards.

B. User Story 8: As a project manager, I want to coordinate with regulatory authorities to obtain the necessary certifications for the new/updated FMS software.

Iteration 5: Deployment and Training

A. User Story 9: As a deployment engineer, I want to install the new/updated FMS software on all seven aircraft.

B. User Story 10: As a trainer, I want to develop and deliver comprehensive training to pilots and maintenance personnel on the new/updated FMS software.

Analysis of Additional Scope and Schedule Elements

Based on the provided practice guides and previous examples of the process to review and capture template and checklist deliverables, several additional scope and schedule elements associated with the AVPM practices were considered by the project team. This was done to ensure comprehensive and effective project management for the Flight Management System (FMS) software development and update.

To ensure a thorough approach, the AirCare team focused first on thoroughly reviewing all primary practices beginning with requirements. Requirements Management is crucial, and this was achieved through the refinement of the Product Backlog. This activity involved ensuring that user stories in the product backlog were well-defined, prioritized, and

Product Requirements Deliverable Template

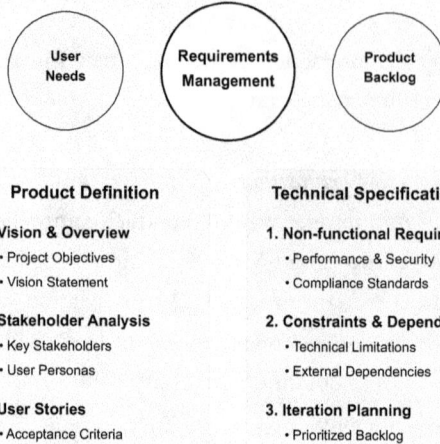

Product Definition

1. Vision & Overview
 • Project Objectives
 • Vision Statement

2. Stakeholder Analysis
 • Key Stakeholders
 • User Personas

3. User Stories
 • Acceptance Criteria

Technical Specifications

1. Non-functional Requirements
 • Performance & Security
 • Compliance Standards

2. Constraints & Dependencies
 • Technical Limitations
 • External Dependencies

3. Iteration Planning
 • Prioritized Backlog

*Figure 5.1 Graphical depiction of Iterative Product Requirements
Management Template*

aligned with project objectives. Additionally, a Traceability Matrix was
developed to link requirements to design, development, and testing activities. See graphical depiction of Iterative Product Requirements Management Template (Figure 5.1).

The review of the Schedule Management practice was also considered
vital by the team. This effort included Risk Mitigation Planning, which
identified potential risks and developed mitigation strategies to address
them proactively. Contingency Planning was also carried out by allocating resources and time for unexpected events or changes in scope.

The AirCare team understood fundamentally that Stakeholder and
Customer Relations Management played a significant role in project success. Regular Communication was considered key, and the team therefore established a communication plan to keep stakeholders informed
about project progress, challenges, and decisions. Feedback Mechanisms
were also implemented including gathering and addressing stakeholder
feedback.

Risk and Safety Management were acknowledged to be critical components of the project as is usually the case in aviation projects. A Safety Assessment was conducted to identify potential hazards and risks associated with the FMS software. Furthermore, ensuring Safety Certification was essential, and milestones and deliverables confirming that the FMS software meets all relevant safety standards and regulations were added to the product backlog and sprint schedules as necessary.

Financial Management concerned the AirCare team throughout the project. This concern led the team to conduct a cost–benefit analysis to evaluate the financial impact of the project and justify investments.

Change-Control Management was also employed to establish a process for managing changes to the project scope and budget.

AirCare, in spite of embarking on its first iterative project, well understood that the iterative lifecycle relies heavily on open communication and teamwork. It is for this reason that the team considered human resource and team management to be vital and ensured that all elements of this AVPM practice were carried out. This included activities such as organizing Teambuilding Activities to enhance collaboration and morale. Performance Evaluation was also implemented to support a system to assess team members' contributions and provide feedback.

Several support practices complement these primary practices. They in turn were carefully evaluated to determine any impact on the product backlog, sprint plans, and overall budget. As one example, Innovation and Research Management involved systematically evaluating the AirCare technology portfolio; tracking emerging technologies and trends, including Research and Development; and, finally, allocating resources for improvement activities. While the AirCare strategic focus on Innovation and Research Management led to the strategic adoption of novel components and processes in the project, the team also considered lower-level tactical concerns involving technology and engineering matters. The Technology and Engineering Management practice developed by the extended organization provided a Technology Roadmap that guided the FMS software evolution. Adhering to relevant Engineering Standards was also a focus so that best practices in Engineering helped ensure quality deliverables.

Supply Chain and Procurement Management required Supplier Evaluations to assess quality, cost, and reliability. Supply Chain Risk Management was also carried out to address supply chain disruption risks. Risks were considered throughout all phases of the iterative lifecycle, and the associated risk management practices included a focus on safety concerns. Aviation Safety Management and its associated practice fostered a Safety Culture within the project team and organization. Regular Safety Audits were carried out and documented in practice templates and checklists to identify and address potential hazards.

Of critical importance to AirCare is to deliver according to the client requirements. Aviation Quality Management involved developing a Quality Assurance Plan and implementing Quality Control Measures. Any additional scope and schedule milestones associated with quality were adopted accordingly into all sprints as necessary. This included Aviation Regulation Compliance and Certification Management that required tracking regulatory compliance and developing a Certification Plan.

Lastly, Environmental and Sustainability Management involved conducting an Environmental Impact Assessment and setting Sustainability Goals.

To incorporate the additional elements emerging from the 14 AVPM practices, the following steps were carried out by the AirCare project team:

1. Updated the product backlog by adding new user stories or tasks related to the identified areas.
2. Adjusted the sprint plan, allocating time and resources for activities related to the additional elements.
3. Refined project documentation to reflect the new scope and requirements.
4. Communicated changes to stakeholders, informing them about the project plan updates and their implications.

By addressing these additional elements, AirCare felt confident that the project would be better managed as well as ensuring that the FMS software meets the highest standards of quality, safety, and compliance.

Sprint Plan for Flight Management System (FMS) Software Development and Update

After converting requirements into the user story scope elements in the product backlog, the team shifted to the development of the sprint plan. The following sprint plan provides the preliminary allocation of backlog elements to the iterative lifecycle.

Sprint 1: Assessment and Planning
  A. Goal: Conduct a thorough assessment of the existing FMS software and define the scope and requirements for the new/updated system.
  B. Tasks:
      a. Review existing FMS documentation and specifications.
      b. Conduct interviews with pilots, maintenance personnel, and other stakeholders.
      c. Identify limitations, areas for improvement, and compatibility with modern avionics systems.
      d. Define the scope and requirements for the new/updated FMS software.

Sprint 2: Core Features Development
  A. Goal: Develop the core features of the FMS software, including advanced navigation capabilities and optimized flight planning.
  B. Tasks:
      a. Design and implement advanced navigation capabilities (RNAV, RNP).
      b. Develop algorithms for optimized flight planning and fuel efficiency calculations.
      c. Create unit tests to ensure the functionality and accuracy of the core features.

Sprint 3: Additional Features Development
  A. Goal: Develop additional features of the FMS software, such as enhanced situational awareness and terrain avoidance.

B. Tasks:
   a. Design and implement enhanced situational awareness features.
   b. Integrate with modern communication and surveillance systems (ADSB, CPDLC).
   c. Create integration tests to verify the interaction between the new/updated FMS software and other avionics systems.

Sprint 4: Testing and Certification
A. Goal: Conduct comprehensive testing of the developed/updated FMS software and obtain necessary certifications.
B. Tasks:
   a. Create and execute comprehensive test cases for the FMS software.
   b. Coordinate with regulatory authorities to obtain certifications.

Sprint 5: Deployment and Training
A. Goal: Deploy the new/updated FMS software on all aircraft and provide training to pilots and maintenance personnel.
B. Tasks:
   a. Install the FMS software on all aircraft.
   b. Develop and deliver training materials and courses.
   c. Provide onsite support for pilots and maintenance personnel.

Product Backlog for Sprint 1: Assessment and Planning

As the AirCare team moved closer to project execution, the project team next prepared the product backlog for Sprint 1 by employing the following user stories and descriptions.

User Story	Description
As a project manager, I want to conduct a thorough assessment of the existing FMS software to identify its limitations, areas for improvement, and compatibility with modern avionics systems.	This user story encompasses the entire scope of the assessment phase of the project. It includes reviewing existing documentation, conducting stakeholder interviews, and identifying key areas for improvement.
As a software architect, I want to define the scope and requirements for the new/updated FMS software, including features like advanced navigation, optimized flight planning, and enhanced situational awareness.	This user story focuses on defining the specific features and functionality of the new/updated FMS system. It will guide the development effort in subsequent sprints.

Schedule for Sprint 1: Assessment and Planning (Final)

As a next step, the AirCare team developed a schedule of key activities required to deliver the Sprint 1 user stories. After completing the schedule for Sprint 1, the team also created preliminary schedules for the product backlog for Sprints 2 through 5 with the understanding that they will be adjusted based on the outcome and feedback from preceding sprints.

Activity	Duration (Days)	Start Date	End Date
Review existing FMS documentation	2	October 14	October 16
Conduct interviews with stakeholders	2	October 17	October 19
Analyze existing FMS limitations and areas for improvement	3	October 20	October 23
Define scope and requirements for new/updated FMS	3	October 24	October 27
Create draft assessment and planning document	2	October 28	October 30
Review and finalize document	1	October 31	October 31

Schedule for Sprint 2: Core Features Development (Tentative, Pending SP1 Outcome)

Activity	Duration (Days)	Start Date	End Date
Design advanced navigation capabilities	3	November 1	November 4
Implement advanced navigation capabilities	5	November 5	November 10
Design optimized flight planning algorithms	2	November 11	November 13
Implement optimized flight planning algorithms	4	November 14	November 18
Create and execute unit tests	2	November 19	November 21

Schedule for Sprint 3: Additional Features Development (Tentative, Pending SP2 Outcome)

Activity	Duration (Days)	Start Date	End Date
Design enhanced situational awareness features	2	November 22	November 24
Implement enhanced situational awareness features	4	November 25	November 29
Integrate with communication and surveillance systems	3	November 30	December 3
Create and execute integration tests	2	December 4	December 6

Schedule for Sprint 4: Testing and Certification (Tentative, Pending SP3 Outcome)

Activity	Duration (Days)	Start Date	End Date
Create and execute comprehensive test cases	5	December 7	December 12
Analyze test results and identify defects	2	December 13	December 15
Remediate defects and retest	3	December 16	December 19
Coordinate with regulatory authorities for certification	3	December 20	December 23
Obtain certification	2	December 24	December 26

Schedule for Sprint 5: Deployment and Training (Tentative, Pending SP4 Outcome)

Activity	Duration (Days)	Start Date	End Date
Develop deployment plan	1	December 27	December 27
Deploy FMS software on all aircraft	3	December 28	December 31
Develop training materials and courses	3	January 1	January 4
Deliver training to pilots and maintenance personnel	5	January 5	January 10
Provide onsite support as needed	2	January 11	January 13

Standup Meeting Minutes

As the project progressed through the five sprints of the project lifecycle, the AirCare team held daily standup meetings following typical sprint guidelines as well as the AVPM iterative lifecycle practice. Select meeting minutes from a standup meeting from each sprint is outlined below:

Sprint 1: Assessment and Planning

Date: October 15, 2024
Attendees: Project Manager, Product Owner, Scrum Master, Developers, Testers

What Did I Do Yesterday?
- Completed a detailed analysis of the existing FMS software, identifying key limitations and areas for improvement.
- Conducted in-depth interviews with pilots and maintenance personnel to gather their insights and requirements.
- Drafted a preliminary requirements specification document, outlining the scope and objectives of the new/updated FMS software.

What Will I Do Today?
- Continue analyzing the identified limitations and explore potential solutions.
- Collaborate with the software architect to define the detailed scope and requirements for the new FMS features.
- Begin outlining the project timeline and resource allocation.

Are There Any Impediments?
- No impediments reported.

Sprint 2: Core Features Development

Date: November 7, 2024
Attendees: Project Manager, Product Owner, Scrum Master, Developers, Testers

What Did I Do Yesterday?
- Finalized the design for advanced navigation capabilities, including RNAV and RNP features.
- Implemented the core components of the RNAV and RNP algorithms.
- Created comprehensive unit tests for the implemented features.

What Will I Do Today?
- Continue implementing the remaining components of the RNAV and RNP algorithms.
- Review and provide feedback on the unit tests.
- Begin integrating the navigation features with the existing FMS architecture.

Are There Any Impediments?
- Developer A is facing an issue with integrating the navigation algorithms. We are working on providing support and guidance to resolve the issue.

Sprint 3: Additional Features Development

Date: December 2, 2024
Attendees: Project Manager, Product Owner, Scrum Master, Developers, Testers

What Did I Do Yesterday?
- Completed the design for enhanced situational awareness features, including terrain avoidance and weather information.
- Implemented the core algorithms for terrain avoidance.
- Integrated the terrain avoidance features with the existing FMS architecture.

What Will I Do Today?
- Continue implementing the remaining components of the terrain avoidance features.

- Begin integrating weather information into the situational awareness display.
- Create and execute integration tests for the additional features.

Are There Any Impediments?
- No impediments reported.

Sprint 4: Testing and Certification

Date: January 10, 2025
Attendees: Project Manager, Product Owner, Scrum Master, Developers, Testers

What Did I Do Yesterday?
- Completed the final round of testing for the FMS software, including system integration and performance testing.
- Prepared the certification documentation for submission to regulatory authorities.

What Will I Do Today?
- Review and address any outstanding issues identified during testing.
- Submit the certification documentation to regulatory authorities.
- Begin planning for the deployment and training phases.

Are There Any Impediments?
- Regulatory authorities have requested additional information for certification. We are working on providing the required documents.

Sprint 5: Deployment and Training

Date: February 3, 2025
Attendees: Project Manager, Product Owner, Scrum Master, Developers, Testers, Pilots, Maintenance Personnel

What Did I Do Yesterday?
- Completed the deployment of the FMS software to all aircraft.
- Conducted initial pilot training sessions on the new FMS features.

What Will I Do Today?
- Continue providing pilot training and support.
- Monitor the performance of the FMS software in real-world operations.
- Gather feedback from pilots and maintenance personnel to identify areas for improvement.

Are There Any Impediments?
- No impediments reported.

> **Note:** These meeting minutes provide more detail on the specific activities and challenges faced during each sprint. They can be further customized to include additional information as needed, such as specific tasks completed, issues resolved, or decisions made.

Sprint Reviews

The AirCare project team held reviews with the client at the end of each sprint. After each review, the team considered the feedback and additional requirements and updated product and sprint backlogs as well as the schedules for the following sprints.

Sprint 1 Review Minutes: Assessment and Planning

Date: October 25, 2024
Attendees: Project Manager, Product Owner, Scrum Master, Customer Representative

Sprint Review Objectives:
1. Present the assessment of the existing FMS software and its limitations.

2. Discuss the proposed scope and requirements for the new/updated FMS.

3. Gather feedback from the customer on the proposed approach.

Key Discussion Points:
1. The customer expressed satisfaction with the thorough assessment of the existing FMS software.
2. The proposed scope and requirements for the new FMS were aligned with the customer's expectations.
3. The customer requested additional features related to [specific feature].
4. The project team agreed to incorporate the requested feature into the product backlog for future sprints.

Action Items:
1. Update the product backlog to include the requested feature.
2. Schedule a follow-up meeting to discuss the detailed requirements for the new feature.

Sprint 2 Review Minutes: Core Features Development

Date: November 19, 2024
Attendees: Project Manager, Product Owner, Scrum Master, Customer Representative

Sprint Review Objectives:
1. Demonstrate the developed core features of the FMS software.
2. Gather feedback from the customer on the functionality and usability of the features.
3. Discuss any identified issues or areas for improvement.

Key Discussion Points:
1. The customer was impressed with the advanced navigation capabilities and optimized flight planning features.

2. Some minor usability issues were identified and will be addressed in the next sprint.
3. The customer requested additional customization options for the flight planning interface.

Action Items:
1. Prioritize the customization options for the flight planning interface in the product backlog.
2. Address the identified usability issues in the next sprint.

Sprint 3 Review Minutes: Additional Features Development

Date: December 6, 2024
Attendees: Project Manager, Product Owner, Scrum Master, Customer Representative

Sprint Review Objectives:
1. Demonstrate the developed additional features of the FMS software.
2. Gather feedback from the customer on the functionality and usability of the features.
3. Discuss any identified issues or areas for improvement.

Key Discussion Points:
1. The customer was satisfied with the enhanced situational awareness and terrain avoidance features.
2. Some minor issues were identified with the integration of weather information.
3. The customer requested additional customization options for the situational awareness display.

Action Items:
1. Prioritize the customization options for the situational awareness display in the product backlog.
2. Address the identified integration issues in the next sprint.

Sprint 4 Review Minutes: Testing and Certification

Date: December 27, 2024
Attendees: Project Manager, Product Owner, Scrum Master, Customer Representative

Sprint Review Objectives:
 1. Present the results of the testing and certification process.
 2. Discuss any identified issues or areas for improvement.
 3. Prepare for the deployment and training phases.

Key Discussion Points:
 1. The customer was satisfied with the overall quality and performance of the FMS software.
 2. Some minor defects were identified and will be addressed before deployment.
 3. The customer requested additional training materials for pilots and maintenance personnel.

Action Items:
 1. Address the identified defects before deployment.
 2. Develop additional training materials as requested by the customer.

Sprint 5 Final Review Minutes: Deployment and Training

Date: February 10, 2025
Attendees: Project Manager, Product Owner, Scrum Master, Customer Representative

Sprint Review Objectives:
 1. Present the status of the deployment and training activities.
 2. Gather feedback from the customer on the initial user experience.
 3. Discuss any ongoing issues or areas for improvement.

Key Discussion Points:
1. The customer was satisfied with the deployment process and the initial user experience.
2. Some minor issues were identified with the user interface.
3. The customer requested additional support resources for pilots and maintenance personnel.

Action Items:
1. Address the identified user interface issues.
2. Develop additional support resources as requested by the customer.
3. Schedule a follow-up meeting to discuss the ongoing performance of the FMS software.

Iterative Practice Deliverables

As the AirCare team carried out the iterative project, care was taken to address all iterative deliverables and checklists supporting the 14 AVPM practices. In the pre-project phase, the focus was on requirements and backlog estimation. See graphical depiction of iterative backlog estimation management (Figure 5.2).

The AirCare team then focused on developing a sprint plan capable of fully delivering the product backlog. See graphical depiction of Sprint Plan Deliverables Template (Figure 5.3).

Once the sprint plan was in place, the next step undertaken by AirCare was to take prioritized items in the product backlog and create the sprint backlog. See graphical depiction of Sprint Requirements Framework Template (Figure 5.4).

The AirCare team carried out standup meetings and prepared minutes for each. As each sprint unfolded, the team focused on the validation of deliverables. See graphical depiction of Validation Deliverables Template (Figure 5.5).

As the sprints unfolded, the AirCare team referred to iterative AVPM practices to verify work and make necessary adjustments. See graphical depictions of Backlog Adjustment Template (Figure 5.6), Iteration Adjustment Deliverables Template (Figure 5.7), and Iterative Verification Deliverables Template (Figure 5.7).

Backlog Estimate Deliverable Template

Backlog Items

Schedule Management

Estimation Techniques

Backlog Definition

1. Overview & Categories
   - Initial Backlog Items
   - Categorization Scheme

2. Estimation Method
   - Techniques Selected
   - Assumptions Made

3. Effort Estimation
   - Story Points/Time Units

Planning Considerations

1. Iteration Planning
   - Iteration Length
   - Capacity Analysis

2. Risk Assessment
   - Uncertainty Factors
   - Mitigation Strategies

3. Stakeholder Input
   - Feedback & Approval

Figure 5.2 Graphical depiction of iterative backlog estimation management

Sprint Number and Duration Framework

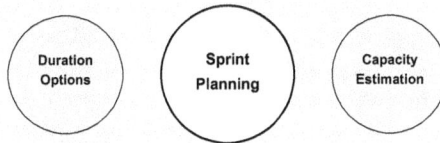

Duration Options

Sprint Planning

Capacity Estimation

Sprint Framework

1. Duration Selection
   - Duration Analysis
   - Selection Rationale

2. Sprint Number Estimate
   - Backlog Assessment
   - Team Capacity Analysis

3. Schedule Overview
   - Timeline & Milestones

Adaptation Framework

1. Flexibility Mechanisms
   - Adjustment Criteria
   - Feedback Integration

2. Stakeholder Engagement
   - Communication Plan
   - Review Participation

3. Approval Process
   - Sign-off Requirements

Figure 5.3 Graphical depiction of Sprint Plan Deliverables Template

Sprint Requirements Deliverable Template

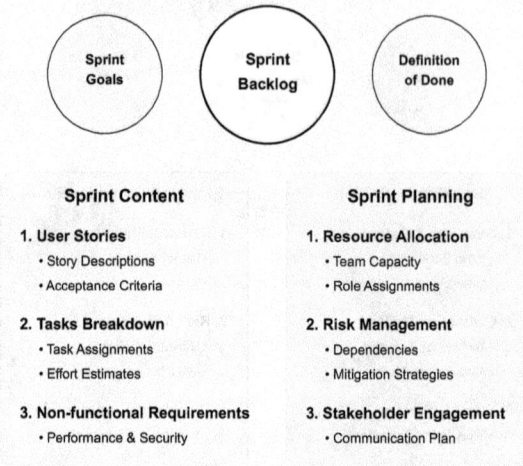

Sprint Goals

Sprint Backlog

Definition of Done

Sprint Content

1. **User Stories**
   - Story Descriptions
   - Acceptance Criteria

2. **Tasks Breakdown**
   - Task Assignments
   - Effort Estimates

3. **Non-functional Requirements**
   - Performance & Security

Sprint Planning

1. **Resource Allocation**
   - Team Capacity
   - Role Assignments

2. **Risk Management**
   - Dependencies
   - Mitigation Strategies

3. **Stakeholder Engagement**
   - Communication Plan

Figure 5.4 Graphical depiction of Sprint Requirements Framework Template

Validation Deliverable Framework

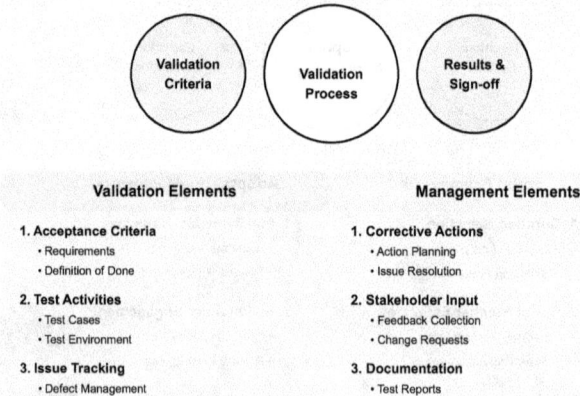

Validation Criteria

Validation Process

Results & Sign-off

Validation Elements

1. **Acceptance Criteria**
   - Requirements
   - Definition of Done

2. **Test Activities**
   - Test Cases
   - Test Environment

3. **Issue Tracking**
   - Defect Management

Management Elements

1. **Corrective Actions**
   - Action Planning
   - Issue Resolution

2. **Stakeholder Input**
   - Feedback Collection
   - Change Requests

3. **Documentation**
   - Test Reports

Figure 5.5 Graphical depiction of Validation Deliverables Template

Backlog Adjustment Framework

Review & Prioritization

Backlog Process

Updates & Approval

Assessment Elements

1. Current Backlog Review
• Backlog Summary
• Key Highlights

2. New Requirements
• New Items
• Changes to Existing Items

3. Prioritization
• Prioritization Criteria
• Adjusted Priorities

Management Elements

1. Backlog Grooming
• Splitting & Merging Items
• Item Removal & Clarification

2. Updated Overview
• Revised Backlog Summary
• Upcoming Sprint Focus

3. Finalization
• Action Items & Next Steps
• Approval & Sign-off

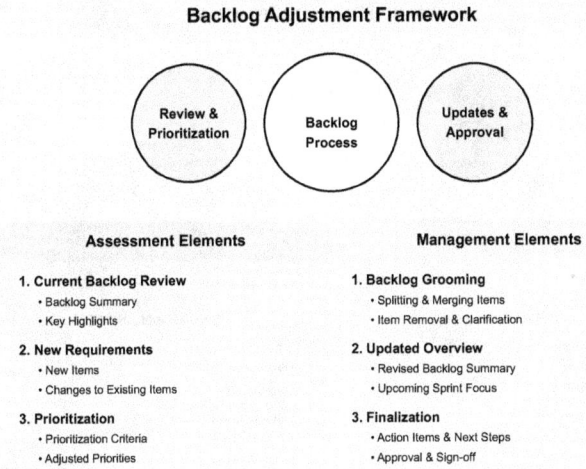

Figure 5.6 Graphical depiction of Backlog Adjustment Template

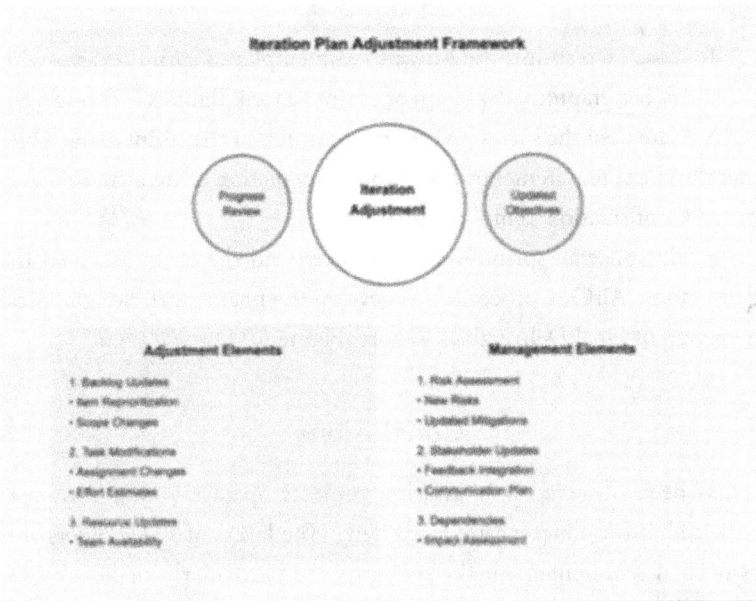

Iteration Plan Adjustment Framework

Progress Review

Iteration Adjustment

Updated Objectives

Adjustment Elements

1. Backlog Updates
• Item Reprioritization
• Scope Changes

2. Task Modifications
• Assignment Changes
• Effort Estimates

3. Resource Updates
• Team Availability

Management Elements

1. Risk Assessment
• New Risks
• Updated Mitigations

2. Stakeholder Updates
• Feedback Integration
• Communication Plan

3. Dependencies
• Impact Assessment

Figure 5.7 Graphical depiction of Iteration Adjustment Deliverables Template

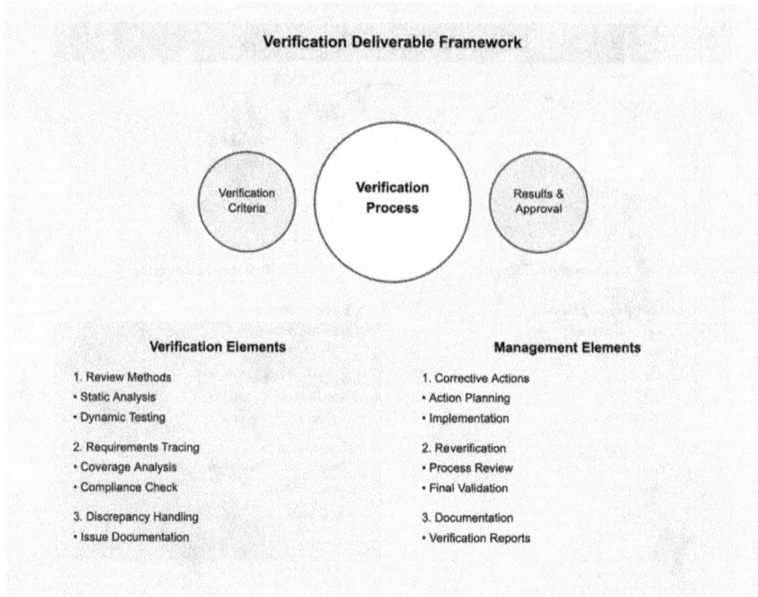

Figure 5.8 Graphical depiction of Iterative Verification Deliverables Template

To close each sprint, the AirCare team employed sprint reviews with the client. See graphical depiction of Sprint Review Template (Figure 5.9).

AirCare used the sprint reviews to confirm that the sprint deliverables met the client requirements. See graphical depiction of Iterative Requirements Confirmation Template (Figure 5.10).

Finally, once all sprints were completed and the client accepted the deliverables, AirCare proceeded to develop the final report. See graphical depiction of Final Deliverables Report (Figure 5.11).

Conclusions

It has been observed that aviation projects operate within extremes. Risk and safety concerns are faced daily. The layers of stakeholders and associated requirements make such projects particularly challenging. It is easy for project managers to leave things out and overlook something essential that could have life-or-death consequences. The AVPM framework helps ensure that nothing important is forgotten. The AVPM

Sprint Review Deliverable Framework

Goals & Achievements

Sprint Review

Sprint Metrics

Review Elements	Management Elements
1. Completed Work	1. Retrospective
• User Stories	• Key Learnings
• Acceptance Criteria	• Action Items
2. Demonstrations	2. Risk Management
• Backlog Items	• New Risks
• Stakeholder Feedback	• Mitigation Plans
3. Incomplete Items	3. Next Steps
• Forward Planning	• Future Goals

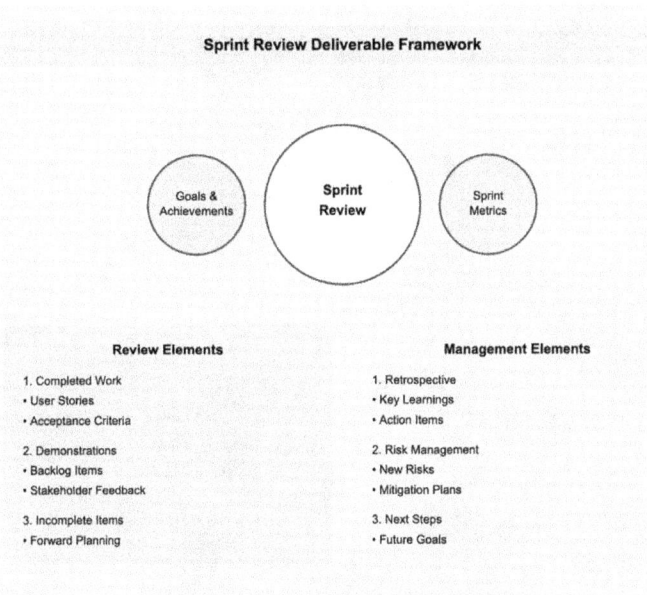

Figure 5.9 Graphical depiction of Sprint Review Template

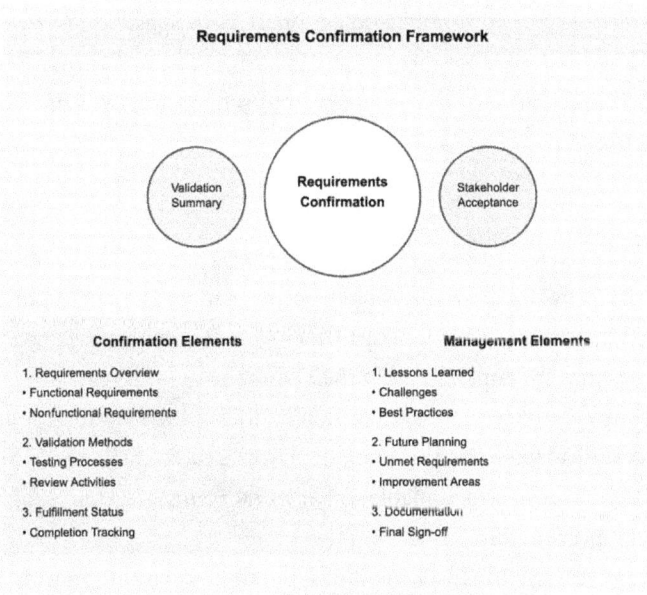

Requirements Confirmation Framework

Validation Summary

Requirements Confirmation

Stakeholder Acceptance

Confirmation Elements	Management Elements
1. Requirements Overview	1. Lessons Learned
• Functional Requirements	• Challenges
• Nonfunctional Requirements	• Best Practices
2. Validation Methods	2. Future Planning
• Testing Processes	• Unmet Requirements
• Review Activities	• Improvement Areas
3. Fulfillment Status	3. Documentation
• Completion Tracking	• Final Sign-off

Figure 5.10 Graphical depiction of Iterative Requirements Confirmation Template

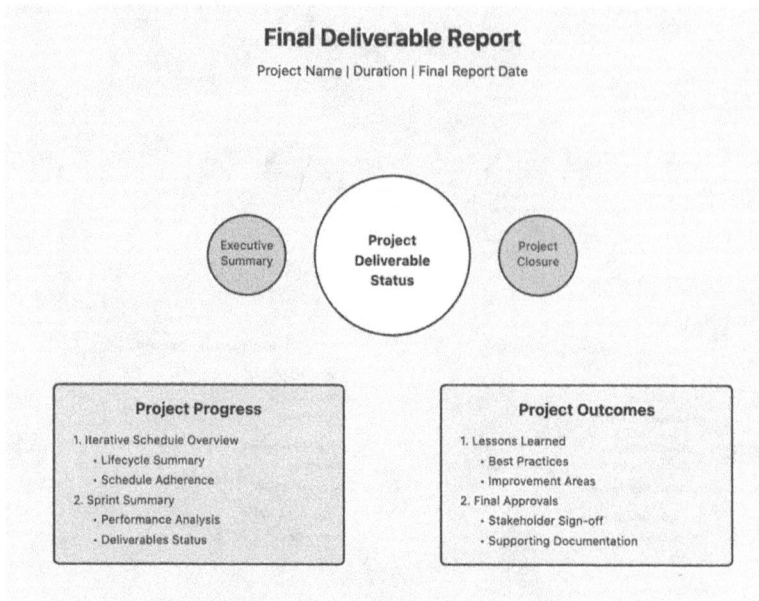

Final Deliverable Report

Project Name | Duration | Final Report Date

Executive Summary

Project Deliverable Status

Project Closure

Project Progress

1. Iterative Schedule Overview
   - Lifecycle Summary
   - Schedule Adherence
2. Sprint Summary
   - Performance Analysis
   - Deliverables Status

Project Outcomes

1. Lessons Learned
   - Best Practices
   - Improvement Areas
2. Final Approvals
   - Stakeholder Sign-off
   - Supporting Documentation

Figure 5.11 Graphical depiction of Final Deliverables Report

practices also outline the big picture of what needs to be done, and these practices unfold in each project phase with specific template and checklist guidance. All of these practices, templates, and checklists contribute to more successful, compliant, and safe projects within the aviation industry.

For the Aviation Community

This book provides a comprehensive toolkit tailored to the unique demands of aviation project management. Aviation professionals face challenges that are unparalleled in their complexity, with regulatory compliance, safety concerns, and stakeholder dynamics requiring constant vigilance and adaptation. This book demystifies these challenges, offering practical solutions and actionable strategies that empower professionals to achieve project success.

Executives will discover methods to align aviation projects with broader organizational strategies, ensuring that initiatives not only meet but also exceed performance expectations. The frameworks presented emphasize efficiency, risk mitigation, and long-term value creation, crucial for navigating the intricacies of aviation projects. Specialists such as engineers and operations managers will benefit from a structured approach to delivering technical outcomes that adhere to the highest safety and quality standards. From procurement decisions to lifecycle management, this book provides a roadmap for managing the technical and operational aspects of aviation projects with precision.

For professionals transitioning into project management within the aviation industry, the book bridges the gap between technical expertise and management acumen. With dedicated sections on stakeholder engagement, regulatory navigation, and risk assessment, transitioning professionals can seamlessly adapt to their new roles while leveraging their technical background. The comprehensive case studies included serve as both instructional guides and sources of inspiration, demonstrating how to apply theory to practice effectively.

This book underscores the critical role of project management in maintaining aviation's reputation for safety and reliability. By integrating project management principles with aviation-specific insights, it ensures that professionals are well-equipped to lead their teams and organizations toward sustained success.

For the Project Management Community

For project managers operating outside the aviation sector, this book provides a rare opportunity to explore the nuances of one of the most demanding industries. The aviation sector presents unique challenges, including intricate regulatory frameworks, high-stakes safety considerations, and multifaceted stakeholder networks. This book offers the tools and insights necessary to adapt generalist project management methodologies to these specialized requirements.

Readers will gain a deeper understanding of aviation's lifecycle complexities, from pre-project planning through execution and closure. The book delves into critical areas such as risk management, safety compliance, and stakeholder alignment, with practical examples and case studies illustrating their application in real-world scenarios. Templates and checklists included in the book provide actionable resources that can be adapted to various project contexts, making this an invaluable companion for project managers seeking to expand their expertise.

For project managers transitioning into aviation, this book acts as a bridge, equipping them with the knowledge to address sector-specific challenges. Detailed guidance on regulatory compliance, lifecycle decision-making, and safety management ensures that managers can seamlessly integrate their skills into aviation projects. By applying the principles outlined, project managers can enhance their adaptability, build cross-industry credibility, and contribute meaningfully to aviation's mission of safety and innovation.

The book's insights into advanced project management practices, such as integrated change-control and iterative lifecycle models, will also appeal to experienced managers looking to refine their skills. Through a blend of theory and practice, it ensures that project managers are prepared to tackle even the most complex aviation projects with confidence and competence.

For the Academic Community

As a cornerstone resource for academic inquiry and instruction, this book is uniquely positioned to shape the next generation of aviation project managers and researchers. Its comprehensive coverage spans the theoretical underpinnings and practical applications of project management in the aviation sector, making it an indispensable textbook for graduate and professional courses.

For educators, the book provides a structured curriculum framework, complete with case studies, templates, and real-world examples that bring theoretical concepts to life. Each chapter is aligned with critical learning objectives, ensuring that students gain not only knowledge but also practical skills applicable to their future careers. Topics such as risk management, safety compliance, and lifecycle decision-making are explored in depth, offering students a holistic understanding of aviation project management.

Researchers will find a treasure trove of inspiration within these pages. The book's exploration of emerging trends, such the integration of artificial intelligence (AI) and digital twin technology in aviation projects, opens new avenues for academic inquiry. The detailed frameworks and methodologies presented can serve as foundational models for dissertations and research papers, advancing the discourse on how to manage complex aviation projects effectively.

Moreover, the book emphasizes the intersection of theory and practice, encouraging collaboration between academia and industry. By highlighting best practices and lessons learned from real-world projects, it provides a roadmap for developing innovative solutions that address aviation's evolving challenges. Whether used as a teaching tool or as a research reference, this book is a catalyst for advancing the field of aviation project management and fostering a culture of excellence within the academic community.

In conclusion, this book is a vital resource for anyone involved in aviation projects, from industry professionals to academics. By addressing the unique challenges of this sector and offering practical solutions, the book fosters a deeper understanding of aviation project management, paving the way for innovation and excellence.

APPENDIX

Aviation-Specific Terms

Aeronautical Information Services: Services that deliver critical information to pilots, including real-time weather updates, air traffic management data, and flight-related information.

Air Traffic Control (ATC): A service that coordinates and directs aircraft movements to ensure safety, efficient use of airspace, and emergency response.

Air Traffic Services: Services provided by air traffic control, including flight planning, navigation, and communication assistance.

Aircraft Maintenance: Tasks performed to ensure an aircraft remains airworthy, including inspections, repairs, and part replacements.

Aircraft Maintenance Records: Documents that record an aircraft's maintenance history, including inspections, repairs, and replacements.

Aircraft Performance: The evaluation of an aircraft's capabilities, including its speed, range, and ability to maneuver.

Aircraft Registration: Official process of registering an aircraft with a national aviation authority, providing it with a unique identifier.

Airworthiness Certification: A formal process confirming an aircraft meets safety standards and regulations, ensuring the aircraft is safe to operate.

Avionics Systems: Electronic systems on an aircraft that provide pilots with information and control functions, including navigation, communication, and flight control systems.

Flight Operations: The coordination and management of flight-related activities, such as flight planning, dispatch, scheduling, and operational control.

Flight Planning: The process of preparing for a flight by determining route, altitude, speed, and accounting for weather and air traffic.

Safety Management: The structured process of identifying, evaluating, and addressing risks and hazards to maintain a safe environment.

Core Project Management Terms

Change Control: The process of managing, evaluating, and approving changes to a project's scope, schedule, or budget.

Cost Management: The process of planning, allocating, and controlling resources to achieve project objectives while optimizing costs.

Earned Value Management (EVM): A methodology for measuring performance by integrating scope, schedule, and cost data.

Project Charter: A formal document that initiates a project, defining its objectives, scope, goals, and key stakeholders.

Project Execution: The process of performing the tasks and activities specified in the project plan.

Project Monitoring and Control: The process of tracking progress and making adjustments to ensure alignment with objectives.

Risk Management: The process of identifying, assessing, and addressing potential risks to minimize negative impacts.

Schedule Management: The process of developing, maintaining, and controlling the project timeline.

Scope Management: The process of defining, documenting, and controlling the project's boundaries and deliverables.

Stakeholder Management: The process of identifying, engaging, and communicating with project stakeholders.

Work Breakdown Structure (WBS): A hierarchical decomposition of project work into smaller, manageable tasks.

Work Package: A manageable subset of project scope, consisting of related tasks and deliverables.

Quality and Compliance Terms

Aerospace Standard (AS): Industry-specific standards of quality used in aerospace and aviation.

Audit: An independent examination of processes or systems to ensure compliance with standards.

Compliance Management: The process of ensuring adherence to laws, regulations, and standards.

Quality Assurance: A systematic process focused on ensuring projects meet defined quality standards.

Quality Control: Activities used to verify that deliverables meet specified requirements.

Quality Management Plan: A document detailing processes to ensure deliverables meet requirements.

Quality Management System (QMS): A framework of processes designed to ensure consistent quality.

Regulatory Compliance: The process of ensuring operations adhere to relevant laws and regulations.

Regulatory Requirements: Laws, regulations, and standards that must be followed.

Safety Certification: Formal verification of compliance with safety standards.

Safety Standards: Industry guidelines established to ensure protection and reduce risks.

Safety System: An organized framework designed to identify and manage risks and hazards.

Technical Systems

Communication Systems: Equipment facilitating voice and data exchange between aircraft and ground.

Emergency Equipment: Specialized tools and devices for responding to emergencies.

Fire Protection Systems: Integrated systems designed to detect and suppress fires.

Flight Management System (FMS): Computer system automating flight planning and navigation.

Hydraulic Systems: Systems managing fluid power generation and distribution.

Navigation Systems: Integrated systems providing real-time position and speed data.

Oxygen Systems: Equipment supplying oxygen to passengers and crew.

Pneumatic Systems: Systems managing compressed air operations.

Radar Systems: Electronic systems for detecting and tracking objects.

Search and Rescue Services: Services for locating and assisting aircraft in distress.

Warning and Alert Systems: Systems notifying pilots of potential hazards.

Weather Radar Systems: Systems detecting and displaying weather information.

Resource and Maintenance Terms

Inventory Management: The process of overseeing and controlling aviation parts and supplies.

Maintenance Lifecycle: Stages involved in ongoing maintenance from deployment through decommissioning.

Maintenance Management: Process of overseeing and coordinating maintenance activities.

Maintenance Repair and Overhaul (MRO): Management of maintenance, repairs, and overhauls.

Maintenance Scheduling: Planning of routine inspections, repairs, and overhauls.

Product Lifecycle Management (PLM): Overseeing a product's lifecycle from concept through disposal.

Resource Allocation: Assigning personnel, equipment, and materials to specific tasks.

Resource Management Plan: Plan detailing how resources will be allocated and managed.

Resource Optimization: Adjusting resource allocation to maximize efficiency.

Supply Chain Management (SCM): Overseeing flow of aviation parts and materials.

Supplier Management: Process of managing relationships with parts and service providers.

Warehouse Management: Overseeing storage and movement of aviation parts and supplies.

Practice Guides

A sample of one each of the primary, supporting, and iterative practice guides are provided below. The complete set of practice guides are documented in the Project Management Resource Center associated with the Embry-Riddle Aeronautical University Worldwide Master of Science in Project Management program that features the complete AVPM framework. The materials presented in this book are sufficient to build aviation project management capabilities within your own organization.

Practice Guides: Primary Practice Example

AVPM: Aviation Project Management Framework Document

Document ID AVPMPGLM1.000	Title **Practice Guide for Lifecycle Management in Aviation Project Management**	Print Date mm/dd/yyyy
Revision 0.0	Prepared By **Preparer's Name/Title**	Date Prepared mm/dd/yyyy
Effective Date mm/dd/yyyy	Reviewed By **Reviewer's Name/Title**	Date Reviewed mm/dd/yyyy
Standard **AVPM 1.0**	Approved By **Final Approver's Name/Title**	Date Approved mm/dd/yyyy

Note: The following practice guide succinctly outlines the key activities and deliverables associated with lifecycle selection and management in the context of aviation project management.

I. Introduction
- **Purpose and Scope**: Provides insights into lifecycle management within aviation projects.
- **Background and Context**: Emphasizes lifecycle management's role in project success.
- **Target Audience**: Project managers and professionals in aviation projects.
- **Deliverables**: Lifecycle Management Strategy, Project Initiation Document.

II. Fundamentals of Aviation Project Management
- **Definition and Objectives**: Outlines lifecycle management's significance in aviation projects.

- ○ **Key Concepts**: Introduces key lifecycle management concepts and terminology.
- ○ **Benefits**: Highlights the benefits of effective lifecycle management.
- ○ **Regulatory Framework**: Reviews relevant regulations and compliance standards.
- ○ **Deliverables**: Compliance Plan, Lifecycle Framework Document.

III. Project Initiation
- ○ **Project Identification**: Identifies and selects aviation projects aligned with goals.
- ○ **Tools and Techniques**: Project Scoring Model, Decision Matrix.
- ○ **Deliverables**: Project Selection Report, Project Portfolio.
- ○ **Stakeholder Analysis**: Analyzes stakeholders' influence and interest.
- ○ **Tools and Techniques**: Stakeholder Analysis Matrix, Power/Interest Grid.
- ○ **Deliverables**: Stakeholder Analysis Report, Engagement Plan.
- ○ **Project Charter**: Develops a charter outlining project scope and objectives.
- ○ **Tools and Techniques**: Project Charter Template, Project Scope Statement.
- ○ **Deliverables**: Project Charter, Scope Document.
- ○ **Risk Assessment**: Identifies and assesses initiation risks.
- ○ **Tools and Techniques**: Risk Register, Risk Probability/ Impact Matrix.
- ○ **Deliverables**: Risk Assessment Report, Mitigation Plan.
- ○ **Resource Allocation**: Allocates resources for initiation activities.
- ○ **Tools and Techniques**: Resource Allocation Matrix, Resource Planning Software.
- ○ **Deliverables**: Resource Plan, Budget Allocation Report.

IV. Planning and Scheduling
- **Work Breakdown Structure (WBS)**: Decomposes activities into tasks.
- **Tools and Techniques**: WBS Templates, WBS Dictionary.
- **Deliverables**: WBS, Task List.
- **Activity Sequencing**: Defines the sequence of project activities.
- **Tools and Techniques**: Network Diagrams, Dependency Determination Techniques.
- **Deliverables**: Activity Sequence Plan, Project Network Diagram.
- **Estimation**: Estimates time, cost, and resources for tasks.
- **Tools and Techniques**: Analogous Estimating, Parametric Estimating.
- **Deliverables**: Estimation Report, Resource Requirements Document.
- **Schedule Development**: Creates a project schedule.
- **Tools and Techniques**: Gantt Charts, Critical Path Method.
- **Deliverables**: Project Schedule, Critical Path Analysis.
- **Budgeting**: Establishes and controls project budgets.
- **Tools and Techniques**: Cost Baseline, Earned Value Management.
- **Deliverables**: Budget Plan, Cost Baseline Document.

V. Execution and Monitoring
- **Project Team Management**: Manages teams for effective execution.
- **Tools and Techniques**: Team Collaboration Software, Team Performance Evaluation.
- **Deliverables**: Team Management Plan, Collaboration Report.
- **Communication**: Implements strategies for stakeholder engagement.
- **Tools and Techniques**: Communication Plan, Communication Matrix.

- **Deliverables**: Communication Strategy, Stakeholder Updates.
- **Risk Monitoring**: Continuously monitors and mitigates risks.
- **Tools and Techniques**: Risk Reporting Tools, Risk Response Plan.
- **Deliverables**: Risk Monitoring Report, Updated Risk Register.
- **Quality Assurance**: Maintains project standards and compliance.
- **Tools and Techniques**: Quality Checklists, Quality Audits.
- **Deliverables**: Quality Assurance Plan, Audit Reports.
- **Safety and Compliance**: Ensures adherence to safety and compliance standards.
- **Tools and Techniques**: Safety Inspections, Compliance Tracking Software.
- **Deliverables**: Safety Compliance Report, Inspection Records.

VI. Procurement and Supply Chain Management
- **Procurement Strategy**: Develops strategies for resource acquisition.
- **Tools and Techniques**: Procurement Management Plan, Make-or-Buy Analysis.
- **Deliverables**: Procurement Strategy, Vendor List.
- **Vendor Selection**: Selects vendors based on project criteria.
- **Tools and Techniques**: Vendor Evaluation Criteria, Request for Proposal (RFP).
- **Deliverables**: Vendor Selection Report, Contract Agreements.
- **Vendor Management**: Manages vendor performance and relationships.
- **Tools and Techniques**: Vendor Scorecards, Performance Reviews.

- ○ **Deliverables**: Vendor Management Plan, Performance Evaluation Report.
- ○ **Supply Chain Logistics**: Manages logistics for material delivery.
- ○ **Tools and Techniques**: Supply Chain Mapping, Inventory Management Software.
- ○ **Deliverables**: Logistics Plan, Inventory Management Strategy.

VII. Safety and Security Measures
- ○ **Safety Management System (SMS)**: Implements SMS for risk mitigation.
- ○ **Tools and Techniques**: Safety Risk Assessment, Safety Incident Reporting System.
- ○ **Deliverables**: SMS Plan, Safety Risk Management Report.
- ○ **Security Protocols**: Establishes security measures for project assets.
- ○ **Tools and Techniques**: Access Control Systems, Security Surveillance.
- ○ **Deliverables**: Security Plan, Security Protocol Documentation.
- ○ **Crisis Management**: Prepares for emergencies and unforeseen events.
- ○ **Tools and Techniques**: Crisis Communication Plan, Emergency Response Procedures.
- ○ **Deliverables**: Crisis Management Plan, Emergency Response Plan.

VIII.   Project Documentation and Recordkeeping
- ○ **Document Control**: Manages project documents and records.
- ○ **Tools and Techniques**: Document Management System, Document Version Control.
- ○ **Deliverables**: Document Control Procedure, Record Retention Policy.
- ○ **Data Management**: Manages project data and reporting systems.

- **Tools and Techniques**: Data Management Plan, Data Visualization Tools.
- **Deliverables**: Data Management Strategy, Reporting System Setup.

IX. Project Closure
- **Evaluation**: Evaluates project performance and captures lessons learned.
- **Tools and Techniques**: Project Evaluation Survey, Lessons-Learned Database.
- **Deliverables**: Project Evaluation Report, Lessons-Learned Document.
- **Handover**: Transfers project deliverables to stakeholders.
- **Tools and Techniques**: Handover Checklist, Knowledge Transfer Sessions.
- **Deliverables**: Handover Documentation, Knowledge Transfer Report.
- **Final Reporting**: Generates final reports for stakeholders.
- **Tools and Techniques**: Project Closure Report Template, Regulatory Compliance Checklist.
- **Deliverables**: Final Project Report, Compliance Report.
- **Post-implementation Review**: Assesses project outcomes and improvements.
- **Tools and Techniques**: Post-implementation Review Template, Performance Analysis Tools.
- **Deliverables**: Post-implementation Review Report, Improvement Recommendations.

X. Continuous Improvement
- **Key** Performance **Indicators (KPIs)**: Measures project performance and success.
- **Tools and Techniques**: KPI Dashboard, Performance Measurement Software.
- **Deliverables**: KPI Report, Performance Improvement Plan.
- **Feedback Mechanisms**: Gathers stakeholder feedback for improvement.

- ○ **Tools and Techniques**: Feedback Forms, Stakeholder Feedback Software.
- ○ **Deliverables**: Feedback Report, Continuous Improvement Plan.
- ○ **Process Optimization**: Identifies and implements best practices.
- ○ **Tools and Techniques**: Process Mapping, Process Improvement Software.
- ○ **Deliverables**: Process Optimization Report, Best-Practice Guidelines.

XI. Case Studies and Examples
- ○ **Real-world Examples**: Showcases successful lifecycle management practices.
- ○ **Lessons Learned**: Shares insights from past projects for future improvements.
- ○ **Deliverables**: Case Study Compilation, Lessons-Learned Summary.

XII. Appendixes
- ○ **Glossary**: Defines terms related to lifecycle management in aviation.
- ○ **Templates and Forms**: Provides resources for project documentation and reporting.
- ○ **Regulations and Guidelines**: Lists relevant regulations and guidelines for aviation projects.
- ○ **Additional Resources**: Offers further materials for exploring lifecycle management.

XIII. Index: Lifecycle Management Phase Deliverable Templates

Lifecycle Management Practice Guide: AVPMPGLM1.000

- • Lifecycle Selection Template: AVPMPLM1.1
- • Project Selection Template: AVPMPLM1.1.2
- • Lifecycle Management Initiation Template: AVPMPLM1.2

- Lifecycle Management Plan Template: AVPMPLM1.3
- Lifecycle Execution Report Template: AVPMPLM1.4
- Lifecycle Control Report Template: AVPMPLM1.5
- Lifecycle Closure Report Template: AVPMPLM1.6

Practice Guides: Supporting Practice Example

AVPM: Aviation Project Management Framework Document

Document ID AVPMPGSAQ 1.000	Title **Practice Guide for Aviation Quality Management in Aviation Project Management**	Print Date mm/dd/yyyy
Revision **0.0**	Prepared By **Preparer's Name/Title**	Date Prepared mm/dd/yyyy
Effective Date mm/dd/yyyy	Reviewed By **Reviewer's Name/Title**	Date Reviewed mm/dd/yyyy
Standard **AVPM 1.0**	Approved By **Final Approver's Name/Title**	Date Approved mm/dd/yyyy

Note: The following practice guide outlines the key activities and deliverables associated with quality management in the context of aviation project management.

Introduction

- Purpose and Scope: This practice guide aims to provide insights and strategies for managing aviation quality effectively within the context of aviation projects.
- Background and Context: Highlights the critical importance of quality management in ensuring the safety, reliability, and compliance of aviation projects with regulatory standards and customer expectations.
- Target Audience: Project managers, quality assurance professionals, aviation engineers, regulators, and stakeholders involved in aviation projects.

I. Fundamentals of Aviation Quality Management
   o Definition and Objectives: Definition of aviation quality management and its role in setting and achieving quality standards.
   o Key Concepts: Introduction to concepts like QMS, quality assurance, and continuous improvement.
   o Benefits: Discussion of benefits such as enhanced safety and customer satisfaction.
   o Regulatory Framework: Overview of relevant regulations and industry standards.
   o Deliverables: Development of a Quality Standards Document tailored to aviation project requirements.
II. Quality Planning and Assurance
   o Quality Planning: Procedures for establishing quality objectives and criteria.
   o Quality Management Systems (QMS): Implementation strategies for QMS frameworks.
   o Quality Audits and Assessments: Schedule and protocols for regular audits.
   o Deliverables: Comprehensive Quality Management Plan, Audit Reports, and Compliance Certifications.
III. Quality Control and Inspection
   o Quality Control Processes: Setup of quality control methodologies.
   o Inspection and Testing: Protocols for conducting thorough inspections and tests.
   o Nonconformance Management: Strategies for addressing quality issues.
   o Deliverables: Quality Control Reports, Inspection Logs, and Nonconformance Reports.
IV. Supplier Quality Management
   o Supplier Qualification: Criteria for evaluating suppliers.
   o Supplier Audits and Performance Monitoring: Systems for continuous supplier evaluation.

- ○ Supplier Collaboration: Mechanisms for enhancing supplier relationships.
- ○ Deliverables: Supplier Audit Reports, Performance Review Documents, and Supplier Improvement Plans.

V. Continuous Improvement and Innovation
  - ○ Quality Metrics and Performance Indicators: Identification and tracking of key performance indicators.
  - ○ Root Cause Analysis: Techniques for identifying the causes of defects or failures.
  - ○ Quality Culture: Strategies for fostering a quality-driven culture within the organization.
  - ○ Deliverables: Performance Dashboards, Improvement Action Plans, and Culture Assessment Reports.

VI. Risk Management and Compliance
  - ○ Quality Risk Assessment: Detailed risk assessment procedures.
  - ○ Regulatory Compliance: Compliance tracking and management.
  - ○ Documentation and Records Management: Systems for maintaining essential documents and records.
  - ○ Deliverables: Risk Management Reports, Compliance Certificates, and Document Registers.

VII. Communication and Stakeholder Engagement
  - ○ Quality Communication: Plans for communicating quality-related information.
  - ○ Stakeholder Engagement: Strategies for engaging stakeholders effectively.
  - ○ Quality Reporting: Procedures for regular quality reporting.
  - ○ Deliverables: Stakeholder Engagement Reports, Quality Newsletters, and Regular Quality Updates.

VIII.   Training and Competency Development
  - ○ Training Programs: Frameworks for delivering targeted training.

- Competency Assessment: Procedures for assessing the competency of personnel.
- Continuous Learning: Opportunities for ongoing professional development.
- Deliverables: Training Records, Competency Assessment Reports, and Professional Development Plans.

IX. Case Studies and Examples
- Real-world Examples: Collection of case studies demonstrating effective quality management.
- Best Practices: Compilation of best practices identified from industry leaders.
- Deliverables: Case Study Compendium, Best Practices Handbook.

X. Appendixes
- Glossary: Definitions of key terms used throughout the guide.
- Templates and Tools: Ready-to-use templates and tools for immediate application.
- References: Curated list of additional resources and literature.
- Index: Detailed index to quickly locate information within the document.

XI. Index

Aviation Quality Management Phase Deliverables Templates
- Aviation Quality Management Practice Guide: AVPMPGSAQ1.000
- Quality Management Strategy Deliverable Checklist: AVPMSAQ1.1
- Quality Systems and Assurance Deliverable Checklist: AVPMSAQ1.2
- Quality Management Plan Deliverable Checklist: AVPMSAQ1.3

AVPM: Aviation Project Management Framework Document

- Quality Control Reports Deliverable Checklist: AVPMSAQ1.4
- Change-Control Deliverable Checklist: AVPMSAQ1.5
- Quality Management Final Report Deliverable Checklist: AVPMSAQ1.6

These additions aim to enhance the guide by explicitly stating the expected outputs and documentation, ensuring that all stakeholders have clear expectations regarding the deliverables at each stage of quality management. This should make the guide more actionable and aligned with the goals of effective project management in the aviation industry.

Practice Guides: The Iterative Practices

AVPM: Aviation Project Management Framework Document

Document ID AVPMPGRM1.000	Title Practice Guide for Requirements Management in Aviation Project Management	Print Date mm/dd/yyyy
Revision 0.0	Prepared By Preparer's Name/Title	Date Prepared mm/dd/yyyy
Effective Date mm/dd/yyyy	Reviewed By Reviewer's Name/Title	Date Reviewed mm/dd/yyyy
Standard AVPM 1.0	Approved By Final Approver's Name/Title	Date Approved mm/dd/yyyy

Note: The following practice guide outlines the key activities and deliverables associated with requirements management in the context of aviation project management.

I. Introduction

Purpose and Scope:

This guide provides methodologies, tools, and best practices for effective requirements management within aviation projects, ensuring alignment with project objectives and stakeholder needs.

Background and Context:

Emphasizes the importance of accurately capturing, analyzing, and managing requirements to ensure project success in the complex and regulated aviation industry.

Target Audience:

Project managers, systems engineers, business analysts, and other stakeholders involved in defining and managing project requirements in aviation.

II. Fundamentals of Requirements Management

Definition and Objectives:

Defines requirements management as the process of eliciting, documenting, analyzing, prioritizing, and tracking requirements throughout the project lifecycle to ensure the final deliverables meet stakeholder expectations.

Key Concepts:

- Requirements Elicitation
- Requirements Documentation
- Requirements Analysis and Prioritization
- Traceability and Change Management

Benefits:

Highlights the benefits of robust requirements management, including reduced project risks, enhanced stakeholder satisfaction, and improved project outcomes.

Regulatory Considerations:

Outlines relevant aviation regulations and standards that impact requirements management, such as FAA and EASA guidelines.

III. Requirements Elicitation and Collection

Techniques for Elicitation:

Describes various techniques for gathering requirements, including interviews, workshops, observation, and document analysis.

Stakeholder Identification:

Guidance on identifying and engaging with stakeholders to understand their needs and expectations.

Tools and Techniques:

- Stakeholder Analysis Matrix
- Elicitation Techniques Overview
- Requirements Gathering Workshops

Deliverables:

- Stakeholder Requirements Document
- Elicitation Report

IV. Requirements Documentation and Analysis

Documentation Standards:

Outlines best practices for documenting requirements, including the use of clear, concise, and unambiguous language.

Requirements Analysis:

Describes methods for analyzing requirements to ensure they are complete, consistent, feasible, and verifiable.

Tools and Techniques:

- Requirements Management Software (e.g., DOORS, Jama)
- Traceability Matrix
- Analysis Checklists

Deliverables:

- Requirements Specification Document
- Traceability Matrix

V. Prioritization and Validation

Prioritization Criteria:

Establishes criteria for prioritizing requirements based on factors such as stakeholder value, regulatory importance, and technical feasibility.

Validation Techniques:

Discusses techniques for validating requirements with stakeholders to ensure alignment with business needs and project objectives.

Tools and Techniques:

- Prioritization Matrix
- Validation Workshops

Deliverables:

- Prioritized Requirements List
- Validation Report

VI. Requirements Change Management

Change-Control Process:

Defines the process for managing changes to requirements, including impact analysis, stakeholder approval, and documentation updates.

Configuration Management:

Outlines the role of configuration management in maintaining the integrity of requirements documents and artifacts.

Tools and Techniques:

- Change Request Form
- Impact Analysis Template

Deliverables:

- Updated Requirements Documents
- Change Log

VII. Traceability and Monitoring

Traceability Strategies:

Explains the importance of establishing traceability from requirements to project deliverables and tests to ensure all requirements are addressed.

Monitoring and Reporting:

Describes methods for monitoring the status of requirements and reporting progress to stakeholders.

Tools and Techniques:

- Traceability Matrix Tools`
- Progress-Tracking Dashboards

Deliverables:

- Traceability Report
- Requirements Status Report

VIII.   Tools, Templates, and Resources

Requirements Management Tools:

Reviews various software tools available for requirements management and their features.

Templates and Checklists:

Provides templates for requirements documents, traceability matrixes, change requests, and other key artifacts.

Additional Resources:

Lists books, articles, and online resources for further study on requirements management in aviation projects.

IX. Case Studies and Best Practices

Real-world Examples:

Presents case studies illustrating successful requirements management in aviation projects.

Best Practices:

Shares insights and best practices from industry experts on effective requirements management.

X. Appendixes

Glossary:

Defines key terms and concepts related to requirements management in aviation projects.

References:

Provides a bibliography of sources cited in the guide and additional reading materials.

Index:

An alphabetical index of topics covered in the guide for quick reference.

XI. Index

Requirements Management Practice Guide: AVPMPGRM1.000

- Sources of Requirements Document Template: AVPMPRM1.1
- Requirements Collection and Statement of Work Template: AVPMPRM1.2
- Scope Development Based on Requirements Document Template: AVPMPRM1.3
- Requirements Validation Report Template: AVPMPRM1.4
- Requirements Measurement and Verification Report Template: AVPMPRM1.5
- Requirements Management Final Report Template: AVPMPRM1.6

About the Authors

Dr. James Marion, PMP, PMI-RMP, is the Department Chair and Associate Professor in the Department of Decision Sciences and Analytics for Embry-Riddle Aeronautical University Worldwide.

Dr. Tracey Richardson, PMP, is a tenured, Associate Professor of Project Management at Embry-Riddle Aeronautical University Worldwide and is a retired USAF Aircraft Maintenance Officer.

Dr. Valerie Denney, PMP, is a tenured Associate Professor of Decision Sciences in the College of Business at Embry-Riddle Aeronautical University Worldwide. Dr. Denney teaches bachelor's and master's degrees in project management and the master's in engineering management.

Dr. Carlos Chaves, PMP, is an Adjunct Professor of Engineering Management at Embry-Riddle Aeronautical University.

Index

www.ingramcontent.com/pod-product-compliance
Lightning Source LLC
Chambersburg PA
CBHW061145220326
41599CB00025B/4367